Lecture Notes in Computer Science 6727

Commenced Publication in 1973
Founding and Former Series Editors:
Gerhard Goos, Juris Hartmanis, and Jan van Leeuwen

T0223409

Klaus Schmid (Ed.)

Top Productivity through Software Reuse

12th International Conference
on Software Reuse, ICSR 2011
Pohang, South Korea, June 13-17, 2011
Proceedings

 Springer

Volume Editor

Klaus Schmid
University of Hildesheim
Institute of Computer Science
Marienburger Platz 22
31141 Hildesheim, Germany
E-mail: schmid@sse.uni-hildesheim.de

ISSN 0302-9743   e-ISSN 1611-3349
ISBN 978-3-642-21346-5   e-ISBN 978-3-642-21347-2
DOI 10.1007/978-3-642-21347-2
Springer Heidelberg Dordrecht London New York

Library of Congress Control Number: Applied for

CR Subject Classification (1998): D.2.13, D.2, D.3, D.1, D.3.3

LNCS Sublibrary: SL 2 – Programming and Software Engineering

Typesetting: Camera-ready by author, data conversion by Scientific Publishing Services, Chennai, India

Printed on acid-free paper

Springer is part of Springer Science+Business Media (www.springer.com)

Preface

This volume contains the proceedings accepted for the International Conference on Software Reuse (ICSR 12) held during June 13–17, 2011 in Pohang, South Korea.

The International Conference on Software Reuse is the premier international event in the software reuse community. It has a long tradition going back 20 years: the first ICSR was held in 1991. During this period reuse has changed the industry significantly on different levels and through different technologies and methods. Examples are feature-based development, product line engineering, or generation-based approaches. Many of these have created their own specific communities. Of course this reflects back on ICSR. Thus, at this conference a healthy mixture of contributions can be found: some are from areas intersecting with other communities, while some either use novel approaches or look at software reuse from a broad angle, which is particularly appropriate for the ICSR conference. Besides being a melting pot for different research directions in software reuse, this year's ICSR also showed that it continues to attract both pure research as well as practical contributions.

We received 43 submissions (excluding withdrawn and incomplete submissions). Each submission was reviewed by at least three, and in several cases four, Program Committee members. The committee decided to accept 16 papers resulting in an acceptance rate of 37%. The program also included invited talks, three workshops, a doctoral symposium and two tutorials. Abstracts of all these are also included in this volume. The program was complemented by tool demos.

This conference was a collaborative effort that could only be realized through many dedicated efforts. First of all I would like to thank Claudia Werner for her work as General Chair. Kyo Kang worked intensively to make this event possible in Pohang. This conference would not have been possible without him. Hong Mei and Greg Kulczycki organized the workshop and the tutorial program. Jeffrey Poulin organized the demonstrations and tools track, and Leonardo Murta was Doctoral Symposium Chair. Hyesun Lee served very well as Web Chair, while Kwanwoo Lee ensured the local organization. Personally, I would also like to thank Leman Sözüçok and Sascha El-Sharkawy for their help in preparing the conference proceedings.

Finally, we would like to thank POSTECH University for its organizational and financial support of the conference, which was instrumental to conducting the conference in Pohang, South Korea.

As the Program Chair of ICSR 2011, I would like to deeply thank the members of the Program Committee and the additional reviewers for their detailed and timely reviews as well as their participation in the intensive discussions of the submissions. I would particularly like to thank those who took upon them additional reviews in order to help clarify the situation in cases of difficult-to-judge papers and those who accepted the additional work as a shepherd and supported promising papers.

April 2011   Klaus Schmid

ICSR 2011 Conference Organization

General Chair	Cláudia Maria Lima Werner (Federal University of Rio de Janeiro, Rio de Janeiro, Brazil)
Program Chair	Klaus Schmid (University of Hildesheim, Germany)
Workshop Chair	Hong Mei (Peking University, China)
Tutorial Chair	Greg Kulczycki (Virginia Tech, USA)
Demonstration and Tools Chair	Jefferey Poulin (Lockheed Martin, USA)
Doctoral Symposium Chair	Leonardo Murta (Fluminense Federal University, Niterói, Brazil)
Publicity Chair	Maurizio Morisio (Politecnico di Torino, Italy)
Local Chair	Kwanwoo Lee (Hansung University, South Korea)
Web Chair	Hyesun Lee (POSTECH, South Korea)
Corporate Donations Chairs	Kyo Kang (POSTECH, South Korea) Eduardo Almeida (Federal University of Bahia, Brazil) Flavio Oquendo (University of South Brittany, France) Okan Yilmaz (NeuStar Inc., USA)

Program Committee

Eduardo Almeida	Federal University of Bahia, Brazil
Colin Atkinson	University of Mannheim, Germany
Paris Avgeriou	University of Groningen, The Netherlands
Ted J. Biggerstaff	Software Generators, USA
Cornelia Boldyreff	University of East London, UK
Jan Bosch	Intuit, USA
Christian Bunse	Univ. Appl. Sciences Stralsund, Germany
Reidar Conradi	NTNU, Norway
Ivica Crnkovic	Mälardalen University, Sweden
Davide Falessi	Simula, Norway
John Favaro	INTECS, Italy
William B. Frakes	Virginia Tech, USA
Birgit Geppert	Avaya Labs Research, USA
Paul Grünbacher	JKU, Linz, Austria
Lothar Hotz	HiTeC and University of Hamburg, Germany
Oliver Hummel	Mannheim University, Germany
Stan Jarzabek	National University of Singapore, Singapore
Isabel John	Fraunhofer IESE, Germany
Kyo C. Kang	POSTECH, Korea
Jaejoon Lee	Lancaster University, UK
Juan Llorens	Univ. Carlos III de Madrid, Spain
Ali Mili	New Jersey Institute of Technology, USA
Maurizio Morisio	Politecnico di Torino, Italy
Dirk Muthig	Lufthansa Systems, Germany
Wolfgang Pree	University of Salzburg, Austria
Jeffrey Poulin	Lockheed Martin, USA
Ruben Prieto-Diaz	Universidad Carlos III de Madrid, Spain
Andreas Rummler	SAP, Germany
Christa Schwanninger	Siemens, Germany
Michael Shin	Texas Tech University, USA
Alberto Sillitti	Free University of Bolzano, Italy
Murali Sitaraman	Clemson University, USA
Michal Smialek	Warsaw University of Technology, Poland
Judith Stafford	Tufts University, USA
Clemens Szyperski	Microsoft Research, USA
Uwe Zdun	University of Vienna, Austria

Additional Reviewers

Yasmine Arafa

Andrea Capiluppi

Hyunsik Choi

Antonio Cicchetti

Charles Cook

Trung Dinh-Trong

Matthias Galster

Peter Hintenaus

Thomas Leveque

Suria R Asai

Frank Roessler

Hampton Smith

Klaas-Jan Stol

Yu-Shan Sun

Josef Templ

Dan Tofan

Anita Vulgarakis

Sponsors

Software Generators, LLC.

Pohang University of Science and Technology

International Society for the Advancement of Software Education

Table of Contents

Evolution

Implementation

Reuse in Practice

Workshops

Tutorials

Understanding Variability
Abstraction and Realization

Krzysztof Czarnecki

Generative Software Development Lab, University of Waterloo, Canada
kczarnec@gsd.uwaterloo.ca

Software product line engineering (SPLE) emerged as a successful software reuse paradigm. The essence of SPLE is the process of factoring out commonalities and systematizing variabilities, that is, differences, among the products in a SPL. In this talk, I will take the position that this process *is* the very act of abstraction. Thus, as suggested by Coplien et al. [8], the purpose of abstraction mechanisms, such as subroutines and inheritance in programming languages and architectural patterns and platforms in architectural design, is to support factoring out commonalities and making variabilities explicit.

Variability modeling is a key discipline in SPLE. It captures the variability realized in the many development artifacts of an SPL, including code, models, and documents, as a separate concern, into distinct variability models.

Variability modeling and abstraction are deeply intertwined. Essentially, any abstraction mechanism achieves variability abstraction because it provides a language to describe and differentiate among instances of an abstraction and a function to map the instances to implementations [11,21].

This talk will explore the design space of languages that capture variability, from feature modeling [15] and decision modeling [19] to highly expressive domain-specific languages (DSLs). This design space embodies a progression of structural complexity, from lists and trees of primitive-type parameters to graphs, which correlates with the increasing closeness to implementation [12].

Further, I will identify a set of basic variability realization mechanisms, including element optionality, alternatives, and substitution, iteration, and value assignment [3,10,14,22,16]. These mechanisms have a natural correlation with different choices in the design space of languages capturing variability; for example, Boolean parameters naturally go with element optionality.

I will illustrate the variability abstraction and realization concepts using Clafer, a modeling language designed to support these concepts using a minimal number of constructs [2]. Further, I will report on the real-world usage of these concepts, based on studies of open-source platforms [5,20] and interviews with practitioners form industry who work on closed-source SPLs. I will also report on the progress towards a Common Variability Language (CVL), the Object Management Group's effort to standardize variability modeling [18], which embodies many of the discussed concepts.

I will close with an outlook on the future research challenges, including the need for (1) a comprehensive theory of variability (some progress has been already achieved, e.g., [3,1,13,6]), (2) a better understanding and guidance related

K. Schmid (Ed.): ICSR 2011, LNCS 6727, pp. 1–3, 2011.
© Springer-Verlag Berlin Heidelberg 2011

to the use of variability mechanisms with existing languages (such as tradeoffs between and the combined use of native and language-external variability mechanisms), and (3) an improved tool support (which requires further progress in reasoning on variability abstraction and realization, e.g. [4,9,17,7]).

References

1. Apel, S., Lengauer, C., Möller, B., Kästner, C.: An algebra for features and feature composition. In: Bevilacqua, V., Roşu, G. (eds.) AMAST 2008. LNCS, vol. 5140, pp. 36–50. Springer, Heidelberg (2008)
2. Bąk, K., Czarnecki, K., Wąsowski, A.: Feature and meta-models in clafer: Mixed, specialized, and coupled. In: Malloy, B., Staab, S., van den Brand, M. (eds.) SLE 2010. LNCS, vol. 6563, pp. 102–122. Springer, Heidelberg (2011)
3. Batory, D., Sarvela, J.N., Rauschmayer, A.: Scaling step-wise refinement. IEEE TSE 30, 355–371 (2004)
4. Benavides, D., Segura, S., Ruiz-Cortés, A.: Automated analysis of feature models 20 years later: a literature review. Information Systems 35(6) (2010)
5. Berger, T., She, S., Lotufo, R., Wąsowski, A., Czarnecki, K.: Variability modeling in the real: a perspective from the operating systems domain. In: ASE (2010)
6. Clarke, D., Helvensteijn, M., Schaefer, I.: Abstract delta modeling. In: GPCE 2010 (2010)
7. Classen, A., Heymans, P., Schobbens, P.Y., Legay, A., Raskin, J.F.: Model checking lots of systems: efficient verification of temporal properties in software product lines. In: ICSE, pp. 335–344 (2010)
8. Coplien, J., Hoffman, D., Weiss, D.: Commonality and variability in software engineering. IEEE Softw. 15, 37–45 (1998)
9. Czarnecki, K., Pietroszek, K.: Verifying feature-based model templates against well-formedness OCL constraints. In: GPCE 2006 (2006)
10. Czarnecki, K., Antkiewicz, M.: Mapping features to models: A template approach based on superimposed variants. In: Glück, R., Lowry, M. (eds.) GPCE 2005. LNCS, vol. 3676, pp. 422–437. Springer, Heidelberg (2005)
11. Czarnecki, K., Eisenecker, U.W.: Generative programming: methods, tools, and applications. ACM Press/Addison-Wesley Publishing Co. (2000)
12. Czarnecki, K., Peter Kim, C.H., Kalleberg, K.T.: Feature models are views on ontologies. In: SPLC (2006)
13. Erwig, M., Walkingshaw, E.: The choice calculus: A representation for software variation. In: ACM TOSEM (to appear, 2011)
14. Haugen, O., Møller-Pedersen, B., Oldevik, J., Olsen, G.K., Svendsen, A.: Adding standardized variability to domain specific languages. In: SPLC (2008)
15. Kang, K., Cohen, S., Hess, J., Nowak, W., Peterson, S.: Feature-oriented domain analysis (FODA) feasibility study. Tech. Rep. CMU/SEI-90-TR-21, CMU (1990)
16. Kästner, C.: Virtual Separation of Concerns: Toward Preprocessors 2.0. Ph.D. thesis, University of Magdeburg (May 2010)
17. Kästner, C., Apel, S., Thüm, T., Saake, G.: Type checking annotation-based product lines. In: ACM TOSEM (to appear, 2011)
18. Object Management Group: Common variability language (CVL) RFP. Document ad/2009-12-03 (2009)

19. Schmid, K., Rabiser, R., Grünbacher, P.: A comparison of decision modeling approaches in product lines. In: VaMoS, pp. 119–126 (2011)
20. She, S., Lotufo, R., Berger, T., Wasowski, A., Czarnecki, K.: The variability model of the Linux kernel. In: VaMoS, pp. 45–51 (2010)
21. Veldhuizen, T.L.: Parsimony principles for software components and metalanguages. In: GPCE (2007)
22. Voelter, M., Groher, I.: Product line implementation using aspect-oriented and model-driven software development. In: SPLC (2007)

Binary-Search Based Verification of Feature Models

Wei Zhang, Haiyan Zhao, and Hong Mei

[1] Key Laboratory of High Confidence Software Technology (Peking University),
Ministry of Education, China
[2] Institute of Software, School of EECS, Peking University, Beijing, 100871, China
zhangw@sei.pku.edu.cn, zhhy@sei.pku.edu.cn, meih@pku.edu.cn

Abstract. The purpose of feature models' verification is to detect deficiencies in feature models, so as to avoid the transmission of these deficiencies into subsequent core-asset and product development activities. Although many researchers have observed that the verification problem of feature models can be transformed into *SAT* problems and proposed to resolve this problem based on third-party's *SAT-solver* or *model-checker* tools, few of them point out how to use these third-party tools efficiently. In this paper, we present a *binary-search* based approach to feature models' verification. Our motivation is to decrease the number of times a *SAT-solver* is invoked during the verification of a feature model, and thus improve the verification efficiency. The basic idea is to change feature models' verification from the linear-search based approach to a binary-search approach, and thereby decrease the number of times to invoke a *SAT-solver*. Preliminary experiments show that as the number of levels in feature models increases, our approach manifests a better scalability than the linear-search based approach. This approach can be easily integrated into any feature modeling environment as its verification component.

Keywords: Feature Model, Verification, Binary Search, SAT Solver.

1 Introduction

Feature models provide an effective approach to manage and reuse requirements in software product lines [2,4]. One important problem related to feature models is called the verification problem. The purpose of feature models' verification is to detect deficiencies in feature models, so as to avoid the transmission of these deficiencies into subsequent core-asset and product development activities. Although many researchers have observed that the verification problem of feature models can be transformed into *SAT* problems and proposed to resolve this problem based on third-party's *SAT-solver* or *model-checker* tools [1,3,7], few of them point out how to use these third-party tools efficiently.

In this paper, we present a binary-search based approach to feature model verification. The motivation of our approach is to decrease the number of times a *SAT-solver* is invoked during the verification of a feature model, and thus improve the verification efficiency. The basic idea is to change feature models' verification from the linear-search based approach to a binary-search approach, and thereby decrease the

K. Schmid (Ed.): ICSR 2011, LNCS 6727, pp. 4–19, 2011.
© Springer-Verlag Berlin Heidelberg 2011

number of times to invoke a *SAT-solver*. In particular, we found that given a refinement path in a feature model, there exists at most one critical point that brings deficiencies into the feature model. For the detection of the critical point in a refinement path, the complexity of a binary-search method is lower than that of a linear-search method; the complexity of the former is $O(log_2n)$, while that of the latter is $O(n/2)$. Preliminary experiments show that as the number of levels in feature models increase, our approach manifests a better scalability than the linear-search based approach. This approach can be easily integrated into any feature modeling environment as its verification component.

The rest of this paper is organized as follows. Section 2 gives some preliminaries of feature models and the verification of feature models. Section 3 presents the binary-search based approach to feature models' verification. Experiments and analysis are shown in Section 4. Related works are discussed in Section 5. Finally, Section 6 concludes this paper with a short summary and future work.

2 Preliminaries

In this section, we introduce some preliminaries of our approach, with the purpose of building a clear understanding of feature models and their verification.

2.1 Feature Models

The motivation behind feature models is to find a practical technique for the modeling and reusing of reusable requirements in a software product line. This motivation is derived from a paradigm for domain-oriented software reuse [15][3], which consists of two basic activities: domain engineering (*a.k.a.* core asset development), and application engineering (*a.k.a.* product development). In the former activity, reusable assets in a software domain are produced or modeled based on existing applications in this domain. In the latter one, these assets are consumed (i.e. reused) to produce new applications/products in this domain. Directed by such a paradigm, feature models are proposed to support the modeling and reusing of reusable assets at the requirements level, that is, to support the modeling and reusing of reusable requirements.

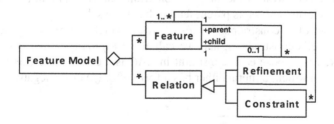

Fig. 1. An abstract metamodel of feature models

The structure of feature models can be generally summarized as *a set of features* with *a set of relations among features* (see Fig. **1**). Each feature encapsulates a cohesive set of individual requirements, and serves as a basic unit in requirements reuse.

There are two common kinds of relation among features: *refinement*, and *constraint*. The purpose of the refinement relation is to organize the usually large number of features in a software product line into a tree structure, in which, high-level abstract features are gradually refined into low-level concrete features. The purpose of the constraints relation is to model the dependencies among features that must be satisfied when doing customization on feature models.

A formal definition of feature models is described in the following definition.

Definition 1. A *feature model* is a 6-tuplet $(F, Root, Refine, BS, RDC, EAC)$[1], where:

- F is a set of n features $\{f_1, f_2, ..., f_n\}$.
- *Root* is feature: $Root \in F$.
- $Refine^{-1}$ is a partial function $F \to F$, which satisfies $\forall f \in F \cdot (f, f) \notin Refine^+$ and $\forall f \in F \cdot (f, Root) \notin Refine$. Through the *Refine* relation, features in F are formed as a tree structure with *Root* as its root node. The physical meaning of a pair $(f_i, f_j) \in Refine^{-1}$ is that f_i is refined from f_j. A *Refine* relation can be further specialized as three subclasses: *decompose*, *specialize*, and *has-an-attribute* [10]. Since the distinguish between three subclasses are irrelevant to the verification of a feature model, we will not explain them furthermore. For convenience, we call f_j the parent of f_i and f_i one of the children of f_j. We use *f.Refine* to denote the feature set consisting of f's children.
- BS is a three-valued predicate $F \to \{true, false, unknown\}$. For a feature f_i, $BS(f_i)$ denotes whether f_i is selected (*true*), removed (*false*) from the feature model, or still undecided (*unknown*). Initially, each feature's <u>b</u>inding-<u>s</u>tate is undecided (and will be changed to selected or removed in later customization activities), except the root feature *Root*, whose binding-state is *selected* initially and can not be changed any more. BS is used to record the customization result of a feature model. The customization of a feature model means to make customization decisions to those undecided features. A customization decision to an undecided feature decides whether to select this feature or to remove it from the current feature model.
- $RDC =_{def} \{ BS(f_i) \Rightarrow BS(f_j) \mid (f_i, f_j) \in Refine^{-1}\}$ is a set of *n-1* constraints. Since these constraints are derived from the *Refine* relation, we call them *refine-derived constraints*. The physical meaning of constraints in *RDC* is that any child feature cannot be selected unless its parent feature has been selected.
- EAC is a set of m constraints $\{c_1, c_2, ..., c_m\}$, which are explicitly added by the feature model's constructors, and we call them *explicitly-added constraints*. For simplicity, we suppose each constraint in *EAC* is a *CNF* clause (i.e. a disjunction of literals), in which, a literal either has a form of $BS(f_i)$ or its negation.

---

[1] It should be pointed out that this definition is a simplified definition of feature models, and the purpose is to make this paper concentrate on the core aspects of feature models' verification. The main simplification is that the *optionality* attribute of features is omitted, and every feature is treated as *optional*, except the root feature that is *mandatory* to every product. Such simplification will not change the essence of feature models' verification, since that any feature model can be easily transformed into a unique feature model conforming to Definition 1, by using the *atomic-set* technique proposed in our previous research [9].

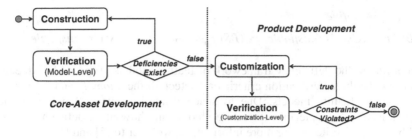

Fig. 2. Reusing requirements in feature models

The reusing of requirements in feature models is usually carried out through a customization-based approach (see Fig. 2). In the core-asset development activity, after a feature model is constructed, the *model-level verification* is carried out to detect possible deficiencies in the feature model. If deficiencies are detected, then the feature model should be reconstructed to eliminate these deficiencies; if no deficiency is detected, then the feature model is allowed to be customized. In the product development activity, after customization, the *customization-level verification* is carried out to detect the violation of constraints. If any constraint is violated, a further customization will be carried out to adjust the current result of customization, and thereby resolve the constraint-violation problem.

2.2 Verification Criteria of Feature Models

In this paper, we only focus on the *model-level verification* of feature models. Based our previous research [8,9], we extract three verification criteria to detect deficiencies in feature models.

Given a feature model $FM = (F, Root, Refine, BS, RDC, EAC)$, if any of the following three criteria is not satisfied, then there must exist deficiencies in FM. In the following, we use Cst to denote the conjunction of all constraints in RDC and EAC. That is,

$$Cst =_{def} \left(\bigwedge_{e \in RDC \cup EAC} e \right).$$

Criterion 1. There exists at least one set of customization decisions to all undecided features in FM that satisfies all constraints in RDC and EAC. That is,

   Cst is satisfiable.

Criterion 2. For each undecided feature $f \in F$, in the premise that f's parent feature is selected without violating any constraint $c \in RDC \cup EAC$, f can be selected without violating any constraint $c \in RDC \cup EAC$. That is,

   $\forall (f_p, f_c) \in Refine \cdot$

   $(BS(f_p) \wedge Cst)$ is satisfiable $\Rightarrow (BS(f_p) \wedge BS(f_c) \wedge Cst)$ is satisfiable.

Criterion 3. For each undecided feature $f \in F$, in the premise that f's parent feature is selected without violating any constraint $c \in RDC \cup EAC$, f can be removed without violating any constraint $c \in RDC \cup EAC$. That is,

$\forall (f_p, f_c) \in Refine \cdot$

$(BS(f_p) \wedge Cst)$ is satisfiable $\Rightarrow$ $(BS(f_p) \wedge \neg BS(f_c) \wedge Cst)$ is satisfiable.

According to the deficiency framework of feature models proposed by Maßen and Lichter [5], the three verification criteria can detect all the *anomaly* and *inconsistency* deficiencies in feature models. Due to space limitation, we will not give further explanations about deficiencies in feature models and how these deficiencies are detected by the three criteria. For more information, we refer to [5] and [10].

2.3 An Intuitive Analysis to *SAT-Solver* Based Verification of Feature Models

Based on their formal definitions, we can easily transform the three verification criteria into a set of *SAT* problems, and thereby check the three criteria by invoking a *SAT-solver*. In the following, we will give an intuitive analysis about the number of times a *SAT-solver* should be invoked in order to check the three verification criteria.

Given a feature model *FM*, suppose it has *n* features, then:

- For Criterion 1, to check whether it is satisfied or not, we need to invoke a *SAT-solver* only *1* time, since this criterion is a *SAT* problem itself.[2]
- For Criterion 2, to check whether it is satisfied or which features violate it, we need to invoke a *SAT-solver* $3 \cdot (n\text{-}1)/2$ times in a general case. The general case is that, for each child feature f_c and its parent f_p, there is a *0.5* possibility that $(BS(f_p) \wedge Cst)$ is satisfiable.
- For Criterion 3, based on the checking result of Criterion 2, to check whether it is satisfied or which features violate it, we need to invoke a *SAT-solver* $(n\text{-}1)/2$ time in the general case.

That is, to detect deficiencies in a feature model with *n* features, in the general case, we need to invoke a *SAT-solver* $2 \cdot (n\text{-}1)$ times.

As far as we have known, the ideas embodied in the analysis above do reflect the common way to feature models' verification used in most (if not all) of those approaches based on third-party's *SAT-solver* or *model-checker* tools. At least, we do not see any of these approaches that propose to use third-party tools in a very different or more efficient way than the way embodied in the analysis above.

3 Verification of Feature Models

In this section, we first introduce two concepts of *refinement paths* and *critical points* in a feature model, and clarify some properties related to the two concepts. After that, we propose a binary-search based method for the verification of Criterion 2, and a simple traversal method for the verification of Criterion 3, respectively.

---

[2] In the following of this paper, we always suppose Criterion 1 is satisfied. Otherwise, if Criterion 1 is unsatisfied, no feature in FM can satisfy Criterion 2 and 3, while the latter two criteria are the real complexity of feature models' verification.

3.1   Refinement Paths and Critical Points

Definition 2. Given a feature model $FM = (F, Root, Refine, BS, RDC, EAC)$ and a feature sequence $P = <p_0, p_1, ..., p_i, p_j, ..., p_l>$, P is called a *refinement path* in FM, iff it satisfies the following two properties:

- $\forall i \in [0, l] \cdot p_i \in F$, and
- $\forall < p_i, p_j >$ in $P \cdot (p_i, p_j) \in Refine$.

Definition 3. Given a feature model $FM = (F, Root, Refine, BS, RDC, EAC)$ and a refinement path $P = <p_0, p_1, ..., p_i, p_j, ..., p_l>$ in FM, P is called a *full refinement path*, iff it satisfies the following two properties:

- p_0 is the *Root* feature, and
- $\forall f \in F \cdot (p_l, f) \notin Refine$.

Fig. 3 gives some examples of *full refinement paths* in a more straightforward way. The right part shows a *Refine* relation and five full refinement paths in this relation. The left part represents the relation through a tree diagram and marks the five refinement paths as four dashed lines. From this figure, we can see that the physical meaning of a full refinement path is actually a path in a tree started with the root node and ended with a leaf node, while a refinement path is just a sub-sequence of a full refinement path.

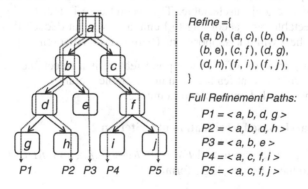

Fig. 3. Examples of full refinement paths

Lemma 1. Given a feature model FM and two features f_a and f_d in FM, suppose $(f_a, f_d) \in Refine^+$ (i.e. f_a is an ancestor of f_d), then

$$(BS(f_d) \wedge Cst) \text{ is satisfiable} \Rightarrow (BS(f_a) \wedge Cst) \text{ is satisfiable}.$$

Proof: Suppose $(BS(f_d) \wedge Cst)$ is satisfiable, that is to say, there exists a set of customization decisions D that satisfies $BS(f_d)$ and all constraints in RDC and EAC. From Definition 1, we can deduce that $Cst \Rightarrow (BS(f_d) \Rightarrow BS(f_a))$, and consequently D also satisfies $(BS(f_d) \Rightarrow BS(f_a))$. As a result, we can conclude that D satisfies both Cst and $BS(f_a)$. Therefore, this lemma is proved.

Lemma 2. Given a feature model *FM* and two features f_a and f_d in *FM*, suppose (f_a, f_d) $\in$ *Refine⁺* (i.e. f_a is an ancestor of f_d), then

$$\neg(BS(f_a) \wedge Cst) \;\Rightarrow\; \neg(BS(f_d) \wedge Cst).$$

Proof: Similar to the proof of Lemma 1.

Definition 4. Given a feature model *FM* and a refinement path *P* in *FM*, a feature in *P* is called a *critical point* iff this feature violates Criterion 2.

Definition 5. Given a feature model *FM* and a feature *f* in *FM*, *f* is called a *selectable* feature, iff $(BS(f) \wedge Cst)$ is satisfiable; *f* is called an *unselectable* feature, iff $(BS(f) \wedge Cst)$ is unsatisfiable.

Obviously, to detect whether a feature is selectable or not, we only need to invoke a *SAT-solver* one time.

Theorem 1. Given a feature model *FM* and a refinement path *P* in *FM*, there exists at most one critical point in *P*.

Proof: Suppose there are two critical points p_{y1} and p_{y2} in *P*. For concise, we use p_{x1} and p_{x2} to denote the parent feature of p_{y1} and p_{y2}, respectively. From Definition 4 and Definition 5, we can know that p_{x1} and p_{x2} are selectable features, while p_{y1} and p_{y2} are unselectable. Without losing the generality, we safely suppose that $(p_{x1}, p_{x2}) \in$ *Re-fine⁺*. Then, there are two possible cases about the relation between p_{y1} and p_{x2}. The first case is that p_{y1} and p_{x2} is the same feature. In this case, we deduce a conflict that p_{y1} is both selectable and unselectable. The second case is that $(p_{y1}, p_{x2}) \in$ *Refine⁺*. Since p_{x2} is selectable, and according to Lemma 1, we can deduce that p_{y1} is select-able, which conflicts with the supposition. Therefore, this theorem is proved.

Corollary 1. Any ancestor of a critical point feature is a selectable feature, and any descendant of a critical point feature is an unselectable feature.
Proof: From Theorem 1, Lemma 1 and Lemma 2.

3.2 Binary-Search Based Verification of Criterion 2

Theorem 2. Given a feature model *FM* = (*F*, *Root*, *Refine*, *BS*, *RDC*, *EAC*), Criterion 2 is *equivalent* to the following logic formula:

$$\forall(f_p, f_c) \in Refine \cdot$$

$(BS(f_p) \wedge Cst)$ *is satisfiable* $\Rightarrow$ $(BS(f_c) \wedge Cst)$ *is satisfiable.*

Proof: To prove this theorem, we only need to prove the following formula is true.

$$\forall(f_p, f_c) \in Refine \cdot$$

$(BS(f_c) \wedge Cst)$ *is satisfiable* $\Leftrightarrow$ $(BS(f_p) \wedge BS(f_c) \wedge Cst)$ *is satisfiable.*

Suppose $(BS(f_c) \wedge Cst)$ is satisfiable, that is, there exists a set of customization decisions *D* that satisfies $BS(f_c)$ and *Cst*. From Definition 1, we know that $(BS(f_c)$ $\Rightarrow BS(f_p)) \in RDC$. Consequently, *D* also satisfies $(BS(f_c) \Rightarrow BS(f_p))$. Since *D* satisfies both $BS(f_c)$ and $(BS(f_c) \Rightarrow BS(f_p))$, we can deduce that *D* also satisfies $BS(f_p)$. As a result, we can conclude that D satisfies $(BS(f_p) \land BS(f_c) \land Cst)$. Therefore, this theorem is proved.

The combination of Theorem 1, Theorem 2 and Corollary 1 points out a binary-search based method to detect the critical point in a refinement path. Fig. 4 demonstrates this method through an illustrative refinement path. This path contains 10 features p_i ($i = 0, 1,.., 9$) and one critical feature p_5 (marked with gray background). Initially, we suppose that p_0 has been detected as a selectable feature. In step 1, p_9 is detected as an unselectable feature. Then, in step 2, p_5 (i.e. a center feature between p_0 and p_9) is detected as unselectable. After that, in step 3, p_3 (i.e. a center feature between p_0 and p_5) is detected as selectable. In step 4, p_4 (i.e. the only feature between p_3 and p_5) is detected as selectable. After step 4, the critical point feature p_5 is finally detected. In such a detection process, the *SAT-solver* is invoked *4* times. Obviously, the complexity of such a binary-search process is $O(\log_2 l)$, while that of a linear-search process is $O(l/2)$ (where, l is the length of a refinement path, i.e. the number of features in the path).

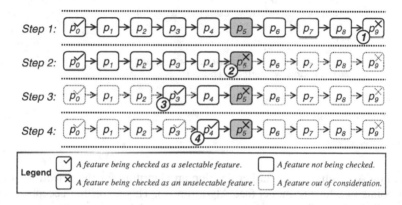

Fig. 4. Binary-search based detection of the critical point in a refinement path

Algorithm 1 gives an implementation of the binary-search based detection method embodied in Fig. 4. This algorithm depends on the invoker providing a *SAT-solver*, and outputs the critical point of the input refinement path.

Algorithm 1. An algorithm of detecting the critical point of a refinement path.

```
Input:
        P   : An refinement path in a feature model, and the first
              element in P has been detected as a selectable
              feature.
       Cst  : The conjunction of all constraints in the feature
              model.
       Sat  : A SAT-Solver object that provide a satisfiable method
              to check whether a propositional formula is
              satisfiable or not.
Output:
  a feature : The critical point of P. A null value means that
              there is no critical point in P.
```

```
Feature detect_critical_point(RefinementPath P,
                                    Constraint Cst, SAT-Solver Sat){
    Feature result = null;
    Feature left, center, right;

    left = P.elementAt(0);
    left.index = 0;
    left.selectable = true;

    right = P.elementAt(p.length-1);
    right.index = P.length-1;
    right.selectable = Sat.satisfiable(Cst∧BS(right));

    if(right.selectable == false){
        while((right.index - left.index) > 1){
            int index = right.index - (right.index-left.index)/2;
            center = P.elementAt(index);
            center.index = index;
            center.selectable = Sat.satisfiable(Cst∧BS(center));

            if(center.selectable == false){
                right = center;
                right.selectable = center.selectable;
                right.index = center.index;
            }else{
                left = center;
                left.selectable = center.selectable;
                left.index = center.index;
            }
        }
        result = right;
    }

    return result;
}
```

Based on Algorithm 1, we further develop an algorithm for the detection of all the critical points in a feature model (see Algorithm 2). This algorithm accepts a set that contains all the full refinement paths in a feature model as one of its input, and outputs all the critical points in the feature model. The detecting process consists of a *while-loop* structure; in each loop, a refinement path is fetched from the refinement path set and then detected for the critical point.

Algorithm 2. An algorithm of detecting critical points in a feature model.

Input:

FRP	:	A set that contains all the full refinement paths in a feature model.
Cst	:	The conjunction of all constraints in the feature model.
Sat	:	A SAT-Solver object as in Algorithm 1.

Output:

A feature set	:	The set contains all critical point features in the feature model.

```
FeatureSet detect_critical_points(RefinementPathSet FRP,
                                    Constraint Cst, SAT-Solver Sat){
    FeatureSet Result = {};
    while(FRP.isEmpty() == false){
```

```
RefinementPath P = FRP.popAnElement();
Feature cp = detect_critical_point(P, Cst, Sat);

if (cp != null){
    Result.add(cp);
    FRP.remove(FRP.getAllPathsContaining(cp));
}

int index = (cp != null) ? P.getIndexOf(cp) : P.length-1;
for(int i = index-1; i > 0; i--){
    Feature f = P.getElementAt(i);
    RefinementPathSet RP = FRP.getAllPathsContaining(f);
    for(each e in RP){
        e.removeElementBefore(f);
    }
}
}

return Result;
}
```

The main characteristic of this algorithm is that it takes advantage of the overlap among refinement paths to optimize the detecting process (i.e. to decrease the number of times to invoke a *SAT-solver*). The optimization involves two cases: *cp-detected* case and *no-cp-detected* case. The former denotes the case that a critical point is detected from a refinement path fetched from the *FRP* set, while the latter denotes the case that no critical point is detected from a fetched refinement path.

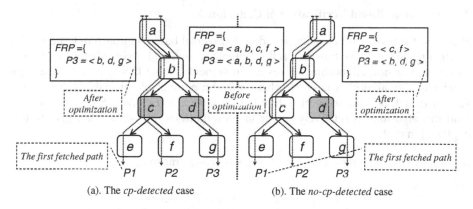

(a). The *cp-detected* case   (b). The *no-cp-detected* case

Fig. 5. Utilizing overlaps among refinement paths in the detection of critical points

In the *cp-detected* case, two optimizing actions are performed:
- The first action is to remove those refinement paths that contain the detected critical point from the *FRP* set, since that these refinement paths do not need to be checked again for the critical point (see Theorem 1). This action will decrease the size of the *FRP* set, and thereby decrease the number of times to invoke a *SAT-solver*.
- The second action is to remove certain elements from some refinement paths in the *FRP* set. That is, for each refinement path *P* in *FRP* that constrains an ancestor of the detected critical point, then all this ancestor's ancestors will be removed from *P*, since that these removed features all are selectable features and

do not need to be checked again for whether selectable or not (see Corollary 1). This action will decrease the length of certain refinement paths in the *FRP* set, and thereby decrease the number of times to invoke a *SAT-solver*.

In the *no-cp-detected* case, an optimizing action similar to the second action in the *cp-detected* case is performed to decrease the length of certain refinement paths in the *FRP* set. That is, for each refinement path *P* in *FRP* that constrains a feature in the fetched refinement path, all this feature's ancestors will be removed from *P*.

Fig. 5 demonstrates the two cases and the effect of the optimizing actions through an illustrative *Refine* relation. The left part shows an instance of the *cp-detected* case, in which, we suppose *c*, *d* are two critical points, and *P1* is the first element fetched from the *FRP* set. As a result, *c* will be detected as a critical point. Before the two optimizing actions are performed, the *FRP* set contains two refinement paths <*a*, *b*, *c*, *f*> and <*a*, *b*, *d*, *g*>, while after optimization, the *FRP* set contains only one path <*b*, *d*, *g*>. That is, after optimization, both the size of *FPR* and the length of elements in *FPR* decrease. The right part shows an instance of the *no-cp-detected* case, in which, we suppose *d* is the only critical point, and *P1* also is the first fetched element. As a result, no critical point will be detected. Before the optimizing action in the *no-cp-detected* case is performed, the *FRP* set contains two paths <*a*, *b*, *c*, *f*> and <*a*, *b*, *d*, *g*>, while after optimization, the *FRP* set contains two reduced paths <*c*, *f*> and <*b*, *d*, *g*>. That is, after optimization, the length of elements in *FPR* decreases.

3.3 Traversal Based Verification of Criterion 3

Based on the verification results, we adopt a traversal based approach to Criterion 3's verification. That is, we traverse each selectable feature and check whether it satisfies Criterion 3 or not. Algorithm 3 gives an implementation of this approach. The complexity of this algorithm is $O(n)$, where n is the number of selectable features in a feature model, and the basic operation is to invoke a *SAT-Solver*. Since the idea behind this algorithm is relatively simple and straightforward, we will not give further explanation of it.

Algorithm 3. An algorithm of detecting features violating Criterion 3.

```
Input:
        Refine  :  The Refine relation of a feature model.
            CP  :  A  set  that  contains  all  critical  points  in  the
                   feature model
           Cst  :  The  conjunction  of  all  constraints  in  the  feature
                   model.
           Sat  :  A SAT-Solver object as in Algorithm 1.
Output:
      A feature  :  The set contains all features that violate Criterion
          set        3.
FeatureSet detect_features_violating_criterion3
                                        (Refine, CP, Cst, Sat){
    FeatureSet Result = {};
    FeatureSet US = CP∪CP.descendants();
```

```
for(each e in Refine){
    if(US.contains(e.parent)||US.contains(e.child)){
        Refine.remove(e);
    }
}
for(each e in Refine){
    if(!Sat.satisfiable(Cst ∧ BS(e.parent) ∧ ¬ BS(e.child))){
        Result.add(e.child);
    }
}
return Result;
}
```

4 Experiments

In this section, we first introduce two families of feature models: the *simple-branch* family and the *binary-branch* family, which serve as the test cases of our experiments, and then apply our binary-search based approach and the *top-down* linear-search based approach to the two families of feature models, respectively, to show the effectiveness of our approach.

4.1 Two Families of Feature Models

Fig. 6 shows the *simple-branch* family of feature models, in which, a feature model only branches at the root level, and all features in the middle level are critical points. There are two parameters m, n to instance a feature model in this family: m is the numbers of levels in a feature model, and n is the number of branches at the root level.

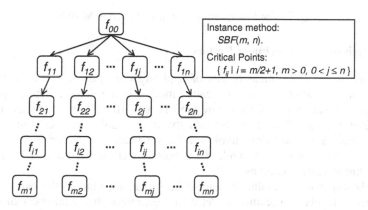

Fig. 6. The *Simple-Branch* Family of Feature Models

Fig. 7 shows the *binary-branch* family of feature models. The characteristic of this family is that any feature model branches at the root level, each feature in the first level has two branches, and all features in the middle level are critical points. Similar to the *simple-branch* family, there are also two parameters m, n to instance a feature model in this family: m is the numbers of levels in a feature model, and n is the number of branches at the root level.

There are two issues that should be pointed out. First, in both of the two families, critical points are all at the middle level. The reason is that we want to make a comparison between our approach and the top-down linear-search approach, for which, it is a general case that critical points appear at the middle of a refinement path. Second, although we cannot see constraints in these two families explicitly, constraints are actually reflected by the critical points – that is, it is the constraints that caused the existence of critical points. And in these two families, for flexibility, we just artificially assign critical points to features. If it is necessary, for every member in the two families, a corresponding feature model with explicit constraints could be constructed, which have the same refinement structure and the same distribution of critical points.

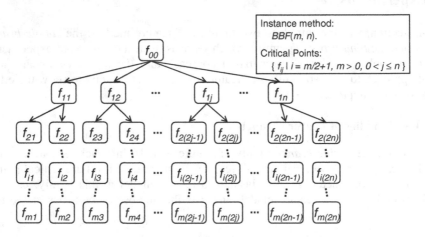

Fig. 7. The *Binary-Branch* Family of Feature Models

4.2 Analysis of the Experiment Results

Table 1 shows the experiment results of applying our approach and the top-down linear-search approach to two sets of feature models in the two families, respectively. Each of the two sets contains 16 feature models with 10 as its n parameter, while the m parameter increases from 1 to 16 gradually. In this table, the B columns show the number of times a *SAT-solver* is invoked in the verification of Criterion 2 by using the binary-search based approach, while the L columns show the number by using the top-down linear-search based method.

From the experiment results, we can observe that, for both of the two familes, as the number of levels in a feature model increases, although the numbers of invoking times in the two methods are both increases, the number in the binary-search based approach increases at a low rate than that of the linear-search based approach. That is, as the number of levels in feature models increase, our approach manifests a better scalability than the linear-search based approach.

Table 1. Experiment Results

Parameter		Simple-Branch Family			Binary-Branch Family		
m	n	B	L	Ratio (B/L)	B	L	Ratio (B/L)
1	10	10	10	100%	10	10	100%
2	10	20	20	100%	15	15	100%
3	10	30	20	150%	25	15	167%
4	10	30	30	100%	30	25	120%
5	10	30	30	100%	30	35	86%
6	10	40	40	100%	35	45	78%
7	10	40	40	100%	35	55	64%
8	10	40	50	80%	40	65	62%
9	10	40	50	80%	40	75	53%
10	10	50	60	83%	45	85	53%
11	10	40	60	67%	40	95	42%
12	10	50	70	71%	45	105	43%
13	10	40	70	57%	40	115	35%
14	10	50	80	63%	45	125	36%
15	10	50	80	63%	45	135	33%
16	10	50	90	56%	50	145	34%

5   Related Work

The approach proposed in this paper is a succeeded work of our previous research on the optimization of feature model verification. In our previous research, we have proposed two techniques to reduce the number of features and constraints to be checked during the verification of a feature model. One is the *atomic-set* technique which treats a set of features as a single feature [9], and the other one is an optimization strategy that removes verification-irrelevant features and constraints from a feature model [8]. It should be pointed that, the approach proposed in this paper is orthogonal to the above two techniques, and thus can be safely integrated with each others in feature models' verification.

Existing approaches to feature models' verification can be generally classified into two categories. One category consists of those approaches based on third-party tools. In these approaches, the verification problem of feature models are firstly transformed into *SAT*, *CSP*, or other kinds of well-resolved formal problems, and then a third-party tool is invoked to find solutions of these transformed problems. The approach proposed in this paper can be classified into this category. However, as far as our knowledge, we do not observe any of these approaches that focus on how use third-party tools in efficient ways.

The other category consists of approaches that develop specific algorithms for feature models' verification. Unfortunately, there exist few approaches in this category. One distinctive approach in this category is a simplified LTMS (Logic Truth Maintenance Systems) algorithm proposed by Batory [1], considering the characteristics of feature models' verification. This algorithm aims to find those features that must be removed or selected in the customization to feature models, through constraints propagation. This algorithm focuses on how to detect customization-level deficiencies, and thus can not detect all kinds of model-level deficiencies. For example, considering the following two constraints: $\neg a \lor b$ and $\neg a \lor b$, this algorithm can not detect that a is an unselectable feature until a user tries to select a. Although a full version LTMS algorithm may detect such kind of model-level deficiencies, the direct invoking on a full version LTMS algorithm is just like invoking on a third-party tool, which still does not focus on the problem of how to invoke third-party tools in efficient ways, while this problem is particularly concentrated in this paper.

6 Conclusions and Future Work

In this paper, we proposed a binary-search based approach to feature models' verification, an approach that employs the binary search method to locate critical points in refinement paths, and thereby possesses a lower complexity. The motivation of this approach is to decrease the number of times a *SAT-solver* is invoked during the verification of a feature model, and thus improve the verification efficiency. Preliminary experiments show that our approach manifests a better scalability than the linear-search based approach, as the number of levels in feature models increases.

Our future work will focus efficient approaches for Criterion 2's verification. That is, how to detect optional features that actually can not be removed when its parent is selected in efficient ways. In our current research, we only take a simple traversal based approach to Criterion 2's verification. The complexity of such an approach is $O(n)$, and we want to find new approaches that have a complexity lower than $O(n)$.

Acknowledgments. The authors would like to thank the anonymous reviewers for their valuable comments and suggestions. This work is supported in part by National Natural Science Foundation of China under Grant No. 60821003, 60703065 and 60873059, National Basic Research Program of China (973) under Grant No. 2009CB320701, and National Key Technology R&D Program under Grant No. 2008BAH32B02.

References

1. Batory, D.: Feature Models, Grammars, and Propositional Formulas. In: Obbink, H., Pohl, K. (eds.) SPLC 2005. LNCS, vol. 3714, pp. 7–20. Springer, Heidelberg (2005)
2. Clements, P., Northrop, L.: Software Product Lines: Practices and Patterns. Addison-Wesley, Boston (2002)
3. Czarnecki, K., Kim, C.H.P.: Cardinality-Based Feature Modeling and Constraints: A Progress Report. In: OOPSLA 2005 International Workshop on Software Factories (2005)
4. Kang, K.C., Cohen, S.G., Hess, J.A., Novak, W.E., Peterson, A.S.: Feature-Oriented Domain Analysis Feasibility Study. Technical Reports, SEI-90-TR-21, Software Engineering Institute, Carnegie Mellon University (1990)
5. von der Maßen, T., Lichter, H.: Deficiencies in feature models. In: Workshop on Software Variability Management for Product Derivation, in Conjunction with the 3rd Software Product Line Conference (2004)
6. Mannion, M.: Using First-Order Logic for Product Line Model Validation. In: Chastek, G.J. (ed.) SPLC 2002. LNCS, vol. 2379, pp. 176–187. Springer, Heidelberg (2002)

7. Trinidad, P., Benavides, D., Durán, A., Ruiz-Cortés, A., Toro, M.: Automated Error Analysis for the Agilization of Feature Modeling. Journal of Systems and Software 81(6), 883–896 (2008)
8. Yan, H., Zhang, W., Zhao, H., Mei, H.: An Optimization Strategy to Feature Models' Verification by Eliminating Verification-Irrelevant Features and Constraints. In: Edwards, S.H., Kulczycki, G. (eds.) ICSR 2009. LNCS, vol. 5791, pp. 65–75. Springer, Heidelberg (2009)
9. Zhang, W., Zhao, H., Mei, H.: A Propositional Logic-Based Method for Verification of Feature Models. In: 6th International Conference on Formal Engineering Methods, pp. 115–130 (2004)
10. Zhang, W., Mei, H., Zhao, H.: Feature-Driven Requirements Dependency Analysis and High-Level Software Design. Requirements Engineering Journal 11(3), 205–220 (2006)

Supporting Consistency Checking between Features and Software Product Line Use Scenarios

Mauricio Alférez[1], Roberto E. Lopez-Herrejon[2], Ana Moreira[1], Vasco Amaral[1], and Alexander Egyed[2]

[1] CITI/Departamento de Informática, Faculdade de Ciências e Tecnologia
Universidade Nova de Lisboa, Caparica, Portugal
[2] Institute for Systems Engineering and Automation
Johannes Kepler University Linz, Austria
{mauricio.alferez,amm,vasco.amaral}@di.fct.unl.pt,
{roberto.lopez,alexander.egyed}@jku.at

Abstract. A key aspect for effective variability modeling of Software Product Lines *(SPL)* is to harmonize the need to achieve separation of concerns with the need to satisfy consistency of requirements and constraints. Techniques for variability modeling such as feature models used together with use scenarios help to achieve separation of stakeholders' concerns but ensuring their joint consistency is largely unsupported. Therefore, inconsistent assumptions about system's expected use scenarios and the way in which they vary according to the presence or absence of features reduce the models usefulness and possibly renders invalid SPL systems. In this paper we propose an approach to check consistency —the verification of semantic relationships among the models— between features and use scenarios that realize them. The novelty of this approach is that it is specially tailored for the SPL domain and considers complex composition situations where the customization of use scenarios for specific products depends on the presence or absence of sets of features. We illustrate our approach and supporting tools using *variant* constructs that specify how the inclusion of sets of *variable features* (that refer to uncommon requirements between products of a SPL) adapt use scenarios related to other features.

1 Introduction

A *Software Product Line* (SPL) can be defined as "a set of software–intensive systems sharing a common, managed set of features that satisfy the specific needs of a particular market segment or mission and that are developed from a common set of core assets in a prescribed way"[7]. In SPLs, requirements are organized by *features* that are useful to express product functionalities concisely [19]. There are *common* features between all the products in the product line (sometimes called *mandatory* features), and there are *variable* features that allow distinguishing between products in a product line. In SPL development the *problem space* focuses on variability modeling and describes the different features available in an SPL and their interdependencies. A common representation to model variability are the *feature models,* where features are realized with correspondent artifacts, for example use scenarios diagrams [8].

K. Schmid (Ed.): ICSR 2011, LNCS 6727, pp. 20–35, 2011.

To produce particular products from a SPL, feature realizations have to be composed according to a specific selection of features from a feature model usually called *product configuration* (also referred to *feature model configuration*). This process requires a mapping between features from a feature model, and artifacts such as use scenarios that realize them. A *use scenario* is a widely used technique that describes, step by step, how an actor is intending to use a system [14]. A number of different approaches have been proposed to create mappings among features and models [13,8,20]. However, ensuring consistency between feature models and recurring requirements specifications techniques such as use scenario modeling has not been thoroughly researched. In this context, by consistency checking we mean the verification of semantic relationships among features and use scenarios. Inconsistent assumptions about system's expected use scenarios and their variations according to the selection of different features, reduce the models usefulness and possibly renders invalid systems. Therefore, it is essential in SPL to determine whether the variability model and its use scenarios defined in the domain requirements specification enable the derivation of any product requirements specification that contains inconsistent requirements.

When a model-based approach is used to represent use scenarios (e.g., in form of use cases or activity diagrams), consistency goes beyond syntactical or semantic errors of each kind of model in isolation. For example, an actor that is not associated with any use case, a dangling node, a loop without exit conditions in activity diagrams or specific set of features that are both simultaneously (and incorrectly) declared as excluding and depending. It means that we aim at taking into account constraints that are not merely expressed in terms of only one language's metamodel which is generally well supported by UML editors in the case of use cases and activity diagrams (e.g., using OCL or hard-coded restrictions particular of each editor) or feature model editors (e.g., using *domain constraints* expressing features interdependencies, and hard-coded restrictions that constrain the construction of the models to conform to their metamodel). In our work, much of consistency checking difficulty lies on maintaining consistency among several, interrelated models. This can become a time-consuming and error prone task given that the number of ways to compose feature realizations grows exponentially with the possible number of SPL features that can be used in a particular product.

In this paper, we present an approach whose driving objective is to enable consistency checking in the problem space between requirements models such as use scenarios and features. It transforms generic constraints expressions between single features to rules specifically tailored for use scenarios and set of features. Then, it employs propositional formulas to relate these specialized rules to the models involved in the creation of customized use scenarios for specific products. These propositional formulas are produced based on the relationships between: i) *domain constraints* that can be obtained from the SPL feature model, ii) the meaning of the relationships between fragments in the use scenarios and SPL features, and iii) a *composition model* that specifies how to vary SPL use scenarios. Checking if all the products in an SPL satisfy consistency constraints is based on searching for a satisfying assignment of a propositional formula. Therefore, our tool translates propositional formulas that can be evaluated by *satisfiability* (SAT) solvers [1]. In case there are constraints that are not satisfied by the SPL, our tool presents to the developer the particular features and fragments of the use scenarios

involved in the violation of the constraint. In our home automation case study this information was useful to take informed decisions about the modifications and additions of
domain constraints, use scenarios and its composition specification. The results of the
application of our approach are encoraging because they did not show scalability and
performance issues, however, we need more extensive validation of our approach with
different case studies.

2   Background and Motivation

To understand consistency between features and use scenarios let us introduce first the
models we use: features model, use case/activity diagrams, mapping model between
features and use cases/activity models, and a composition specification model. After
this, we exemplify inconsistency using these models.

2.1   Models Involved in Consistency Checking

Feature Model.   A feature model describes a set of all possible valid product configurations [8]. A configuration specifies a concrete product in terms of its features.

Figure 1-1 shows a sample feature model of part of our running example, the *Smart
Home* SPL [18]. Smart Home has four optional features, AUTOMATED WINDOWS(AW),
AUTOMATED HEATING (AH), REMOTE HEATING CONTROL (RHC) and INTERNET
as a mean to control the heater and other devices remotely. Also, it has a set of common
features, such as MANUAL WINDOWS and MANUAL HEATING that will be included
in all the target products to be produced using the Smart Home SPL.

Specific product configurations can be defined selecting optional features in the feature model 1-1. Figure 1-2 shows a sample product configuration of the Smart Home
SPL called PRODUCT-1 that will be used to illustrate consistency problems between
features and use scenarios. PRODUCT-1 has all features except AUTOMATED WIN-
DOWS (AW). Domain constraints in the feature model such as the REQUIRES relationship from RHC to INTERNET, can be added incrementally and in parallel with the
creation of use scenarios (discussed below).

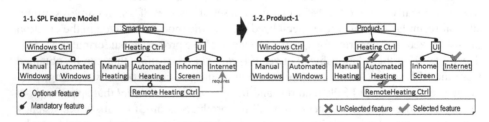

Fig. 1. (1) Simplified sample of the Smart Home feature model; (2) Sample SmartHome configuration that excludes the Automated Windows feature

Use Scenarios. Features can be realized with other models such as use scenarios. To model use scenarios we employ use case and activity diagrams because they are commonly used in mainstream UML-based methods such as RUP [16] and, in contrast to mere free-form textual scenario descriptions, they help to reduce ambiguity in the specifications [19].

Use case and activity diagrams provide a description of what products in the domain should do. Feature models determine which functionality can be selected when engineering new products from the SPL. Therefore, product requirements specifications consist of customized use cases diagrams and specific paths through those use cases represented in activity diagrams. The customization is guided by a composition specification discussed in next subsection.

Figure 2-1 (Left) shows part of the final target model composed for PRODUCT-1. The INCLUDES relationship describes the case where one use case, the *base* use case, includes the functionality of another use case, the *inclusion* use case. The INCLUDES relationship supports the reuse of functionality in a use case diagram and is used to express that the behavior of the *inclusion* use case is common to two or more use cases. Note that INCLUDES relationships between use cases may constrain the relationship between the features related to them. For example, the INCLUDES relationship between the base use case CTRLTEMPREMOTELY that includes the use case OPENANDCLOSEWINAUTO may imply that feature REMOTEHEATINGCNTRL(SH) requires feature AUTOMATED-WINDOWS (AW). We discuss this and other consistency constraints in Section 3.

Figure 2-1 (Right) shows an activity diagram that depicts the possible scenarios for the use case CNTRLTEMPREMOTELY that comprises activities for the use cases OPENANDCLOSEWINAUTO, CALCENERGYCONSUMPTION and ADJUSTHEATER-VALUE. Within this activity diagram it is possible to select several scenarios that correspond to different paths. Two of all the possible scenarios are: Scenario i) includes reaching the in-home temperature and save energy by means of closing some windows, and Scenario ii) to use the heater to reach the desired in-home temperature. It is important to note that the customization of activity diagrams and scenarios depends on the features chosen for the SPL product and also on the relationship with the use case model. For example, in PRODUCT-1 the feature AUTOMATEDWINDOWS was not selected, therefore the WINACTUATOR actor in the use case diagram as well as the swimlane (also called activity partition) related to WINDOWSACTUATOR should not appear in any diagram. Therefore, scenarios such as i) are not realizable because of the lack of windows actuators. This and other constraints will be discussed in Section 3.

Composition Specification. To evidence consistency problems between features and use scenarios we employ a composition process (also called, derivation process) for use cases and activity diagrams. Languages such as the VML4RE (Variability Modelling Language for Requirements) [20,4] help to specify how use scenarios can be customized.

Figure 3 illustrates a composition specification that guides the specification of the transformation of requirements specifications of products in the SmartHome SPL. VML4RE [20,4] is a textual language that allows associating *actions*, that wrap a set of model transformations for specific requirements models such as use cases and activity

2-1. Use Scenarios: Customized SPL Use case diagram (Left) and Activity diagrams (Right) for Product-1

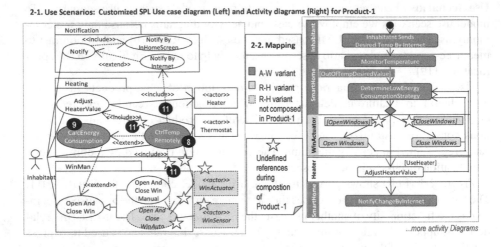

...more activity Diagrams

Fig. 2. (1) Referencing undefined model fragments during composition for PRODUCT-1 in the Use Case model (left side) and in the Activity Diagram for the CntrlTempRemotely scenario (right side). (2) Mapping variants to model fragments.

diagrams, to combinations of features written as logic expressions that we call *feature expressions*. Feature expressions can be i) *atomic* that represent single features such as "Automated Windows" in Figure 3, Line 1, and ii) *compound* that also contain logic operators such as AND, NOT and OR such as "And ("Remote Heating Ctrl","Automated Heating","Internet")" in line 7. Feature expressions evaluation works as follows: if AU-TOMATEDHEATING, REMOTE HEATING CTRL, AUTOMATED HEATING and INTER-NET features are selected in a product configuration, the feature expression associated to the variant named "R-H" (i.e., the compound feature expression: And ("Remote Heating Ctrl","Automated Heating","Internet")) will be evaluated to TRUE. The consequence of this is that the actions that are inside the "R-H" variant block (Figure 3, lines 6-13) will be processed and applied to a base model. For example, the CNTRLTEM-PREMOTELY use case will be inserted into the package HEATING and then it will be related to other use cases using INCLUDES and EXTENDS relationships. If more than one feature expression is evaluated to TRUE, the default composition order follows a top-down sequence (which corresponds to a left-right sequence in Figure 3).

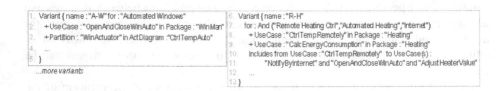

Fig. 3. Composition specification of variants A-W and R-H

Mapping Model. Figure 2-1 (Left) and (Right) show use case and activity diagrams fragments, such as actors and use cases, related with the variants shown in Figure 3. The base mechanism to relate requirements model fragments to features is to use a correspondence table (or mapping table), as presented by [11], [19] and [3]. In our case, we parse the composition specification to generate the mapping between variants and parts of the use cases, therefore, for example if variant named A-W inserts the OPENANDCLOSEWINAUTO use case, we link A-W to OPENANDCLOSEWINAUTO. To facilitate the visualization of such relationships with the models, in the figure we assign different gray tones to the models fragments according to the features that they are related to (see mapping in Figure 2-2). Please note that specific model fragments could be related also to more than one variant. This may be considered as a m-to-n (m and n >= 1) mapping between variants and model fragments and is not illustrated in Figure 2.

2.2   Consistency Checking Motivation

Consistency checking has to ensure that inconsistent requirements do not become part of the requirements specifications of a given product. Our work aims at guaranteeing that *all* the products that could be derived from a feature model indeed have consistent requirements specifications. This is achieved through the description and verification of semantic relationships between feature model and use scenarios. One of the possible inconsistencies between features and use scenarios in the Smart Home SPL happens between the relationship of variants R-H and A-W, and the INCLUDES relationship between the use cases CNTRLTEMPREMOTELY and OPENANDCLOSEWINAUTO which are related to R-H and A-W variants respectively. The domain requirements are:

R1- Only one, none or both R-H and A-W variants can be included in a product. (This is implicit in the feature model and composition model because all the features in the feature expression of R-H variant are optional (i.e., REMOTE HEATING CNTRL, AUTOMATED HEATING and INTERNET are optional features), and the only feature in the feature expression A-W is also optional (i.e., the AUTOMATED WINDOWS feature is optional)); and

R2- If the use case CNTRLTEMPREMOTELY is provided in a product then the use case OPENANDCLOSEWINAUTO must be provided too, (This is implicit in the includes relationship from the use case CNTRLTEMPREMOTELY to OPENANDCLOSEWIN-AUTO in the use case diagram in Figure 2-1 (Left)).

Figure 2-1 shows PRODUCT-1 built using the composition model shown in Figure 3. In PRODUCT-1 the feature expression of variant R-H (3, line 7) evaluates to TRUE. However, because Figure 1-2 does not include the AUTOMATED WINDOWS feature, the feature expression of variant A-W (i.e., AUTOMATED WINDOWS) (3, Line 1) evaluates to FALSE and the actions inside its variant block are not processed. We annotated the diagrams with numbers that represent the line in Figure 3 where a composition action is specified. Note that we omitted some of the actions, for example, the insertion of some actors such as WINSENSOR and WINACTUATOR and some partitions such as HEATER.

PRODUCT-1 presents inconsistent requirements *R1* and *R2*. This is evident during composition of use scenarios. See lines 10-11 when the action "Includes from UseCase

: "CtrlTempRemotely" to UseCase(s) : "NotifyByInternet" and "OpenAndCloseWin-Auto" and "AdjustHeaterValue" " references elements such as the use case OPENAND-CLOSEWINAUTO that do not exist in the model. In this case, PRODUCT-1 fulfills requirement *R1*, but not requirement *R2*. The result is that the functionality provided by OPENANDCLOSEWINAUTO will not be present in the requirements of PRODUCT-1 and therefore it will not be taken into account in later stages of its development process.

It is not too difficult to check consistency manually in small examples with a reduced number of features such as the one mentioned previously. One solution to solve the inconsistency for our example would be to guarantee the presence of the feature AUTOMATED WINDOWS when AUTOMATIC HEATING or REMOTE HEATING CTRL are selected, in every possible feature model configuration using a domain constraint REQUIRES. Another solution is to establish that AUTOMATED WINDOWS will be a mandatory feature in the SPL. However, the number of possible feature combinations may grow exponentially with the number of features of the SPL. The result of this explosion is that it becomes unfeasible to manually check the consistency of all the products.

To guarantee that all the products that could be derived from a feature model indeed have consistent requirements specifications we take into account the relationships between domain requirements specified using use scenarios and feature models to propose rules and constraints to support consistency checking in SPLs use scenarios as it is shown in the next section.

3   Consistency Checking between Features and Use Scenarios

While some product configurations of a feature model may generate consistent use scenarios, other product configurations based on the same feature model could lead to inconsistencies in the requirements specifications. In this section we present our approach for consistency checking between SPL features and use scenarios.

3.1   Approach Overview

Figure 4 presents an overview of our approach. Section 2 explained and exemplified the specification of a feature model, use scenarios (Figure 4, Step 1), and the mapping between variants and fragments of the use scenarios (Step 2). Based on previous work [17], we have developed a consistency checking approach for use scenario composition based on variants. This approach relies on the domain evaluation of feature expressions, written as propositional formulas that are associated to a *variant* and transformations of use scenarios called *actions*. We denote D_f the domain constraints that can be derived from a feature model of an SPL and are expressed in terms of atomic features f (Step 3), and C_{VAR_f} denote composition constraints that will be derived in next section (Step 4) and are expressed in terms of variants (VAR_f). We use propositional logic to express and relate D_f and C_{VAR_f} (Step 5). Because we are interested in verifying that all members of the product line satisfy a given composition constraint, Equation 1 should not be "satisfiable". If it is satisfied, it means that there is a product of the product line that does not meet constraint C_{VAR_f}. The violating product configurations can be identified

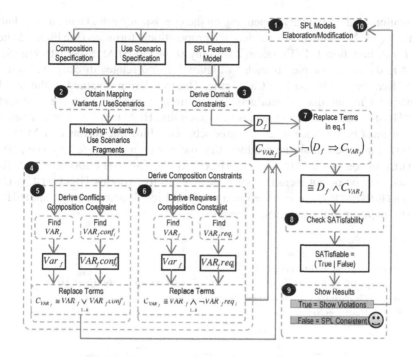

Fig. 4. Overview of Our Consistency Checking Approach

using a SAT solver (Step 7 and 8). This can support the developer to take informed decisions on modifications of the initial SPL models, for example, creating or modifying domain constraints (Step 10).

$$\neg \left(D_f \Rightarrow C_{VAR_f} \right) \tag{1}$$

Section 2-1 shows that at least one product (i.e., PRODUCT-1) from the products that can be configured based on the feature model of the Smart Home SPL is inconsistent. In that case, *composition constraints* (also called *implementation constraints*) between the elements in use scenarios such as the INCLUDES between use cases, imply the application of domain constraints for example, turning the AUTOMATEDWINDOWS feature from optional to mandatory or creating a REQUIRES dependency (also called domain constraint) from AUTOMATEDHEATING to AUTOMATEDWINDOWS. That particular inconsistency that will help to explain our approach can be defined as:

– *Rule Required Inclusion Use Case:* at least one variant ($VAR_f req_i$), defines an inclusion use case that must be selected in every feature configuration that contains the variant (VAR_f) which introduces a base use case linked to the inclusion use case.

3.2 Deriving Domain Constraints (D_f)

Figure 4 - Step 3 shows that the domain constraints are derived from a SPL feature model. Therefore the D_f in a SPL is the same for all the possible products configurations and do not vary depending on the consistency rule. Using a well-known translation table between feature models and propositional formulas (see Figure 5) helps to get D_f in Equation 1. In Equation 2 we only show the HEATING-CTRL branch because it is the most complex branch in Figure 1-1 and relates directly with our exemplar "Required Inclusion Use Case" rule. The translation obtained in the first line of Equation 1 means that all products unconditionally must contain the root feature SMARTHOME. The second line means that given that HEATING CTRL is a mandatory feature, it must be included in all the products. The third line means that MANUAL-HEATING is included in all the products that include their parent feature (i.e., HEAT-INGCTRL), in contrast to AUTOMATEDHEATING and REMOTEHEATINGCTRL (lines 3-4), that may be or not included when their respective parents HEATINGCTRL and AUTOMATEDHEATING are included in a product. Line 5 means that REMOTEHEAT-INGCTRL *requires* of the INTERNET feature.

1. $(SmartHome \Leftrightarrow TRUE) \land$
2. $(SmartHome \Leftrightarrow HeatingCtrl) \land$
3. $(HeatingCtrl \Leftrightarrow ManualHeating) \land (AutomatedHeating \Rightarrow HeatingCtrl) \land$
4. $(RemoteHeatingCtrl \Rightarrow AutomatedHeating) \land$
5. $(RemoteHeatingCtrl \Rightarrow Internet)$

$$(2)$$

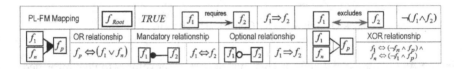

Fig. 5. Mapping from Feature Model to Propositional Logic [6]

In this section we addressed D_f, the first part of Equation 1. Next section presents C_{VAR_f} that comprises a set of constraints that are essential for consistency between use scenarios and the set of domain constraints expressed in Equation 2.

3.3   Deriving Composition Constraints (C_{VAR_f})

Composition constraints act as consistency rules describing the semantic relationships that must hold among the different models. Figure 4-4 shows two kinds of composition constraints that can be expressed in propositional logic. We classified them according to the type of domain constraint that they relate with: i) a constraint that implies a REQUIRES relationship between features that therefore implies dependencies between variants (Figure 4- Step 4), and ii) a constraint that implies a EXCLUDES relationship (Figure 4- Step 6) between features and therefore implies incompatibilities between variants (Figure 4- Step 5). This section shows those constraint equations expressed in propositional logic.

EXCLUDES Relationship: Let VAR_f be a variant that defines a model element e. A variant $VAR_f conf_1$ conflicts with VAR_f if $VAR_f conf_1$ defines a model element c

which cannot be present in the same requirements specifications of a product where element e is also present. Therefore, because of the incompatibility between elements e and c, if variant VAR_f is selected then variant $VAR_f conf_1$ should not be selected in the same product configuration. This is denoted in the following expression where k represents the number of variants in the composition specification:

$$C_{VAR_f} \equiv VAR_f \Rightarrow \neg \left(\overset{\vee}{_{1..k}} (VAR_f conf_i) \right) \equiv \neg VAR_f \vee \neg \left(\overset{\vee}{_{1..k}} (VAR_f conf_i) \right) \quad (3)$$

$$\equiv VAR_f \wedge \overset{\vee}{_{1..k}} VAR_f conf_i$$

REQUIRES Relationship: Let VAR_f be a variant that refers to a model element e defined by another variant. To be consistent, the requirements specifications of a product that includes variant VAR_f must also include at least one other variant $VARreq_i$ (required variant) where element e is defined. This is denoted in the following expression where k represents the number of variants in the composition model:

$$C_{VAR_f} \equiv VAR_f \Rightarrow \overset{\vee}{_{1..k}} (VAR_f req_i) \equiv \neg VAR_f \vee \overset{\vee}{_{1..k}} (VAR_f req_i) \quad (4)$$

$$\equiv VAR_f \wedge \overset{\wedge}{_{1..k}} \neg VAR_f req_i$$

The rule "Required Inclusion Use Case" mentioned at the beginning of this section is an example of this last kind of constraint expression. An instance of this constraint is found in our motivation example related to the use scenario of CNTRLTEMPRE-MOTELY. For example, given that the variant VAR_f = R-H is selected (i.e., a product with REMOTE HEATING CNTRL, AUTOMATED HEATING and INTERNET features), and it is related to the base use case CTRLTEMPREMOTELY, we want to guarantee that there are at least one variant (e.g., $VAR_f \ req_1$ = A-W) related to the inclusion use case OPENANDCLOSEWINAUTO (i.e., model element e = use case OPENANDCLOSEWIN-AUTO), and that its feature expression evaluates to TRUE in all possible feature model configurations. This way, we guarantee the presence of the functionality required by CTRLTEMPREMOTELY, such as to include a WINDOWSACTUATOR that regulates the temperature opening and closing windows. Thus, we can get a constraint instance replacing the variants by their corresponding feature expressions:

$$(RemoteHeatingCntrl \wedge AutomatedHeating \wedge Internet) \quad (5)$$

$$\wedge \neg (AutomatedWindows)$$

3.4   Replacing Terms in Equation

The replacing step depicted in Figure 4- Step 7 depends on the kind of constraint that we created in previous section. If we replace C_{VAR_f} of Equation 4 in Equation 1 and perform some logic manipulation to translate expressions of the form $x \Rightarrow y$ to $\neg x \vee y$, and $x \vee y$ to $\neg x \wedge \neg y$ respectively, we obtain the expression in Equation 6.

$$REQUIRES: \neg \left(D_f \Rightarrow \left(VAR_f \wedge \overset{\wedge}{_{1..k}} \neg VAR_f req_i \right) \right) \equiv D_f \wedge VAR_f \wedge \overset{\wedge}{_{1..k}} \neg VAR_f req_i$$

$$(6)$$

Similarly, if we replace C_{VAR_f} of Equation 3 in Equation 1, and perform some logic manipulation, we obtain the expression in Equation 7.

$$EXCLUDES : \neg \left(D_f \Rightarrow \left(VAR_f \wedge \bigvee_{1..k} VAR_f conf_i\right)\right) \equiv D_f \wedge VAR_f \wedge \bigvee_{1..k} VAR_f conf_i$$

(7)

3.5   Checking SATisfability

Figure 4- Step 8 shows that the input for satisfability checking are expressions such as the ones in 6 and 7. Each expression to be checked is instantiated with:

i) the specific domain constraints, D_f of the SPL produced in Equation 2,

ii) the feature expressions related to the variants VAR_f and either the set of required variants $VAR_f\ req_i$, or the set of conflictant variants $VAR_f\ conf_i$.

Equation 4 evaluates to true when any action inside variant VAR_f requires an element or set of *required elements* that are not composed in the use scenarios. It happens because none of the correspondent variants $VAR_f\ req_i$ that introduce the *required elements* was selected in the product configuration. Also, expression 3 evaluates to false when variant VAR_f defines an element or set of elements that are introduced in the use scenarios that also contain elements defined by other variant(s) $VAR_f\ conf_i$.

3.6   Show Results and SPL Models Modification

The possible results generated by a SATisfability checker for each expression (Figure 4- Step 9) can be TRUE (satisfiable) or FALSE (insatisfiable). In case we obtain FALSE for all the expressions, we know that the SPL is consistent because there are not inconsistencies between the relationships and dependencies (e.g., excludes, optional, mandatory, requires) between features depicted in the SPL feature model, and the use scenarios. In case we obtain a TRUE in an expression, our tool based on the mapping between variants and model elements in the use scenarios shows a list of the variants and the model fragments related to the inconsistency. Taking the example of the Smart Home feature model depicted in Figure 1, the result of the SAT solver for the Rule - Required Inclusion Use Case is that it is satisfiable (i.e., it evaluates to TRUE). Which means that there is an inconsistency between the features and use scenarios. An example of the type of message generated by our tool to the user 4 is:

"...Inconsistent use scenario(s) [CTRLTEMPREMOTELLY] and feature(s) in feature expression(s) of variant(s) [A-W], [R-H]. The Action: [Includes from UseCase: "Ctrl-TempRemotely" to Use Case(s) "OpenAndCloseWinAuto"] implies a [REQUIRES] relationship between variant [R-H] and required variant(s) [A-W] that is not enforced in the SPL feature model...".

Based on this information, for the SAT solver to evaluate to FALSE, the developers may consider for example to:

- Modify the feature model: the set of SPL domain constraints that can be extracted from the feature model can be modified for example creating a REQUIRES relationship for AUTOMATEDHEATING feature to AUTOMATEDWINDOWS, or changing the AUTOMATEDWINDOWS feature from optional to mandatory.

- Modify use scenarios and composition model: for our particular rule, developers may want to check if in fact the INCLUDES association between use cases CTRLTEMPREMOTELY and OPENANDCLOSEWINAUTO is mandatory for every single product or not.

4   Tool Support

Tools for consistency checking can be highly effective for detecting errors in SPL requirements specifications. Such tools not only can find errors people miss, but also they can alleviate developers from the tedious and error-prone task of checking requirements specifications for consistency. Our tool prototype Variability Consistency Checker for Requirements (VCC4RE) [2] was designed to support the process described in Section 3.1 and consist on several components: (i) composition models editor for the VML4RE language, (ii) two translators: one from propositional formulas in prefix notation to conjunctive normal (CNF) form in DIMACS format [1], and the other from the CNF clauses provided by the feature model editor to DIMACS format; and finally (iii) the consistency checker.

We created the *composition model editor* using EMFTEXT [1]. It provides the software infraestructure to derive an initial concrete syntax and plug-in based on the metamodel of our VML4RE language written in Ecore[2]. We employ this technology mostly because of two reasons: first, it separates concrete syntax and abstract syntax which eases the maintenance of the language, and second, it provides a default Human Usable Notation (HUTN)[3] as concrete syntax. Using the HUNT concrete syntax in comparison with our previous tool version [20] allows a more usable and suitable notation for describing requirements composition.

We created a *translator for feature models* created with the SPLOT editor[4]. We chose SPLOT because it allows us to share and edit our models collaboratively via web, and because it generates the CNF formula that represents the domain constraints (D_f) in our equations that later we transform to a widely accepted standard format for boolean formulas in CNF called DIMACS.

Also, we created another *translator* to obtain the feature expressions related to each variant in $VAR_f \wedge \bigwedge_{1..k} \neg VAR_f req_i$ and $VAR_f \wedge \bigvee_{1..k} VAR_f conf_i$ from our composition model. It translates from a prefix notation of propositional formulas of our composition specification, to CNF formulas in DIMACS format. Composition model, consistency rules, as well as the use cases and activity diagrams modelled in any Ecore-based UML tool are interpreted by our consistency checker to produce a set of constraints expressions in CNF DIMACS format. Then, it is possible to use a standard SAT solver to determine the satisfability of each formula. In our case, we experimented with PicoSAT[5] and SAT4J[6].

5   Evaluation

The complete Smart Home SPL was used to evaluate our approach. We chose this case study because, despite of being a large-scale embedded system, this can be understood

---

[1] http://www.emftext.org/: Concrete syntax mapper.

[2] http://www.eclipse.org/modeling/emf/: Eclipse Modelling Framework based on Ecore.

[3] http://www.omg.org/spec/HUTN/: The OMG HUTN specification.

[4] http://www.splot-research.org/: Software Product Line Online Tools.

[5] http://fmv.jku.at/picosat/: PicoSAT: Pico satisfability solver.

[6] http://sat4j.org/: SAT for Java.

by a general reader given its application in everyday's life. Also, we had previous experience modelling variability and part of the use scenarios of the Smart Home supported by one of our industrial partners who set the requirements of the system [18].

Table 1. Evaluation results using VCC4RE in the Smart Home SPL

Features	59	Variants	27
CNF clauses	79	Rules	6
Use Cases	36	Rule instances checked	74
Activity Diagrams	13	Domain constraints created after consistency checking	16
Scenarios	48	Time taken in consistency checking in milliseconds	810

Table 1 summarizes some information about the evaluation. The Smart Home has 59 features and comprises significant aspects of modern home automation domain such as security, HVAC (Heating, Ventilating, and Air Conditioning), illumination control, fire control and multiple user interfaces. These features describe variability at the use scenarios therefore, it is relevant to all kind of SPL stakeholders which are not necessarily experts in domotics and its implementation technologies. When mapped to propositional formulas the feature model produced 79 clauses in CNF format.

We modelled the use scenarios manually using an open source Ecore-based UML tool called Papyrus[7]. In total we modelled 36 use cases, 13 activity diagrams that can represent 48 different possible scenarios, and an initial set of 6 rules for use scenario consistency that follow a very similar reasoning than the rule *Required Inclusion Use Case* explained in Section 2. They vary only in the kind of model elements and their relationships with other model elements, for example: inclusion, generalization, specialization, aggregation and mapping between activity diagram partitions to actors and use cases. Based on the scenarios and feature model we specify 27 *variant* modules using VML4RE. Before applying our approach for consistency checking, we found that using the Smart Home feature model it was possible to generate ONE BILLION product configurations. This information can be obtained using the feature model analyzer provided by the SPLOT tool and allows us to evidence the complexity of checking consistency without any approach and tool support such as the one that we proposed in this paper.

In our experiments we found in total 74 rules instances to check. Using this information we created 16 domain constraints, mainly dependencies of type REQUIRES between features in the feature model that finally help us to solve consistency between use scenarios and features. 16 errors is a significant number taking into account mainly two things: i) Use scenarios, feature model and composition were first carefully modeled and before applying our approach they were apparently "perfect", and ii) The large number of possible combinations of features, the number of variants and use scenarios makes this task challenging, however our approach and tool support gives results in a "blink of an eye". The time taken to evaluate consistency rules using the Pico SAT solver and produce the results is in the order of milliseconds when run on an Intel

---

[7] http://www.eclipse.org/modeling/mdt/?project=papyrus : Papyrus.

Core-Duo i5 at 2.4 Ghz. Given that in VCC4RE, feature models and constraints are mapped to clauses, the performance and scalability of our approach are proportional to the efficiency of the SAT solvers which are able to handle large number of clauses in industrial applications. However, though encouraging results, the scalability of our approach needs to be more extensively validated with more complex case studies and probably using more consistency rules. Doing that is part of our future work.

6   Discussion and Related Work

An issue in the development of SPLs is the lack efficient approaches for consistency checking among all the artifacts, including requirements specifications. In model-driven development this becomes a crucial issue as software is built by means of a chain of transformations. This can start from assets such as requirements specification models, to code-based assets that typically depend on a particular implementation technology. In this setting, the quality of the final code of target products depends mostly on (i) the transformations, (ii) the source models of each transformation and (iii) the information added after each transformation. Therefore, to create constraints helps not only to compose models that helps to understand the intended products to the SPL stakeholders, but also to obtain good quality source models that are the base for deriving good quality code.

The idea of this paper was to explore whether it was possible to use so called "hard" methods for consistency checking as early as requirements analysis. Usually such methods are used much later in the development. We believe now that they can be used much earlier and therefore some inconsistencies do not have to be left until later to be detected. The use of these methods is transparent for the SPL developer and therefore, it does not add extra complexity to the modeling process. SAT solvers are implemented by libraries that are used internally by VCC4RE.

The effective use of use scenarios in SPL demands mechanisms for consistency checking that cope with variability. However, to the best of our knowledge, this issue has not been extensively researched except by Czarnecki, et al [9]. They observed that implementation constraints should follow from domain constraints. Their findings apply to a different composition technique that uses model templates to generate concrete models for product configurations. That work ensures that no ill-structured template instances (i.e., concrete models of products) will be generated from a correct product configuration. In comparison with that work, we check consistency between use scenarios and feature models of domain requirements specifications and we do not assume that the feature model contains all domain constraints since its creation as it usually happens in incremental SPL development processes. In fact, our approach benefits from the semantic of the use scenarios to deduce domain constraints.

There are different research areas related to our work and that have been taken into account the importance of consistency constraints in models. In the field of well-formedness of models for example Egyed [10]. Also, for single systems modeling, Jacobson [15] used aspect-oriented use case models. However, none of those works check consistency of SPL models, and their composition mechanism does not support model weaving of model fragments as it is possible with a requirements-tailored composition language as VML4RE.

Previous work [17] addressed consistency in composition in multi-view modeling in SPL following a FOSD [5] approach for models closer to the product implementation. Also, Harhurin and Hartmann [12] provided denotational semantics and a notation called *Service Diagram* to describe system functionality and variability. Both works focus only on depedencies between atomic features. Our work addresses composition of requirements specifications and an advanced way for model composition based on an aspect-oriented framework VML4RE that is capable to manage variants in addition to atomic features.

7 Conclusions and Future Work

This paper establishes constraints and presents tool support for consistency checking between use scenarios and features in the SPL domain, using feature models and VML4RE. However, our approach does not depend on the use of VML4RE. We use it because its actions facilitate expressing the composition in use scenarios. The objective of checking consistency is to guarantee that all the products that could be derived from a feature model indeed have consistent requirements specifications. This means without omitting information or containing conflicting requirements that eventually may cause errors when transformed and implemented into more platform dependent models and code.

The feasibility of our approach was evaluated using a prototype tool and a home automation case study. The results show that performance and scalability were not an issue. However, these aspects need further assessment with larger and more complex SPLs and consistency rules. Such assessment is part of our future work.

We think that the application of constraints is necessary but do not satisfy completely the problem of consistency checking of models. This problem also depends on the composition order of the variants and in the application order of the actions inside each variant block. Currently, we are researching algorithms to calculate the precedence order between variants and its application in non-monotonic composition. Our proposal here is a proof of concept. Our strategy can be extended for other models, for example to model variability of system qualities, that is not within the scope of our paper and is part of our future work. Here, we are addressing part of the problem for some models.

Acknowledgements

This work was partially supported by the CITI, Portugal, the European project AMPLE, contract IST-33710 and the grant SFRH/BD/46194/2008 of Fundação para a Ciência e a Tecnologia, Portugal. It was also partially funded by the Austrian FWF under agreement P21321-N15 and Marie Curie Actions—IEF project number 254965. We thanks to Alexander Nöhrer for its Java interface for PicoSAT.

References

1. Int. confs. on theory and applications of satisfiability testing, http://www.satisfiability.org/
2. Alférez, M.: Variability consistency checking for requirements tool, http://citi.di.fct.unl.pt/prototype/prototype.php?id=116

3. Alférez, M., Kulesza, U., Sousa, A., Santos, J., Moreira, A., Araújo, J., Amaral, V.: A model-driven approach for software product lines requirements engineering. In: SEKE, pp. 779–784 (2008)
4. Alférez, M., Santos, J., Moreira, A., Garcia, A., Kulesza, U., Araújo, J., Amaral, V.: Multi-view composition language for software product line requirements. In: van den Brand, M., Gašević, D., Gray, J. (eds.) SLE 2009. LNCS, vol. 5969, pp. 103–122. Springer, Heidelberg (2010)
5. Batory, D.: Ahead tool suite, http://www.cs.utexas.edu/users/schwartz/ATS.html
6. Benavides, D., Segura, S., Cortés, A.R.: Automated analysis of feature models 20 years later: A literature review. Inf. Syst. 35(6), 615–636 (2010)
7. Clements, P., Northrop, L.: Software Product Lines: Practices and Patterns. Addison-Wesley, Boston (2002)
8. Czarnecki, K., Eisenecker, U.W.: Generative programming: methods, tools, and applications. ACM Press/Addison-Wesley Publishing Co., New York (2000)
9. Czarnecki, K., Pietroszek, K.: Verifying feature-based model templates against well-formedness ocl constraints. In: Proc. of the GPCE 2006, Portland, Oregon, USA, pp. 211–220. ACM, New York (2006)
10. Egyed, A.: Fixing inconsistencies in UML design models. In: Proc. of the 29th Int. Conf. on Software Engineering, ICSE 2007, pp. 292–301. IEEE Computer Society, Washington, DC, USA (2007)
11. Gomaa, H.: Designing Software Product Lines with UML: From Use Cases to Pattern-Based Software Architectures. Addison Wesley Longman Publishing Co., Inc., Redwood City (2004)
12. Harhurin, A., Hartmann, J.: Towards consistent specifications of product families. In: Cuellar, J., Sere, K. (eds.) FM 2008. LNCS, vol. 5014, pp. 390–405. Springer, Heidelberg (2008)
13. Heidenreich, F., Kopcsek, J., Wende, C.: Featuremapper: mapping features to models. In: Companion of the 30th Int. Conf. on Software Engineering, ICSE Companion 2008, Leipzig, Germany, pp. 943–944. ACM, New York (2008)
14. Jacobson, I.: Object-Oriented Software Engineering: A Use Case Driven Approach. Addison Wesley Longman Publishing Co., Inc., Redwood City (2004)
15. Jacobson, I., Ng, P.-W.: Aspect-Oriented Software Development with Use Cases (Addison-Wesley Object Technology Series). Addison-Wesley Professional, Reading (2004)
16. Kruchten, P.: The Rational Unified Process: An Introduction, 3rd edn. Addison-Wesley Longman Publishing Co., Inc., Boston (2003)
17. Lopez-Herrejon, R.E., Egyed, A.: Detecting inconsistencies in multi-view models with variability. In: Kühne, T., Selic, B., Gervais, M.-P., Terrier, F. (eds.) ECMFA 2010. LNCS, vol. 6138, pp. 217–232. Springer, Heidelberg (2010)
18. Morganho, H., Gomes, e.a.: Requirement specifications for industrial case studies. Deliverable D5.2, Ample Project (2008), www.ample-project.net
19. Pohl, K., Böckle, G., Linden, F.J.v.d.: Software Product Line Engineering: Foundations, Principles and Techniques. Springer-Verlag New York, Inc., Secaucus (2005)
20. Zschaler, S., Sánchez, P., Santos, J., Alférez, M., Rashid, A., Fuentes, L., Moreira, A., Araújo, J., Kulesza, U.: VML* – A family of languages for variability management in software product lines. In: van den Brand, M., Gašević, D., Gray, J. (eds.) SLE 2009. LNCS, vol. 5969, pp. 82–102. Springer, Heidelberg (2010)

Towards a More Fundamental Explanation of Constraints in Feature Models: A Requirement-Oriented Approach

Wei Zhang, Haiyan Zhao, Zhi Jin, and Hong Mei

[1] Key Laboratory of High Confidence Software Technology (Peking University),
Ministry of Education, China
[2] Institute of Software, School of EECS, Peking University, Beijing, 100871, China
zhangw@sei.pku.edu.cn, zhhy@sei.pku.edu.cn,
zhijin@sei.pku.edu.cn, meih@pku.edu.cn

Abstract. One basic construct in feature models (FMs) is the constraints between features, which play the role of ensuring the consistency and completeness of any configuration of a FM. However, most of the existing research about FMs views constraints between features as a kind of black-box entities, and cares little about more fundamental problems relating to them, such as what are the origins of them, and whether there is an insight explanation for their existence. In this paper, we try to provide a more fundamental explanation of constraints between features. The basic idea is that constraints among features are not imposed by external, but rooted in the nature of features – that is, a feature is a kind of container for requirements, and the constraints between features naturally inherit from the constraints between requirements. Following this idea, we identify two general situations that usually relate different requirements, and introduce a set of constraint-patterns based on the different compositions of the two general situations. The value of this research is that it provides a requirement-oriented approach to reflecting our current understanding of constraints in FMs, and also provides us with more theory support to identify, specify and explain constraints between features.

Keywords: Feature Model, Constraint, Semantic.

1 Introduction

One basic construct in feature models (FMs) is the constraints between features, which play the role of ensuring the consistency and completeness of any configuration of a FM. For example, for two features a and b, if there is a *requires* constraint between them (i.e. *a requires b*), and if in a configuration a is selected and b is removed, then we can confirm that this configuration is incomplete, since that b is not included in this configuration. If there is an *excludes* constraint between the two features (i.e. *a excludes b*), and if in a configuration both of the two features is selected and bound, then we can confirm that this configuration is inconsistent, since that two conflicting features are bound in the same time. By explicitly identifying constraints between features, feature models can be configured and reused more easily and efficiently.

K. Schmid (Ed.): ICSR 2011, LNCS 6727, pp. 36–51, 2011.

However, most of the existing research about FMs view constraints between features as a kind of black-box entities – that is, they treat constraints between features as accomplished facts, and care little about more fundamental problems relating to them, such as what are the origins of them, and whether there is a theoretical explanation for their existence. For example, for a *requires* constraint between two features *a* and *b* (i.e. *a requires b*), most of the existing research cares only the surface meaning of this constraint – that is, if *a* is selected then *b* should also be selected. Such a kind of black-box view on constraint certainly is not wrong itself, since that it is sufficient for the purpose of ensuring the consistency and completeness of configurations of a FM. But if we want to extend our confidence from the configurations of a FM to the FM itself – for example, to evaluate whether a constraints in a feature model is right or wrong, such a kind of black-box view will be insufficient, and we have to transform our focus to more essential aspects of constraints – that is, the origins that cause the existence of constraints between features.

In this paper, we try to give a more fundamental explanation of constraints in feature models. The basic idea is that constraints among features are not imposed by external, but rooted in the nature of features. A lot of existing research has pointed out that a feature essentially denotes a cohesive set of individual requirements [20,21,14,22]; in other words, a feature is a kind of requirement container. Based on this understanding of features, we believe that the constraints between features are actually caused by the constraints between requirements – that is, the constraints between features naturally inherit from the constraints between requirements. Following this belief, we investigate the nature of requirements from a phenomenon-based view, identify two general situations that usually relate different requirements, and introduce a set of constraint-patterns based on the different compositions of the two general situations. The value of this research is that it provides a requirement-oriented approach to reflecting our current understanding of constraints in FMs, and also provides us with more theory support to identify, specify and explain constraints between features.

The rest of this paper is organized as follows. Section 2 introduces some preliminaries. Section 3 gives two general situations about how different requirements could be related with each other. Section 4 presents seven patterns that cause constraints between features by composing the two general situations in different ways. Section 5 discusses related work. Finally, Section 6 concludes this paper with a short summary and further work.

2 Preliminaries

In this section, we introduce some preliminaries, including a phenomenon-based understanding of requirements, a classification of phenomena, and three kinds of roles that requirements plays to their referenced phenomena. We also give a simple example containing four requirements, and show how these requirements reference to a set of phenomena.

2.1 An Understanding of Requirements

In our research, we adopt a phenomenon-based understanding of requirements, which is independently proposed by Jackson [11] and Parnas et al. [16], and then formalized by Gunter et al. [10]. Generally, a phenomenon is something that is observed to happen in a time point or exist in a period of time. The core of this understanding is the distinction between *requirements*, *specifications*, and *domain properties*. The commonality of the three concepts is that all of them describe properties between phenomena involved in a software system, and the differences between them exist in two aspects, which are the different types of phenomena referenced by the three concepts, and the different enforcers of the properties captured by the three concepts. Properties between phenomena specify how two or more phenomenon are related with each others – for example, causality is a kind of properties between phenomena, which shows that the occurrence of one phenomena will lead to the occurrence of other phenomena.

Generally, phenomena involved in a software system can be partitioned into four types: E_h, E_v, S_v and S_h. The explanations of them are given in Table 1.

Table 1. Four types of phenomenon

Phenomenon Types	Explanation
E_h	$\forall p \in E_h$, p is controlled by the environment, and not visible to the software.
E_v	$\forall p \in E_v$, p is controlled by the environment, and also visible to the software.
S_v	$\forall p \in S_v$, p is controlled by the software, and also visible to the environment.
S_h	$\forall p \in S_v$, p is controlled by the software, and not visible to the environment.

Table 2 shows the differences between the three concepts. The phenomena that *specifications* can reference are those that are visible both to the software and the environment, and the properties captured by *specifications* are enforced by the software. That is, specifications describe the software's behavior at the interface between the software and the environment. The phenomena that *requirements* and *domain properties* can reference are those that are visible to the environment. The differences between them is that the properties described by *domain properties* are enforced by the environment , while the properties captured by *requirements* are desired by software stakeholders and could be enforced only after the software is successfully deployed into the environment.

The relations between the three concepts could be expressed by the following formula (in which, D, S and R denote domain properties, specifications and requirements,

Table 2. Differences between requirements, specifications, and domain properties

Concept	Referenced Phenomena	Enforcer
Domain Properties	$E_h \cup E_v \cup S_v$	*Environment*
Requirements	$E_h \cup E_v \cup S_v$	*The conjunction of software and environment*
Specifications	$E_v \cup S_v$	*Software*

respectively): $D, S \models R$. The meaning of this formula is that *requirements* can only be satisfied when *domain properties* and *specifications* are both satisfied. For more detailed information, we refer to [10], [11] and [16].

2.2 A Classification of Phenomena

As stated in Section 2.1, requirements capture desired properties between phenomena – that is, these properties don't exist naturally or previously, but will be exist if an appropriate software system is developed and deployed. In the following, we give a brief introduction to a simplified classification of phenomena. The original complete classification is proposed by Jackson, and more information about it could be found in [12].

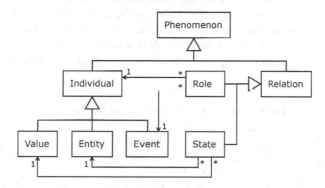

Fig. 1. A classification of phenomena

Fig. 1 shows an overview of this classification, in which, phenomena are partitioned into two subclasses: *individuals* and *relations*. An individual is something that *can be named and reliably distinguished from other individuals* [12]. Individuals are further partitioned into three subclasses: *entities*, *events* and *values*. An entity is an individual that exists over a period of time, and the states of an entity can be changed with time. An event is an indivisible individual that occurs at a specific time point. A value is a constant individual that is independent of time and space, such as numbers and characters.

A relation is "a set of associations among individuals" [12]. Relations are further partitioned into three subclasses: *states* and *roles*. A state is a relation between entities and values. A role is a relation between events and individuals, which captures individuals participating in events.

2.3 Roles of Requirements to Their Referenced Phenomena

A requirement often plays different roles to their referenced phenomena. In this paper, we distinguish three kinds of reference role.

Read-only (ro) reference: When a requirement references a phenomenon in a read-only way, it means that the requirement is just an observer of the phenomenon, and does not impose any constraint on the phenomenon.

Functional constraining (fc) reference: When a requirement references a phenomenon in a functional constraining way, it means that the requirement imposes certain temporal sequence constraints on the phenomenon (For example, the phenomenon should occur only after the occurring of some other phenomenon).

Non-functional constraining (nfc) reference: When a requirement references a phenomenon in a non-functional constraining way, it means that the requirement imposes certain constraints on the phenomenon that cannot be represented by temporal sequences between phenomena, such as the timing constraints between phenomena and the throughput constraints of software systems.

2.4 An Example

In the following, we introduce four requirements, and show the different reference roles that they play to phenomena. The four requirements will be used in the rest of this paper as a running example to demonstrate our main ideas. We could find the four requirements in a software system that allows multiple users to log in to. Table 3 lists the four requirements. Fig. 2 shows the phenomena referenced by the four requirements.

Table 3. Four requirements and their descriptions

ID	Description
REQ-01	*If a user provides correct user name and password, the system should allow the user to log in.*
REQ-02	*After a user logs in to the system, a welcome message should be send to the user.*
REQ-03	*The average interval between a user's log-in and the welcome message's appearing should less than 5 seconds.*
REQ-04	*The system should allow at least 5000 users in the log-in state at the same time.*

From *REQ-01*'s description, we can identify an entity phenomenon: *user*, two value phenomena: *name* and *password*, and a state phenomenon: *log-in-state*. *REQ-01* references the former three phenomena in a read-only way – that is, *REQ-01* does not impose any restriction on who can try to log in, or which user name or password should be provided, and anyone can freely provide any user name and password. But *REQ-01* does impose a functional constraint on the log-in-state phenomenon. That is, after a user provides the correct name and password, the user's log-in-state should be changed from false to true.

From *REQ-02*'s description, we can find that it has two *ro-references* to the entity phenomenon *user* and the event phenomenon *log-in*, and two *fc-references* to the entity phenomenon *wel-msg* and the state phenomenon *sending-state* (That is, after a user's log-in, a wel-msg should be constructed, and its sending-state should be made to be true by sending the wel-msg to the user).

REQ-03 and *REQ-04* show two examples of *nfc-references*, respectively. One is a *nfc-reference* to the *occurring-time* (a role phenomenon) of the event *wel-msg-send-out*. The other is a *nfc-reference* to the *log-in-state* of users.

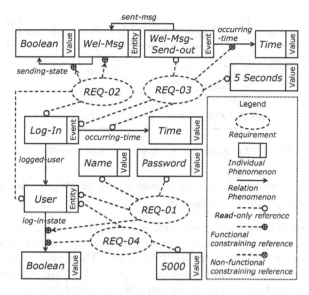

Fig. 2. Phenomena referenced by the four requirements

3   Two Elementary Situations

In this section, we give two elementary situations of how different requirements are related with each other through those phenomena referenced by them.

3.1   Situation 1: Multiple References to the Same Phenomenon

The first situation we have observed is that *two or more requirements reference the same phenomenon*. Fig. 3 illustrates such a situation, in which, two requirements *REQ-A* and *REQ-B* both reference the phenomenon *pheno-x*.

This situation varies at two dimensions: the type of the referenced phenomenon, and the type of reference role of involved requirements. For example, *pheno-x* could be an entity or a state phenomenon, and *REQ-A* may have a *ro-reference* to *pheno-x*, while *REQ-B* may have a *fc*- or *nfc*- reference to *pheno-x*.

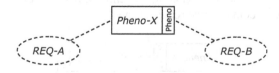

Fig. 3. Multiple references to a same phenomenon

In a paper on requirements triage [6], Davis provides two simple requirements to show the constraints between them. Here we investigate the two requirements from a different view, and show how they fit into the situation illustrated in Fig. 4. The two requirements are:

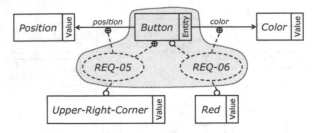

Fig. 4. *REQ-5*, *REQ-6* and their referenced phenomena

- *REQ-05*: *The system shall provide a stop button in the upper right corner*, and
- *REQ-06*: *The stop button shall be red.*

Fig. 4 shows how the two requirements reference a set of phenomena, in which, the *button* is referenced by both of them, but with different roles; one is a *fc-reference*, and the other is a *ro-reference* (see the filled area). The former exists because that *REQ-05* requires to import a *button* into the system, and the latter exists because that *REQ-06* only requires to set the *color* state of a pre-imported *button*.

3.2   Situation 2: Separated References to Related Phenomena

The second situation is that two requirements reference two different phenomena respectively, and the two phenomena are related in a certain way. Fig. 5 illustrates such a situation, in which, *REQ-A* and *REQ-B* reference two related phenomena *pheno-x* and *pheno-y* respectively.

Besides the two dimensions as in *situation 1*, this situation also varies at the third dimension of how those referenced phenomena are related. In our research, we identify two ways. The first way is that, two phenomena are related by the connection between their semantics. One example of this case exists between the event phenomenon *log-in* and the state phenomenon *log-in-state* (see Fig. 2). *Log-in-state* denotes the relation between *users* and *boolean* values. The occurring of a *log-in* event means that a certain *user*'s *log-in-state* is changed from *false* to *true*. When some constraints are applied on *log-in-state* (for example, to satisfy *REQ-01*), a *log-in* event may also occur correspondingly.

The second way is that, two phenomena are related by domain properties. One example of this case could be found in the *time-alarming* service of most mobile phones. This service contains two requirements:

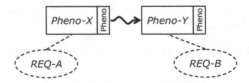

Fig. 5. Separated references to related phenomena

- *REQ-07*: *When a pre-defined time point arrives, the bell should ring.*
- *REQ-08*: *When the off-button is pressed, the bell should stop ringing.*

Fig. 6 shows how the two requirements reference a set of phenomena, in which, *REQ-07* has a *fc-reference* to the *bell*'s *ringing-state*, while *REQ-08* has a *ro-reference* to the *button-pressed* event (see the filled area). The two phenomena *ringing-state* and *button-pressed* are related through the following process: when the *bell*'s *ringing-state* is true, its sound will pass through the atmosphere into the user's ears, and the user will be woken up and then press the *off-button*, which further causes the occurring of a *button-pressed* event. This process is supported by the following three domain properties: the atmosphere's physical property of transferring sounds, the user's physiological property of being woken up by sounds, and the user's rational decision of pressing the *off-button* to stop the ringing.

In addition, there are also relations between *REQ-07* and *REQ-08* that fit into *situation 1*. That is, both of them reference to the two phenomena: *bell* and *ringing-state*, but impose different constraints on the *ringing-state*.

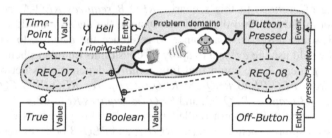

Fig. 6. *REQ-07, REQ-08* and their referenced phenomena

4 Patterns for Constraints between Features

In this section, we present a set of patterns developed by composing the two situations above in different ways, and show how these patterns cause constraints between requirements. We first introduce two set of constraint patterns for the *requires* and the *excludes* constraints, respectively. After that, we show how these patterns could be further extended to cover more complex constraints between features.

4.1 Patterns of the *Requires* Constraints

For two requirements *REQ-A* and *REQ-B*, "*REQ-B requires REQ-A*" means that the selection of *REQ-B* requires the selection of *REQ-A*. That is, it will have no sense to introduce *REQ-B* into a software system, if *REQ-A* is not introduced.

We have identified four patterns that induce the *requires* constraints. Fig. 7 shows the first pattern (called *pattern 1*). This pattern is developed from *situation 1* and captures such a scenario: *REQ-A* imports an *entity-x* into the software system, and *REQ-B* has a *ro*-reference to the *entity-x* and a *fc*-reference to the *entity-x*'s *state-z*. In this scenario, *REQ-B requires REQ-A*. The reason for this *requires* constraints is obvious: if *REQ-A* is not introduced, the *entity-x* would not be imported into the system, and thus *REQ-B* would never have a chance to apply his constraint on the *entity-x*'s *state-z*.

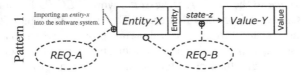

Fig. 7. *Pattern 1* of the *requires* constraints

Guided by *pattern 1*, we could find a *requires* constraint between *REQ-05* and *REQ-06*, that is, *REQ-06 requires REQ-05*.

Fig. 8 shows the second pattern (called *pattern 2*). This pattern is developed from *situation 2* and captures such a scenario: *REQ-A* applies a constraint on the *entity-x*'s *state-z*, *REQ-B* has a *ro-reference* to the *event-u*, and the changing of *state-z* induces the occurring of *event-u*. In this scenario, *REQ-B requires REQ-A*, because that if *REQ-A* is not introduced into the software system, the *event-u* would not occur, and thus *REQ-B* would never have a chance to reference the *event-u*, to say nothing of how *REQ-B* would use the *event-u* to apply its constraints on other phenomena.

Guided by *pattern 2*, we could find four *requires* dependencies between those requirements from *REQ-01* to *REQ-08*: *REQ-02 requires REQ-01*, *REQ-03 requires REQ-01*, *REQ-03 requires REQ-02*, and *REQ-08 requires REQ-07*.

Fig. 9 shows the third pattern (called *pattern 3*). This pattern is developed from *situation 1* and captures such a scenario: *REQ-A* and *REQ-B* both reference the *entity-x*'s *state-z*, but impose different constraints on it: the former changes the *entity-x*'s *state-z* from a default value to other values, while the latter recovers the *entity-x*'s *state-z* to its default value. In this scenario, *REQ-B requires REQ-A*, because that if *REQ-A* is not introduced into a software system, the *entity-x*'s *state-z* would always

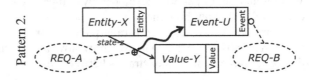

Fig. 8. *Pattern 2* of the *requires* constraints

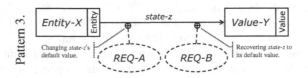

Fig. 9. *Pattern 3* of the *requires* constraints

keep its default value, and thus it would be unnecessary to introduce *REQ-B* to recover the *state-z* to it default value.

Guided by *pattern 3*, we could find the *requires* constraint between *REQ-07* and *REQ-08*, that is, *REQ-08 requires REQ-07*. It is interesting to observe that this constraint could be identified either from *pattern 2* or from *pattern 3*.

Fig. 10 shows the fourth pattern (called *pattern 4*). This pattern is developed from *situation 1* and captures such a scenario: *REQ-A* and *REQ-B* both reference the *pheno-x* in a constraining way, but with different types: one is a *fc-reference*, the other is a *nfc-reference*. In this scenario, *REQ-B requires REQ-A*, because that the non-functional constraining usually bases itself on the functional constraining (for example, imposing quality requirements on the functional constraining). This kind of dependency conforms to the general relationships between functional and non-functional requirements [19].

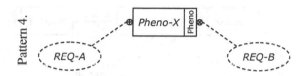

Fig. 10. *Pattern 4* of the *requires* Constraints

Guided by pattern 4, we could find the *requires* constraint between *REQ-01* and *REQ-04*, that is, *REQ-04 requires REQ-01*.

4.2 Patterns of the *Excludes* Constraints

For two requirements *REQ-A* and *REQ-B*, "*REQ-A excludes REQ-B*" means that when both of them are introduced into a software system, there may exist a scenario, in which, the two requirements can not be satisfied at the same time, or the satisfaction of both of them can lead to unexpected negative behavior of the software system.

We have identified three patterns that induce the *excludes* constraints. Fig. 11 shows the first pattern (called *pattern 5*). This pattern is developed from *situation 1* and captures such a scenario: both of *REQ-A* and *REQ-B* have a *ro-reference* to the *event-x*, but impose conflicting constraints on the *pheno-y*. In this scenario, *REQ-A excludes REQ-B*, because that when the *event-x* occurs, their constraints on the *pheno-y* could not be satisfied at the same time.

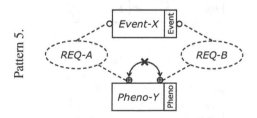

Fig. 11. *Pattern 5* of the *excludes* constraints

One instance of *pattern 5* could be found between the two requirements *show-caller-ID* and *block-caller-ID* in the telecommunication systems [8]. *Show-caller-ID* requires that *"the caller's phone number should be shown to the recipient"*, while *block-caller-ID* requires the inverse. When there is a call from one user who subscribes to *block-caller-ID* to the other user who subscribes to *show-caller-ID*, the two requirements can not be both satisfied.

Fig. 12 shows the second pattern (called *pattern 6*). This pattern is also developed from *situation 1*, and captures such a scenario: *REQ-A* has a *ro*-reference to the *event-x*, and imposes a constraint on the *entity-v*'s *state-r*; while *REQ-B* has a *ro*-reference to the *entity-y*'s *state-u*, and imposes a constraint on the *entity-v*'s *state-r*, a constraint conflicting with the one that *REQ-A* imposes on. *REQ-A* and *REQ-B* will conflict with each other, when the *event-x* occurs and at the same time, the *entity-y*'s current *state-u* causes *REQ-B* to keep its constraint on the *entity-v*'s *state-r*.

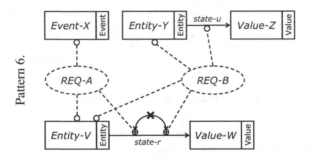

Fig. 12. *Pattern 6 of the excludes constraints*

One instance of *pattern 6* could be found between the *time-alarming* service and the *meeting-silence* service of mobile phones. Two requirements involved in the two services show the potential of conflicting with each other. One is *REQ-07*, which has been introduced in Section 3.2. The other is a requirement in the *meeting-silence* service:

• *REQ-09*: *When the mobile phone is in the meeting state, the bell should not ring.*

The two requirements exclude each other in the following scenario: a pre-defined time point arrives, while the phone is in the meeting state.

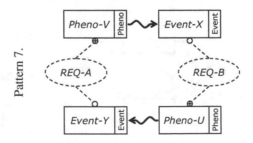

Fig. 13. *Pattern 7 of the excludes constraints*

A common kind of negative behavior of a software system is live lock – that is, the system runs into an infinite loop. Based on this observation, we identify the third pattern (called *pattern 7*, see Fig. 13). This pattern is developed from *situation 2*, and captures such a scenario: *REQ-A* has a *ro-reference* to the *event-y*, and imposes a constraint on the *pheno-v*, while *REQ-B* has a *ro-reference* to the *event-x*, and imposes a constraint on the *pheno-u*. These two requirements may run into an infinite loop in the following scenario: *REQ-A* applies its constraint on the *pheno-v*, which causes the occurring of *event-x*, and then *REQ-B* applies its constraint on the *pheno-u*, which further causes the occurring of *event-y* and *REQ-B*'s constraint applying action again.

4.3 Extended Patterns

The seven patterns introduced above can be extended in two ways. One way is to extend each requirement in the seven patterns into a set of requirements, and each of them has similar references with the original requirement.

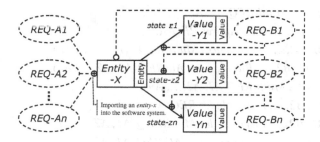

Fig. 14. An extension to *pattern 1*

Fig. 14 shows an extension to *pattern 1* following this way. In this new pattern, *REQ-A* is extended into a set of requirements, and each of them has the capacity to imposing a new *entity-x* into the software system. *REQ-B* is also extended into a set of requirements, and each of them imposes on a constraint on one of the *entity*'s state. Guided by this pattern, we could identify a new kind of *requires* constraint with the following form: *Multi(REQ-B1, B2,..., Bn) requires Multi(REQ-A1, A2,..., An)*. The meaning of such a constraint is that when one or more requirements in the left are introduced, one or more requirements in the right should also be introduced; it will have no sense to just introduce the left requirements without any of the right requirements.

Another way is to extend each requirement in the four patterns into a set of requirements, but only the conjunction of all of them has similar references with the original requirement.

Fig. 15 shows such an extension to *pattern 1*. Guided by this extension, we could get another new kind of *requires* with the following form: *All(REQ-B1, B2,..., Bn) requires All(REQ-A1, A2,..., An)*. The meaning of such a dependency is that when all the left requirements are introduced, all the right requirements should also be introduced.

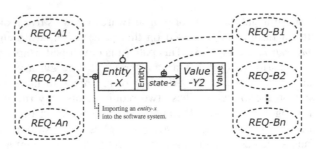

Fig. 15. Another extension to *pattern 1*

Based on the two ways above, the seven patterns in Section 4.1 and 4.2 can be extended in more flexible styles. For example, only apply one of the two ways to one of the two requirements in original patterns, or apply the two ways to the two requirements respectively. Consequently, we could get more kinds of extended *requires* and *excludes* constraints, such as:

- *REQ-B requires Multi(REQ-A1, A2,..., An)*,
- *All(REQ-B1, B2,..., Bn) requires REQ-A*,
- *All(REQ-B1, B2,..., Bn) requires Multi(REQ-A1, A2,..., An)*,
- *Multi(REQ-B1, B2,..., Bn) requires All(REQ-A1, A2,..., An)*.
- *REQ-B excludes Multi(REQ-A1, A2,..., An)*,
- *All(REQ-B1, B2,..., Bn) excludes REQ-A*,
- *All(REQ-B1, B2,..., Bn) excludes Multi(REQ-A1, A2,..., An)*,
- *Multi(REQ-B1, B2,..., Bn) excludes All(REQ-A1, A2,..., An)*.

5   Related Work

Our work is inspired in part by Jackson's research on *problem frames* [12]. Especially, our understanding of requirements and the classification of phenomena are directly based on his work and other related research [10, 16]. The difference between our work and the research on problem frames is that: while the latter focuses on those reusable patterns existed in a single requirement or a set of closely-related requirements (called a *problem*), our work concentrates much on how different requirements are related with each other. Such a difference also points out the possible combination of the two approaches. For example, our approach could be used to analyze the dependencies between those requirements contained in a problem, and thus make a deep understanding of the problem. Similarly, our approach could also be used to analyze dependencies between problems and evaluate how these problems could be composed to resolve a more complex problem. In addition, we extend the constraining references in the *problem frames* into two distinct subclasses: *functional* and *non-functional* references. Although in some contexts, a requirement may describe both functional and non-functional constraints (For example, an requirement such as "*after the occurring of event A, event B should occurs in five seconds*"), we think that the explicit distinction between them could attain a high degree of *separation of concerns* in requirements specifications. The distinction also makes it possible to investigate the dependencies between functional and non-functional requirements.

In software reuse, feature models [13,9,3] are proposed to improve the customizability of requirements. For this purpose, a feature model usually contains a set of *requires* or *excludes* constraints between features. Pohl et al [18,1] pointed out the importance of constraints between features for the variability modeling of software product lines. In addition, many researchers also identified the value of constraints/dependencies between requirements in other software development activities. For example, Moisiadis [15] and Davis [6] observed that the using of constraints makes the requirements prioritizing activity more efficient and reduces effort in later maintenance activities. Based on an industrial survey, Carlshamre et al. [2] identified a set of dependency types (including *requires* and *excludes* dependencies), and showed their influence on the release planning activity. In our previous research [23], we found that the constraints could be used to identify interactions between components. Ferber et al. [7] also showed the constraints's value in the reengineering of legacy software product lines. Our work in this paper could be used to improve the above research by provide them a systematical way to identifying the constraints.

Much effort has also been made towards a systematic modeling framework for different types of requirements dependency. The most significant work in this direction is conducted by Dahlstedt and Persson [4, 5]. In their research, they made an extensive survey of different types of requirements dependencies in literature, and classified them into a set of fundamental dependency types, based on a general dependency model proposed by Pohl [17]. Dahlstedt and Persson also pointed out that although we have recognized the importance of requirements dependencies for software development, there are still many fundamental or practical problems relating to requirements dependencies, such as what are the origins of requirements dependencies, and how to identify requirements dependencies. Our research in this paper does not try to resolve all these unresolved problems, but only focuses on a specific type of requirements dependency, namely, the constraints. We locate the constraints' origin in the nature of requirements (that is, it is the requirements themselves that cause the constraints between them), and introduce a set of patterns that cause constraints between requirements, based on a phenomenon-based understanding of requirements.

6 Conclusions and Future Work

In this paper, we present our preliminary research on the understanding of constraints in feature models, from a requirement-oriented approach. We view features as a kind of requirements container, and believe that constraints between features naturally inherit from constraints between requirements. Based on this viewpoint, we conclude two elementary situations of how different requirements are related with each other, develop seven concrete by composing the two elementary situations in different ways, and show how these patterns induce the constraints between requirements/features.

Our future work will focus on the automatic identification of the constraints between requirements/features. The key problem in attaining this goal is to find a formal method to specify the relations between phenomena, and to specify the relations between requirements/features and their referenced phenomena. Based on such a formal method, patterns inducing constraints could also be formalized, and algorithms could be developed to identify those patterns automatically.

Acknowledgments. The authors would like to thank the anonymous reviewers for their valuable comments and suggestions. This work is supported in part by National Natural Science Foundation of China under Grant No. 60821003, 60703065 and 60873059, National Basic Research Program of China (973) under Grant No. 2009CB320701, and National Key Technology R&D Program under Grant No. 2008BAH32B02.

References

1. Buhne, S., Lauenroth, K., Pohl, K.: Modelling Requirements Variability across Product Lines. In: 13th IEEE International Conference on Requirements Engineering (RE 2005), pp. 41–52. IEEE Computer Society, Los Alamitos (2005)
2. Carlshamre, P., Sandahl, K., Lindvall, M., Regnell, B., Nattoch Dag, J.: An Industrial Survey of Requirements Interdependencies in Software Product Release Planning. In: 5th IEEE International Symposium on Requirements Engineering (RE 2001), pp. 84–91. IEEE Computer Society, Los Alamitos (2001)
3. Chastek, G., Donohoe, P., Kang, K.C., Thiel, S.: Product Line Analysis: A Practical Introduction. SEI-2001-TR-001, Software Engineering Institute, Carnegie Mellon University (2001)
4. Dahlstedt, A.G., Persson, A.: Requirements Interdependencies - Moulding the State of Research into a Research Agenda. In: 9th International Workshop on Requirements Engineering - Foundation for Software Quality (REFSQ 2003), Klagenfurt/Velden, Austria, June 16-17, pp. 55–64 (2003)
5. Dahlstedt, A.G., Persson, A.: Requirements Interdependencies: State of the Art and Future Challenges. In: Engineering and Managing Software Requirements, pp. 95–116. Springer, Heidelberg (2006)
6. Davis, A.M.: The Art of Requirements Triage. IEEE Computer 36(3), 42–49 (2003)
7. Ferber, S., Haag, J., Savolainen, J.: Feature Interaction and Dependencies: Modeling Features for Reengineering a Legacy Product Line. In: Chastek, G.J. (ed.) SPLC 2002. LNCS, vol. 2379, pp. 235–256. Springer, Heidelberg (2002)
8. Fife, L.D.: Feature Interaction-How It Works in Telecommunication Software. IEEE Potentials 15(4), 35–37 (1996)
9. Griss, M.L., Favaro, J., d'Alessandro, M.: Integrating Feature Modeling with the RSEB. In: 5th International Conference on Software Reuse, pp. 76–85. IEEE Computer Society, Los Alamitos (1998)
10. Gunter, C.A., Gunter, E.L., Jackson, M., Zave, P.: A Reference Model for Requirements and Specifications. IEEE Software 17(3), 37–43 (2000)
11. Jackson, M.: Software Requirements and Specifications: A Lexicon of Practice, Principles and Prejudices. Addison-Wesley, Reading (1995)
12. Jackson, M.: Problem Frames: Analyzing and Structuring Software Development Problems. Addison-Wesley, Reading (2001)
13. Kang, K.C., Cohen, S.G., Hess, J.A., Novak, W.E., Peterson, A.S.: Feature-Oriented Domain Analysis Feasibility Study. Technical Reports, SEI-90-TR-21, Software Engineering Institute, Carnegie Mellon University (1990)
14. Mehta, A., Heineman, G.T.: Evolving Legacy System Features into Fine-Grained Components. In: 24th International Conference on Software Engineering, Florida, pp. 417–427 (May 2002)

15. Moisiadis, F.: The Fundamentals of Prioritising Requirements. In: Systems Engineering/Test and Evaluation Conference, SETE 2002 (2002)
16. Parnas, D.L., Madey, J.: Functional Documents for Computer Systems. Science of Computer Programming 25(1), 41–61 (1995)
17. Pohl, K.: Process-Centered Requirements Engineering. John Wiley & Sons, Inc., Reading (1996)
18. Pohl, K., Böckle, G., van der Linden, F.J.: Software Product Line Engineering: Foundations, Principles and Techniques. Springer, Heidelberg (2005)
19. Sommerville, I.: Software Engineering. Addison-Wesley, Reading (2000)
20. Turner, C.R., Fuggetta, A., Lavazza, L., Wolf, A.L.: A Conceptual Basis for Feature Engineering. Journal of Systems and Software 49(1), 3–15 (1999)
21. Wiegers, K.E.: Software Requirements. Microsoft Press, Redmond (1999)
22. Zhang, W., Mei, H., Zhao, H.: A Feature-Oriented Approach to Modeling Requirements Dependencies. In: 13th IEEE International Conference on Requirements Engineering (RE 2005), pp. 273–282. IEEE Computer Society, Los Alamitos (2005)
23. Zhang, W., Mei, H., Zhao, H., Yang, J.: Transformation from CIM to PIM: A Feature-Oriented Component-Based Approach. In: Briand, L.C., Williams, C. (eds.) MoDELS 2005. LNCS, vol. 3713, pp. 248–263. Springer, Heidelberg (2005)

Towards Feature-Oriented Variability Reconfiguration in Dynamic Software Product Lines

Liwei Shen, Xin Peng, Jindu Liu, and Wenyun Zhao

School of Computer Science, Fudan University, Shanghai, China
{shenliwei,pengxin,09212010014,wyzhao}@fudan.edu.cn

Abstract. Dynamic Software Product Line (DSPL) provides a new paradigm for developing self-adaptive systems with the principles of software product line engineering. DSPL emphasizes variability analysis and design at development time and variability binding and reconfiguration at runtime, thus requires some kinds of variability mechanisms to map high-level variations (usually represented by features) to low-level implementation and support runtime reconfiguration. Existing work on DSPL usually assumes that variation features can be directly mapped to coarse-grained elements like services, components or plug-ins, making the methods hard to be applied for traditional software systems. In this paper, we propose a feature-oriented method to support runtime variability reconfiguration in DSPLs. The method introduces the concept of role model, an intermediate level between feature variations and implementations to improve their traceability. On the other hand, the method involves a reference implementation framework based on dynamic aspect mechanisms to implement the runtime reconfiguration. We illustrate the process of applying the proposed method with a concrete case study, which helps to validate the effectiveness of our method.

Keywords: Dynamic software product line, self-adaptation, dynamic AOP, variability binding, reconfiguration.

1 Introduction

Software-intensive systems in areas like pervasive computing and online service systems are required to be more adaptive nowadays. Rather than behaving constantly, these systems, also called self-adaptive systems, can automatically adapt their behaviors at runtime based on the environment and guided by objectives and needs of stakeholders [1].

In the software reuse community, Dynamic Software Product Line (DSPL) [2] has been proposed as an effective paradigm to develop self-adaptive systems with the principle of software product line (SPL) engineering. DSPL identifies the reusable and dynamically reconfigurable core assets at development time which are explicitly modeled as dynamic variability. At runtime, DSPL application proposes to configure and reconfigure runtime instances by the variability customization, which means to adapt the binding decisions of the variations within the current system during execution. The business logic of a DSPL application covers the adaptable behaviors which

K. Schmid (Ed.): ICSR 2011, LNCS 6727, pp. 52–68, 2011.
© Springer-Verlag Berlin Heidelberg 2011

can be represented as a domain model, usually as a feature model [10, 11]. As a result, the dynamic reconfiguration strategies can be obtained and specified in a higher feature level rather than the lower program level, which makes it easily be validated and understood by the system users.

In order to implement the feature-oriented variability reconfiguration, DSPL requires some kinds of variability mechanisms to map high-level feature variations to low-level implementations. Existing work usually assumes that variation features can be directly mapped to coarse-grained implementation elements like services [7, 8], components [4] or plug-ins [3]. However, the variability traceability from features to implementations in the traditional software systems may be more complicated. For example, a single feature can be implemented by multiple program units, while a program unit may also contain the functions for several features. Existing feature-based methods do not provide the traceability naturally due to the big gap between the problem space and the solution space [12, 13]. Thus, the program-level reconfiguration driven by the feature level variation binding is hard to be performed.

In this paper, we propose a feature-oriented method to support runtime variability reconfiguration in DSPLs. The method introduces the concept of role model, an intermediate level between feature variations and implementations to improve their traceability. In a role model, each feature is implemented by a set of roles as well as various role interactions, and roles will be further instantiated by elements in the implementation level. In particular, a special type of roles, called control roles, is introduced to manage the dynamic reconfiguration upon feature variations. On the other hand, our method involves a reference implementation framework based on dynamic aspect mechanisms to implement the runtime reconfiguration. Currently, we adopt *JBoss-AOP* [18], a popular mechanism supporting dynamic aspect weaving. Following our method, we conducted a concrete case study on a course selection system, and the preliminary results help to validate the effectiveness of our method.

The remainder of this paper is organized as follows. Section 2 gives a background introduction to the DSPL and analyzes research problems in feature-oriented variability reconfiguration. Section 3 describes the role model as well as its capability to support the runtime reconfiguration. Then Section 4 introduces our reference implementation framework based on dynamic aspect mechanisms. Section 5 presents the case study with the discussion, and Section 6 introduces related work. Finally Section 7 draws the conclusion and plans our future work.

2   Background and Problems for Variability Reconfiguration

In this section, we will first briefly introduce the background of a DSPL. Then the working example of a course selection system will be given out to derive the research problems when realizing the feature variability reconfiguration.

2.1   Background of DSPLs

Complying with a traditional SPL, the feature model of a DSPL provides an integrated business view emphasizing on possible variations and changes in its runtime behaviors. Thus, the variability in DSPLs is bound or unbound during runtime and the binding decisions on the variations may change several times in its lifetime [2].

In our method, we consider two kinds of variation points (i.e. adaptation points at runtime) in feature models which are optional and alternative. Since the binding status of the variations can be changed several times during execution, all of their corresponding implementations should be incorporated into the application initially. At runtime, whether they are available will depend on the reconfiguration strategies generated from the adaptation rules in a specific context.

We think an important engineering principle that DSPL can bring to self-adaptive systems is the feature dependency and constraint mechanism. By feature constraints, we can represent *require* or *exclude* dependencies among feature variations, and combine them into runtime adaptation controls to help to ensure consistent and complete feature bindings and reconfigurations.

2.2 DSPL Example of a Course Selection System (CSS)

The Course Selection System is a DSPL example whose feature model (in Figure 1) as well as its adaptation rules (in Table 1) is identified before the system is running. The system is endowed with the capability of self-adaptation so that it can provide a stable online service facing the course-selecting demand from thousands of students in a campus. The adaptation capabilities are formalized as the ECA (*On* Event *If* Condition *Do* Action) [16] rules which indicate the operations upon the dynamic variation points in the feature model.

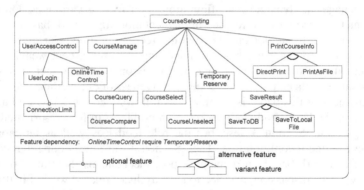

Fig. 1. Feature model of the course-selecting system

The self-management capability helps to generate the variations in the business model which represents the possible configurations that the system may behave at runtime. For example in the figure, the feature *OnlineTimeControl* is an optional feature that can be bound or unbound according to the changing concurrent accessing number specified in the first rule. *TemporaryReserve* which can keep the unsaved user operations for a period of time if the user is disconnected is required by *OnlineTime-Control*. It means the former cannot be bound if the latter is not bound. *ConnectionLimit* is another optional feature whose binding status depends on the available server memory. *SaveResult* is an alternative feature whose variants are *SaveToDB* and *SaveToLocalFile* separately. Thus, the saving mode can be changed at runtime conforming to the availability status of the database which is evaluated through the response time shown in the third rule. *PrintCourseInfo* is similar with the previous

Table 1. The ECA rules for CCS

ON	IF	DO
the concurrent accessing number (CAN) changes	CAN > 500	bind *OnlineTimeControl*
	CAN < 450	unbind *OnlineTimeControl*
the memory utilization (MU) changes	MU > 90%	bind *ConnectionLimit*
	MU < 80%	unbind *ConnectionLimit*
database response time (DRT) changes	DRT > 3s	bind *SaveToLocalFile*
	DRT < 1s	bind *SaveToDB*
printer state (PS) changes	PS = out-of-service	bind *PrintAsFile*
	PS = in-service	bind *DirectPrint*

alternative feature that its binding strategy of its variants depends on the availability of the printer (the forth rule).

2.3 Research Problems in Feature-Oriented Variability Reconfiguration

During runtime, the DSPL application should monitor the current situation and activate the corresponding feature variability reconfiguration specified by the ECA rules. However, when transferring the reconfiguration from the feature level to the implementation level, the following problems may emerge.

On the one hand, the complex mapping between the features and the implementation artefacts poses difficulty for the dynamic reconfiguration. Under the circumstance, a feature is not directly mapped to the coarse-grained component, service or plug-in. However, a single feature variation may influence several fine-grained program units. For example, if the feature *OnlineTimeControl* is bound to be available, it will first introduce a list which is used to store the remaining online time of each access to the module implementing *UserAccessControl*. Furthermore, it will also append an operation to start the timing as soon as a new access is permitted. In addition, the feature will activate a thread which checks the time list all the time to find out and stop the overtime access. Thus, without a clear traceability between the two levels, what to do to reconfigure in the program artefacts is hard to be specified.

On the other hand, the underlying runtime collaboration between the features may also influence the execution of the dynamic reconfiguration. For instance, if *ConnectionLimit* is bound, it can modify the behavior of *Userlogin* by determining whether to execute it or not although the collaboration is not explicitly illustrated in the feature model. If it is not bound, the constraint will not take effect. Another example is that *UserAccessControl* may invoke *OnlineTimeControl* to initialize the timing for an access if the latter feature is bound. The collaborations especially between the common features and the variable features vary in different scenarios and can be dynamically established or revoked during runtime. Therefore, without a comprehensive description of the various feature collaboration, the reconfiguration is hard to be applied in the program level, i.e. what kind of collaborations and how they can be reconfigured.

Existing coarse-grained mapping methods are not suitable for capturing the decomposition of the feature's responsibility as well as the underlying collaborations. Therefore, an effective mapping method which provides explicit traceability from the business model to the implementation artefacts is desired. In addition, a mechanism towards the program level adaptation driven by the dynamic feature binding is consequently necessary.

Based on the considerations, we will introduce the role model as well as the reference implementation framework in Section 3 and 4 separately.

3 Role Model of DSPLs

In this section, we will first introduce the basic concepts of the role model by illustrating its meta-model. The included role interactions and their semantics are identified. Then we will present the role-level interaction reconfiguration which is supported by the special control roles.

3.1 The Role Meta-Model

Role model is the logic design model for the implementation of features [18]. It is regarded as a type of domain architecture which relates the business features to the actual program artefacts. Figure 2 depicts the role meta-model together with the features and the code implementations.

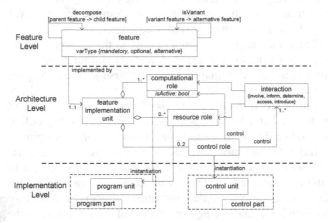

Fig. 2. Meta-model of the role model

In the feature model, feature is the basic element which represents the business operation of a DSPL. Mandatory features, optional features and alternative features are expressed separately. Usually, parent features can be decomposed into the child features which are organized in a tree-like style. Furthermore, variants are specific features that are related to the parent alternative feature with the relationship *isVariant*.

In the architecture level, a feature is implemented by a feature implementation unit which is combined with different kinds of roles. The concept of role here is similar to the *responsibility* in [12] and the *role* in [9]. Compared with features, roles reserve the knowledge of features as well as endow features with the implementation aspects, so it can support the mapping from features to program artefacts in a more natural way [19].

From the meta-model, there are three kinds of roles with separate design concerns. Firstly, a computational role denotes a logical unit or a responsibility which should be taken by the program units for feature implementation. It refines the function of a feature into a finer-grained level so that the existing feature tangling and scattering problems can be alleviated. Furthermore, a computational role has a property *isActive* which claims that the role runs in a recurrent way and requests other's services if the value is true, otherwise to be invoked by others if the value is false. An active role is common in an information system that a lot of specific events are triggered by the active inspection. Secondly, a resource role represents the specific internal or external entity necessary for the implementation of a feature. It is usually cooperated with other computational roles to fulfill a certain business goal. For example, it can be a widget in the user interface and then a computational role can specify its content, or a data structure used to store information which can be read or written by other computational roles. Thirdly, a control role is of much difference with the previous two roles. It takes the responsibility in two respects. On one hand, it helps to manage the status of the interactions (they will be described later) between the previous two roles. Thus, it can control whether a specific interaction can be established or revoked during runtime. On the other hand, it can also influence the active role to determine its running status, i.e. to start it or to suspend it.

A feature may be implemented by a set of identified roles which organize a feature implementation unit. Usually, a feature is certainly to be refined as one or more computational roles. It also involves some resource roles on condition that the feature works on some entities (UI widget, data structure, etc). The control role is not an indispensable element. It exists only if the feature implementation unit corresponds to a feature with variability. This kind of roles takes effect according to the binding strategy of the features.

Furthermore, we do not define the variability property to the roles in the metamodel since all the roles should be included in the product but available at different times. However, for the sake of clearness, we distinguish the roles as base roles and variability-related roles. The former resides in the feature implementation unit which relates to a mandatory feature, while the latter is refined from the variation features.

In the implementation level, the computational roles as well as the resource roles can be instantiated by program artefacts which compose the program part of a DSPL application. The artefacts may be components, classes, methods, code segments or configuration files with various granularities. However, they should be organized as an encapsulated entity especially for the fine-grained units. Sometimes several roles will be instantiated with the artefacts contained in a same encapsulation which is the result of feature tangling. On the other hand, the control role is instantiated by the control unit that contains the operations for managing the role interactions and the active computational roles. It resides in the control part within the DSPL implementations.

Furthermore, there exist various kinds of interactions between the roles. They indirectly denote the underlying collaborations between the features in order to reach the system business goals. Following our previous work in [18], we list the five identified interactions as well as their descriptions in Table 2. The *involve* and *inform* interactions are the functional dependencies between two computational roles, however in different invoking mode. The *determine* interaction is special that it is used to manage the normal execution of the target role by means of the semantic of the source role. The *access* and *introduce* interactions are built between a computational role and a resource role with opposite directions.

It should also be noticed that the *control* links from a control role are not regarded as a kind of role interaction as liste. In fact, it is of great importance for the role-level

Table 2. Descriptions of the role interactions [18]

role interaction	description
involve	a computational role requires a function from another computational role in a synchronous mode
inform	a computational role activates the executing of another computational role in an asynchronous mode
determine	a computational role decides the behavior of another computational role by allowing or rejecting the operation of the target role
access	a computational role accesses a resource role by reading, writing or modifying it
introduce	a resource role is introduced into an implementation unit of another computational role to be a sub-element

interaction reconfiguration based on the feature-level variability reconfiguration which will be represented in the next subsection.

3.2 Role-Level Interaction Reconfiguration

During the adaptation process, the feature variation reconfiguration is further mapped to the role model. Under this circumstance, the variability-related roles can be adapted to be available or unavailable when the runtime reconfiguration is performed. Since the roles cannot be removed from the running application, the management of the role interactions supports the reconfiguration, i.e. the interactions are variable and the dynamic establishing or revoking of the role interactions can change the application's behavior during runtime. For example, if a base role A has an involve interaction towards an optional-related role B, the interaction should be built when the optional feature is bound. Otherwise, the interaction should be removed since the relationship target does not exist anymore.

In our method, the interaction reconfiguration is supported by the control roles. Figure 3 depicts the role-level interaction reconfiguration patterns by the control roles which are related to the two kinds of variation points in the feature model.

For the sake of simplicity, we assume that each feature is implemented by one computational or resource role. Furthermore, in the corresponding feature implementation unit, there exists a control role (CRx) if the feature is of variability. The semantics of the patterns are as follows.

The pattern for the optional feature: Suppose Fb is an optional feature whose parent feature is Fa. Under the separate situations of the interaction scenarios and the

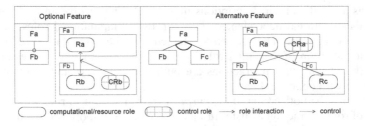

Fig. 3. Role-level reconfiguration patterns by control roles

role types, there may exist all the five types of interactions between Ra and Rb, e.g. usually Ra involve/inform/access Rb, or Rb determine/introduce Ra. The control role CRb manages the existence of the interaction during execution, i.e. establish it when feature Fb is bound, or revoke it when Fb is unbound.

The pattern for the alternative feature: Suppose Fa is an alternative feature and its variants are Fb and Fc. Since the invocation to Fa may be transferred to any of its variant, Ra can have involve or inform interactions towards Rb and Rc. However, the underlying constraint indicates that the two interactions are mutually exclusive, which means only one interaction can be established at a specific time. Therefore, the switch between the interactions is controlled by CRa. Its operation includes two respects of actions, i.e. remove the interaction towards one role and establish the interaction towards another role.

Furthermore, the feature dependency should also be considered. It has nothing to do with the reconfiguration patterns but to put the dependent reconfigurations together in order to reach a valid runtime instance. For example, if an optional feature requires another optional feature, the dependency will indicate that the reconfigurations of the different feature implementation units should be performed at the same time.

Besides, the control role also takes the responsibility to start or suspend an active role in a variability-related feature implementation unit. For example, an active role Ra is refined from an optional feature Fa, and Ra continuously checks the modification of an information list to trigger the events to be handled. Supposing Fa is not bound, Ra's running is meaningless and also wastes the system resource. Thus, it should be stopped or suspended. On the contrary, if Fa is to be bound, Ra should be started as soon as possible. Thus, it is the control role that manages the running status of an active role.

4   The Reference Implementation Framework of DSPLs

The feature-oriented variability reconfigurations should be realized in the implementation layer with the support of the role model. In this section, we will describe the referent implementation framework which adopts *JBoss-AOP* as the dynamic aspect mechanism.

4.1   Dynamic-AOP in *JBoss-AOP*

Dynamic AOP is a powerful technique to realize the dynamic program adaptation [14, 15]. Similar with the traditional static AOP, it also involves the concepts of the binding from advice to pointcut. However, the key characteristic is that the binding can be decided during runtime, i.e. the inclusion of the binding can be changed.

In our method, we adopt *JBoss-AOP* [15] as the underlying mechanism for the dynamic aspect weaving. In *JBoss-AOP*, an aspect is defined by an interceptor and a pointcut. The interceptor is the same as the advice and it is programmed as a *Java* class. The aspect bindings are prepared to be included.

When the dynamic aspect is to be woven, *JBoss-AOP* will dynamically insert or remove the aspect binding through *AspectManager*. The binding establishing process can be described in the following steps: 1) create a new aspect binding by a given name; 2) declare the pointcut of the base program in the created binding; 3) declare the interceptor to the binding. On the other hand, the existing named aspect can also be removed by means of the *AspectManager*.

4.2 Implementation-Level Composition Patterns

The roles are instantiated by the program units or control units. As mentioned in Section 3, the program units can be any artefact in different granularity, including the encapsulated components, classes, or scattered code segments. In our method, we claim the following development principles for the implementations in order to support the runtime reconfiguration. Firstly, the base roles and the variability-related roles should be instantiated by different program units. In particular, different base roles can reside in the same unit while different variability-roles are suggested to be located in separate entities. Secondly, the base roles are requested to correspond to the program artefacts whose granularity is bigger than method so that they can be woven by aspects, i.e. the pointcut can be defined around the methods declared. Thirdly, the program which instantiates a variability-related role should be encapsulated as an interceptor which is a regular *Java* class and implements the *Interceptor* interface.

When preparing a dynamic aspect, the expression of the pointcut as well as the content of the interceptor depends on the type of the role interactions. Table 3 illustrates the composition patterns for the program artefacts separated by the various interaction types. In this mapping, we simply assume that each role is instantiated by a corresponding code encapsulation.

The direction of the aspect weaving (from the interceptor to the pointcut) does not always conform to the direction of the original interaction. For example in the first two rows, if *Ra* has an involve or inform interaction towards *Rb*, *Ia* is woven which means *Ib* is able to adapt the behavior of *Ia* by appending additional functions in an obliviousness way. However, the woven logic can be performed in different modes. Usually, if a role is involved, the base program has to be suspended until the finishing of the interceptor's execution. On the contrary, the base program notifies the interceptor to run in a new thread and continuous its execution if a role is informed.

Table 3. Composition patterns for different role interactions

role interaction	composition pattern	*JBoss-AOP* implementation
Ra —involve→ Rb	Ia ←before/after execution— Ib	pointcut: before or after the execution of *Ia* interceptor: *Ib*, runs in a synchronous mode (the same thread)
Ra —inform→ Rb	Ia ←before/after execution— Ib	pointcut: before or after the execution of *Ia* interceptor: *Ib*, runs in an asynchronous mode (a new thread)
Ra —determine→ Rb	Ia —around execution→ Ib	pointcut: around the execution of *Ib* interceptor: *Ia*, decides whether to proceed *Ib*'s execution or not
Ra —introduce→ Rb	Ia —after execution→ Ib	pointcut: after the execution of *Ib* interceptor: *Ia*, added into *Ib* as a new member, be declared and instantiated after the execution (constructor) of *Ib*
Ra —access→ Rb	Ia ←before/after execution— Ib	pointcut: before or after the execution of *Ia* interceptor: *Ib*, the direct accessing of the resources

In particular, the introduce interaction adopts a simple weaving mode since there is no *intertype* support in *JBoss-AOP* like that in *AspectJ* [17]. Thus, the resource is introduced to be a member of the target unit by appending the code segment which is used to declare and instantiate the resource after the execution of the target implementation, usually after the constructor.

During runtime, the interactions between the roles can be established or revoked. Therefore, the binding statuses of the dynamic aspects towards the various interactions are decided by the implementations of the control roles.

4.3   The Reference Implementation Framework

The reference implementation framework based on *JBoss-AOP* is depicted in Figure 4. It is noticeable that the framework only works for the reconfiguration realization. Therefore, how as well as when the adaptation needs are generated is out of scope.

When encountering a situation that triggers reconfiguration, the strategy of the feature variability reconfiguration is obtained based on the predefined ECA rules. The strategy is the input to the framework and is handled by the two special ingredients which are the global aspect manager and the local aspect manager.

Each local aspect manager is the instantiation of the control role in a single feature implementation unit. It is responsible for establishing or removing the dynamic aspect binding through the steps mentioned in Section 4.1. The local aspect manager is an encapsulated entity composed of a set of operations. The semantics of the operations follow the reconfiguration patterns in Figure 3. For example, in the case of an optional feature, a local aspect manager has one operation to bind the dynamic aspect and the other operation to remove it. As for an alternative feature, each operation has to first remove the existing aspect binding and then to weave the one related to the selected variant in a sequence. In addition, the local aspect managers should be implemented before the system is running. Which operation will be invoked depends on the reconfiguration strategy which is managed by the global aspect manger.

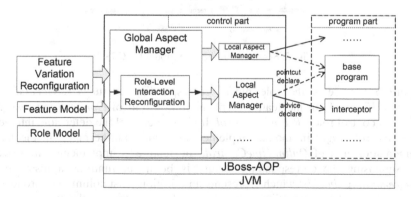

Fig. 4. The reference implementation framework based on *JBoss-AOP*

The global aspect manager, on the other hand, is an independent entity that is responsible for distributing the reconfiguration tasks. As soon as it receives the strategy of the feature variability reconfiguration, the global aspect manager validates the strategy based on the feature model as well as the feature dependencies defined. Then the strategy is transferred to derive a set of role-level interaction reconfigurations. The local aspect managers in the corresponding feature implementation units can be identified based on the feature traceability knowledge. Finally it automatically invokes the corresponding operations to implement the reconfiguration at the program level by managing the dynamic aspects.

5 Case Study

In this section, we will go back to the course selection system in Figure 1 to give out the role model for the DSPL application. Based on it, the program level artefacts following the reference implementation framework are also illustrated.

5.1 The Role Model for the Course Selection System (CCS)

Based on the role meta-model introduced in Section 3, we have constructed the role model for CCS, whose segments are depicted in Figure 5.

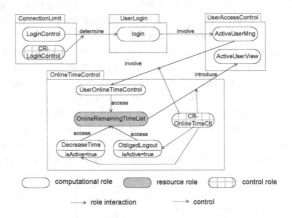

Fig. 5. Segments of the role model for CSS

Figure 5 represents the role model corresponding to the *UserAccessControl* sub-tree in Figure 1. In the feature implementation unit of *ConnectLimit*, we have identified a control role *CR-LoginControl*. It aims to control the determine interaction towards the role *login* in another implementation unit. Furthermore, in the feature implementation unit of *OnlineTimeControl*, the feature is implemented into several roles. Supposing the corresponding feature is bound at runtime, a resource role *OnlineRemainingTimeList* which represents an additional list column is introduced to *ActiveUserView*. The interaction indicates to add a column to the list in the form where the system administrator can check the left time for each user connection. In addition, *UserOnlineTimeControl* is involved by *ActiveUserMng* once there is a new connection. When it is invoked, it will access *OnlineRemainingTimeList* to insert a record of the new access along with its maximal remaining time such as 15 minutes.

On the other hand, *ObligedLogout* is an active role which will continuously access *OnlineTime* to discover the connection that has expired. *DecreaseTime* is also an active role whose responsibility is to modify the time value in the list every three minutes. In the feature implementation unit, the two interactions as well as the two active roles are managed by *CR-OnlineTimeCtl*.

5.2 Reconfiguration Based on the Reference Implementation Framework

Before the DSPL application is running, the artefacts for the dynamic reconfiguration should be implemented. As discussed in Section 4.2, the variability-related roles should be instantiated by the interceptors. We take the resource role *OnlineRemainingTimeList* as an example. Figure 6 depicts the code snippet of the interceptor which instantiates the role.

```
public class TimeListInterceptor implements Interceptor {
    @Override
    public String getName() {
        return "TimeListInterceptor";
    }
    @Override
    public Object invoke(Invocation invocation) throws Throwable {
        Object result = invocation.invokeNext();
        //get the target object usersList
        Object object = invocation.getTargetObject();
        if (object instanceof UsersList) {
            UsersList usersList = (UsersList) object;
            //introduce the limit time column to the show table
            TableColumn loginDateColumn = new TableColumn(usersList.userlistTable, SWT.LEFT);
            loginDateColumn.setText("LimitTime");
            loginDateColumn.setWidth(130);
            //initialize the OnlineTimeList
            AspectPanel.OnlineTimeList.clear();
            Object[] userNames = usersList.getUsers().keySet().toArray();
            for (Object userName : userNames) {
                AspectPanel.OnlineTimeList.put(userName.toString(), AspectPanel.defaultTime);
            }
        }
        return result;
    }
}
```

Fig. 6. Code snippets of the role *OnlineRemainingTimeList* (as an interceptor)

The resource role is introduced into a user-visible form which is developed by SWT (the Standard Widget Toolkit for *Java*). The interceptor then includes a method that appends the codes about the declaration and initialization of the widget after the execution of the pointcut.

On the other hand, *CR-OnlineTimeCtl* should be instantiated as a local aspect manager which contains the operations to establish or revoke the related aspect bindings. Figure 7 depicts the code snippet for the control role.

The local aspect manager is instantiated as a Java class. It first references to the single instance of *AspectManager* provided by the *JBoss-AOP* API (it is not the same as the global aspect manager in the framework). The two operations are represented by the two methods, i.e. *bindOnlineTime* and *unbindOnlineTime*. In the former method, two new aspect bindings are created which can be seen in the first two steps. In sequence, the last two steps offer the instructions to start the programs which instantiate the active roles. On the other hand, the latter method is responsible for removing the named bindings and stopping the active roles' execution.

```
public class CR_OnlineTimeControl {
    AspectManager manager = AspectManager.instance();
    //This function wave two Interceptor.
    public void bindOnlineTime() throws ParseException {
        //1.bind the OnlineTimeInterceptor
        //Here the pointcut is instrument using JBoss AOP expression "execution(...)"
        AdviceBinding timeBinding = new AdviceBinding("OnlineTimeInterceptor",
            "execution(public void swt.UsersList->registerUser(*))", null);
        timeBinding.addInterceptor(OnlineTimeInterceptor.class);
        manager.addBinding(timeBinding);
        //2.bind the "TimeListInterceptor"
        AdviceBinding timeListBinding = new AdviceBinding("TimeListInterceptor",
            "execution(public * swt.UsersList->userToArray(*))", null);
        timeListBinding.addInterceptor(timeListInterceptor.class);
        manager.addBinding(timeListBinding);
        //3.begin to force users who are timeout to logout
        startObligedLogout();
        //4.start to count down users' online time
        startDecreaseTime();
    }
    //This function remove the bindings and stop timer
    public void unbindOnlineTime() throws ParseException {
        //1.stop forcing users out
        stopObligedLogout();
        //2.stop timer
        stopDecreaseTime();
        //3.remove the binding of OnlineTimeInterceptor
        if (manager.getBindings().containsKey("OnlineTimeInterceptor"))
            manager.removeBinding("OnlineTimeInterceptor");
        //4.remove the binding of timeListInterceptor
        if (manager.getBindings().containsKey("timeListInterceptor"))
            manager.removeBinding("timeListInterceptor");
    }
    // startDecreaseTime(), stopDecreaseTime(),startObligedLogout() and stopObligedLogout() are eliminated here
}
```

Fig. 7. Code snippets of the control role (*CR_OnlineContrl*)

During execution, we assume the situation that the concurrent accessing number to CCS has exceeded 500. Therefore, the adaptation is triggered and the action of the first ECA rule in Table 1 (bind *OnlineTimeControl*) is to be performed. On the same time, due to the feature dependency, the optional feature *TemporaryReserve* should also be bound.

The feature variability reconfiguration strategy is input into the framework and the reconfiguration is handled by the global aspect manager. During the process, it firstly identifies the local aspect managers for *OnlineTimeControl* and *TemporaryReserve*. Then it invokes the corresponding methods to accomplish the target of the runtime reconfiguration, e.g. invokes *bindOnlineTime* method for realizing the binding of *OnlineTimeControl*. As a result, the behavior of the DSPL has been modified without recompiling the application.

5.3 Discussion

Based on the preliminary results from the case study, the proposed method can be regarded as an effective way to help the feature-oriented variability reconfiguration in DSPLs.

First, the role model helps to establish the dynamically reconfigurable artefacts based on the refinement of the features. At the same time, it is also used to clarify the complex mapping between the features and the implementation programs. When refining, we use the computational and resource roles to cover the responsibility of a feature. After that, the roles are instantiated by program artefacts. Thus, at the application construction time, the role model can indicate the developers about the artefacts that should be prepared for the dynamic reconfiguration, e.g. implementation for the role *OnlineRemainingTimeList* as an interceptor and the implementation for the control role *CR-OnlineTimeCtl*. In addition, during the reconfiguration process, the artefacts can be located based on the clear traceability so that the reconfiguration in the implementation level can be correctly implemented conforming to the feature level strategy.

Second, the role interactions in the model contribute to clarify the underlying runtime collaboration between the features. Besides the identified feature dependencies, the semantic relationships between the features should also be captured. Therefore, the role interactions describe the behavior of the application and explain how the features can be collaborated to achieve the business goal in a finer-grained view. On the other hand, we conclude the patterns for the different role interaction types based on the AOP technique (see in Table 3) although the binding directions as well as the definitions of the aspect elements vary between each other. Thus, the reconfiguration on the feature variations can be transferred into the role level as the decision on the binding status of a set of unified dynamic aspects, further identifying the reconfiguration scope in the program level. Furthermore, the special control roles are necessary in the DSPL applications that they help to interpret the reconfiguration from the features to the roles.

In a word, the benefits provided by the role model help us to draw a systematic process for the realization of the runtime adaptation, i.e. from the feature-level variation reconfiguration, to the role-level interaction reconfiguration, and finally to the implementation-level code adaptation.

We also propose a reference implementation framework to support the reconfiguration realization. The framework claims the program patterns for the role interactions including the interceptors and the local aspect managers which should be developed before the system is running. Based on it, the program-level reconfiguration can be performed in a manageable way. On the other hand, the dynamic aspect mechanism of *JBoss-AOP* is able to change the application's behavior without intervening the system running.

However, the method introduced still has several limitations. First, it may have difficulty for managing the artefacts when encountering large scale applications. Under the circumstances, the domain model may contain thousands of features, which will make the number of the roles as well as the program artefacts expand to a degree hard to handle. Second, the role model is designed in an ad-hoc way. Furthermore, the codes for the dynamic aspect binding are also developed by experienced developers with the knowledge of *JBoss-AOP*. So, it lacks a supporting tool which can ease the job for practical use. Third, the example DSPL application in our paper is simple that it cannot cover all the applied capability for adaptation. In fact, we have not considered the scenarios where conflicts will emerge in the reconfiguration process.

6 Related Works

The method in this paper is the extension of our previous work in [18]. In that work, the role model is introduced to ease the product derivation in the product line with static variability. The role interactions are classified and implemented using *AspectJ*.

However, our method applies the role model for a single DSPL application where there is also the problem of the complex mapping between the features and the program implementations. Under the circumstance, some new characteristics have been addressed. First, we introduce a new kind of control role which is of great importance to the role-level reconfiguration. Second, we adopt the dynamic-AOP technique (*JBoss-AOP*) to support the implementation-level adaptation since *AspectJ* lacks the capability for the dynamic aspect weaving. Third, we propose a reference implementation framework for the realization of the runtime reconfiguration.

Our work is close to the dynamic product reconfiguration. Lee et al. [5] propose a systematic approach to developing dynamically reconfigurable core assets in product line engineering as well as a reconfigurator model to manage the product configuration at runtime. In their method, the feature binding analysis takes an important role in identifying the granularity of the configuration units and the corresponding binding time. On the other hand, the reconfigurator including the master and local configurators is introduced to perform the consistent feature variation binding during runtime. In addition, Lee et al. [6] further provide a formal representation mechanism to analyze and specify the features that may vary as a part of reconfigurations within a family of products, thus supporting the consistent reconfiguration. Our method also aims at the goal of the dynamic product reconfiguration driven by the feature variation binding. However, it differs in the following aspects: We focus on the reconfiguration of a single DSPL application and all the feature variations are incorporated into the product initially. Furthermore, we also involve the activity to analyze features but in an opposite direction that we refine them to imply the program artefacts in the finer granularity level based on the role model.

There are other works concentrating on the dynamic reconfiguration upon the different kinds of program artefacts driven by the feature variation bindings. Trinidad et al. [4] propose a method to map the feature models onto the component architecture for building a DSPL. The mapping is direct and the self-adaptation can be realized by the dynamic connection between the specific components. Wolfinger et al. [3] propose their method to support adaptation by means of the combination of the product line engineering and the plug-in techniques. The adaptation is then realized by loading and unloading the plug-ins at runtime. Lee and Kotonya [7, 8] introduce their work on the service-oriented product line, where the features can be mapped to the workflow or dynamic services through the service analysis. Thus, the variation of the features can be dynamically bound during runtime by means of selecting the services with right quality levels. These works are based on the clear mapping between the features and the program artefacts with a well-designed feature model. However, the solution to the complex mapping problem is not addressed. Our method takes it into consideration and thus proposes the role model to clarify the complex mapping as well as identify the program implementation in a finer-grained level.

7 Conclusion and Future Work

DSPL provides a new paradigm for developing and managing self-adaptive systems by introducing the principles and techniques proposed in SPL engineering. By DSPL, we can use feature models to capture runtime variations (i.e. adaptation points), as well as their dependencies, to provide a high-level business view for adaptations. Similar to product derivation in SPL engineering, DSPL requires some kinds of variability mechanisms to map feature reconfigurations to implementation-level adaptations. In this paper, we propose a feature-oriented method to support runtime variability reconfiguration in DSPLs. In the method, the role model is introduced to clarify the complex mappings between features and implementation elements. Furthermore, a reference implementation framework based on dynamic aspect mechanisms is also proposed to implement runtime reconfigurations. As a result, the runtime adaptation can be realized in a more systematic way, from the feature-level variation reconfiguration, to the role-level interaction reconfiguration, and finally to the implementation-level code adaptation adopting dynamic AOP.

As for our future work, we will mostly concentrate on improving the limitations discussed in 5.3. More concretely, we will take the tool and runtime infrastructure development as the first step in our plan. The tool and infrastructure are anticipated to support role modeling, feature traceability specification, and automatic code generation for dynamic aspect bindings.

Acknowledgments. This work is supported by National Natural Science Foundation of China under Grant No. 90818009.

References

1. Ganek, A.G., Corbi, T.A.: The dawning of the autonomic computing era. IBM Systems Journal 42(1), 5–18 (2003)
2. Hallsteinsen, S., Hinchey, M., Park, S., Schmid, K.: Dynamic Software Product Line. Computer 41(4), 93–95 (2008)
3. Wolfinger, R., Reiter, S., Dhungana, D., Grunbacher, P., Prahofer, H.: Supporting Runtime System Adaptation through Product Line Engineering and Plug-in Techniques. In: International Conference on Composition-Based Software Systems (ICCBSS), pp. 21–30 (2008)
4. Trinidad, P., Ruiz-Cortes, A., Pena, J., Benavides, D.: Mapping Feature Models onto Component Models to Build Dynamic Software Product Lines. In: International Workshop on Dynamic Software Product Line, DSPL 2007 (2007)
5. Lee, J., Kang, K.C.: A Feature-Oriented Approach to Developing Dynamically Reconfigurable Products in Product Line Engineering. In: International Software Product Line Conference (SPLC), pp. 131–140 (2006)
6. Lee, J., Muthig, D.: Feature-Oriented Analysis and Specification of Dynamic Product Reconfiguration. In: Mei, H. (ed.) ICSR 2008. LNCS, vol. 5030, pp. 154–165. Springer, Heidelberg (2008)
7. Kotonya, G., Lee, J., Robinson, D.: A Consumer-Centred Approach for Service-Oriented Product Line Development. In: Working IEEE/IFIP Conference on Software Architecture (WICSA), pp. 211–220 (2009)
8. Lee, J., Kotonya, G.: Combining Service-Orientation with Product Line Engineering. IEEE Software, 35–41 (2010)
9. Jansen, A.G.J., Smedinga, R., van Gurp, J., Bosch, J.: First class feature abstractions for product derivation. IEE Proc.-Softw. 151(4) (2004)

10. Kang, K.C., Cohen, S.G., Hess, J.A., Novak, W.E., Peterson, A.S.: Feature-oriented domain analysis feasibility study. In: Technical reports, SEI, Carnegie Mellon University (1990)
11. Kang, K.C., et al.: FORM: A feature-oriented reuse method with domain-specific architecture. Annals of Software Engineering 5, 143–168 (1998)
12. Zhang, W., Mei, H., Zhao, H.: Feature-driven requirement dependency analysis and high-level software design. Requirements Eng. 11, 205–220 (2006)
13. Riebisch, M., Brcina, R.: Optimizing Design for Variability Using Traceability Links. In: International Conference on Engineering of Computer Based Systems, pp. 235–244 (2008)
14. Bockisch, C., Haupt, M., Mezini, M., Ostermann, K.: Virtual Machine Support for Dynamic Join points. In: International Conference on Aspect-Oriented Software Development, AOSD 2004 (2004)
15. Khan, D.: JBoss-AOP (2008), http://www.jboss.org/jbossaop/
16. Dittrich, K.R., Gatziu, S., Geppert, A.: The Active Database Management System Manifesto: A Rulebase of ADBMS Features. In: Sellis, T.K. (ed.) RIDS 1995. LNCS, vol. 985, pp. 3–20. Springer, Heidelberg (1995)
17. AspectJ Team. AspectJ Project, http://www.eclipse.org/aspectj/
18. Peng, X., Shen, L., Zhao, W.: Feature Implementation Modeling Based Product Derivation in Software Product Line. In: Mei, H. (ed.) ICSR 2008. LNCS, vol. 5030, pp. 142–153. Springer, Heidelberg (2008)
19. Shen, L., Peng, X., Zhao, W.: A comprehensive feature-oriented traceability model for software product line development. In: Australian Software Engineering Conference (ASWEC), pp. 210–219 (2009)

Reuse by Placement: A Paradigm for Cross-Domain Software Reuse with High Level of Granularity

Yingxiao Xu[1,2], Jay Ramanathan[2,*], Rajiv Ramnath[2], Nisheet Singh[2], and Shubhanan Deshpande[2]

[1] Software School, Fudan University, 200433, Shanghai, China
[2] CETI, Computer Science and Engineering, The Ohio State University, 43210, Columbus, OH, U.S.A.
`xu.667@osu.edu`, `{jayram,ramnath,singhni}@cse.ohio-state.edu`, `deshpande.34@osu.edu`

Abstract. It is a challenge to reuse existing software at a high level of granularity across different domains. Inspired by product placement for advertising in markets, where a movie can be "reused" for advertising without losing the function of the movie, this paper proposes a new paradigm for software reuse: "reuse by placement". This concept is illustrated in this paper using serious games. A framework based on virtual interactions is presented to provide dynamic placement points with reusable services to facilitate implanting new requirements intoop games in educational and human computation domains.

Keywords: Reuse, placement, implanting, human computation, serious game.

1 Introduction

"Software reuse is the process of creating software systems from existing software rather than building software systems from scratch"[1]. The reuse granularity of software may be at multiple levels – at a low level (i.e. reuse of design patterns), mid-level (i.e. reuse of the software framework), or high level (such as when product line techniques are used to identify reusable components). The higher the level of granularity, the more difficult it is to reuse software across different domains. Consider as an example, the fact that product lines typically only support reuse within the same product family.

As software needs become complex, software reuse at a higher level of granularity *across different domains* enables these needs to be met better and more cost-effectively. For example, an educational software developer might lack skills to design software that is enjoyable and attractive for students. Since many enjoyable and attractive games already exist, it would be of great benefit if the educational software developer can reuse games for the purpose of education. This reuse is in fact, exhibiting itself in the domain of serious games [2]. Another example of cross-domain reuse is in the use of crowdsourcing or human computation [3] to solve computationally

---

* Corresponding author.

K. Schmid (Ed.): ICSR 2011, LNCS 6727, pp. 69–77, 2011.

complex problems. Here, computationally difficult problems are broadcast to humans (that make up the "crowd") who use their unique abilities to generate solutions. For example, in an optical character recognition (OCR) program, scanned characters that are difficult to recognize may be delegated in real time to a human crowd, which does the recognition. This technique is currently being used via security applications [4], and games[5, 6] that use aggregated user responses in their decision making.

However, although there are examples of such reuse in serious games[6] and human computation[4, 5] fields, this type of reuse has not been comprehensively studied. Such an approach has not yet been formally proposed as a reuse paradigm, and no tools exist to facilitate reuse from this perspective. In this paper, we propose a new paradigm that we call "reuse by placement" as a start towards such a comprehensive study.

The underlying idea is analogous to product placement [7, 8], an approach widely used in the advertising market. A key problem to be addressed in designing an advertisement is to make it reach its (hopefully large) target population. Product placement leverages movies and television programs have already attracted these populations, by placing or "implanting" the advertisement in them. Note that the advertisers are not building a similar movie, or applying the additional skills required to turn a movie into a revenue source. The movies and television programs are being reused as it is, but are providing some points (or "hooks") where different products may be advertised without affecting the normal function of movie or television program.

This concept is what we propose to generalize into the conceptual model for "reuse by placement". We explore this generalization in Section 2, along with giving some examples from the educational and human computation domains. In Section 3, we develop a framework that facilitates the placement of education and human computation elements in reusable games. In Section 4 we provide a "case study" on how the framework may be utilized for reuse. Section 5 describes related work, while Section 6 concludes the paper and motivates future work.

2   Conceptual Model for Reuse by Placement

Figure 1 illustrates the conceptual model behind reuse by placement. Here, an existing piece of software meets a requirement in Domain 1. However, it also exhibits an attribute (for example, the use of crowd-sourcing) that is a need within software to be written for Domain 1. A placement point that exposes this attribute allows it to be reused in Domain 1. Thus, when a new software capability in Domain 1, but with

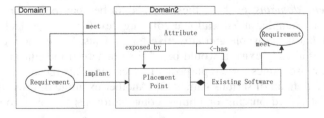

Fig. 1. Conceptual Model of Reuse by Placement

the attribute exposed from Domain 2, is needed, the developer implants the requirement from Domain 1 into the existing system in Domain 2 through use of the placement point.

We illustrate this concept through examples of placement drawn from the educational and human computation domains:

- Reuse of a "dress up game" for memory improvement

In the traditional dress-up game, players can dress up models with clothes, hats, and other apparel and accessories. This game has a significant following. To reuse this for an educational purpose, like improving memory, we can refactor the game by configuring each object (cloth, hat etc.) with different pop-up descriptions that are to be associated with a particular model and name. From a game perspective, the game now becomes more challenging as the player has to determine and then remember a set of clothes that the particular model likes, instead of choosing clothes arbitrarily (note that the essential nature of the game has not changed; it is still a dress-up game). However, the game can now be used to train users in memorization or assess their ability to remember, because it requires matching the descriptions (configured to clothes) with the concepts (configured to the model).

The placement point in this game is exposed through a configuration file. This file configures in concepts from the memorization domain and implants it into the game user-interface (in the pop-up dialogs that enable dress or accessory selection) and the game logic (determined by the rules that determine whether a dress selection is allowed).

- Reuse of existing "minesweeping game" for improving factual recall

In traditional minesweeping game, the player looks for mines by reasoning about the information (i.e. the numbers of surrounding in the adjacent squares) about an uncovered square. In order to make this game more enjoyable, a game developer (who is the entertainment expert) may create a three-dimensional version of this game, have objects in the game environment provide cryptic clues as to mine locations, and have mine variants that require the player to select an appropriate tool to sweep the mine. This game may now be used as an educational program for improving factual recall. The game can also now be used for training or assessing knowledge by associating (through configuration) different images for each type of mine and configuring different names for each tool. Now, in order to impart medical training related to cells, for example, an image of a simple cuboidal epithelium may be configured to a mine. When the player finds the mine, three sweep tools could appear, each configured with a different name, "Simple squamous epithelium", "Simple cuboidal epithelium" and "Simple columnar epithelium" respectively. Through the act of selecting a tool to sweep the mine, the player may be trained or assessed in the ability to recognize the different kinds of tissues in the images. In fact, this game may be taken even further to achieve individualized training, because history data of players could be retained and analyzed to control which images are configured in a game for the current player at a given time. In this way, the game can be used to teach students in accordance with their aptitude.

Note that the placement point of this game is also a configuration file (that controls the game user interface and game logic as in the previous example).

● Reuse of a game to achieve human computation features

The minesweeping game may be (further) reused for medical diagnosis by incorporating human computation. For example, there could be photographs of tissues that need to be recognized and categorized. This is a problem for which it is hard to find reliable computer algorithms. However, the human brain can do this task well (when it already has the relevant knowledge). Assuming the minesweeping game has the property that a lot of students use it to train in anatomy courses, we can further reuse the educational game for recognizing otherwise difficult to characterize tissue photographs. This can be done by recording all the data during the game lifetime and analyze the performance of all the players. For example, if a photo is recognized as a simple columnar epithelium by 90% of students, and these students get a high score in most examinations, then it is very likely that these students are correct, and the image is that of a simple columnar epithelium. Here also, the placement point is implemented by a configuration file.

Note that, in these three examples, the original software is reused as a whole, and at a very high level of granularity. Figure 2 (below) shows where reuse by placement fits as a overall reuse paradigm.

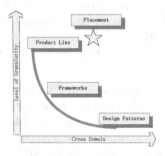

Fig. 2. Illustrating the Reuse by Placement Approach on the Axes of Granularity and Extension Across Domains

Note that the examples above have similarities in the technique used in the implementation of the placement point and in the framework services needed. These similarities indicate why we believe that that a generic framework for placement-based reuse may be possible. We describe this generic framework next. This framework will focus on developing applications in the education and human computation domains, through placement-based reuse of functionality in games in the gaming domain.

3 A Framework for Reuse-by-Placement in the Gaming Domain

Products and advertisement placements in movies only seek to show the product to the audience as part of the movie narrative, which does not have change in order to showcase the product or the advertisement. The challenge with placement-based reuse of applications is that the satisfactory use of the placement point by other applications could need changes to the user-interface and the logic of the original application. For example, applications in the education and human computation domains need a high degree of participation from humans, not to mention a lot of data analysis. Thus, the reuse framework needs to take into account human interaction and instance data needs.

We show an architecture for a reuse-by-placement framework in the gaming domain in Fig. 3. We developed this architecture by abstracting the core (or stable) part of the application and separating it from the reusable aspects of the application that make for the placement points. The core of the framework is the game layer that abstracts or "virtualizes" the game interactions. This layer makes its user-interface and data-management layers reusable by adopting the concept learning objects [9] (thus defining a knowledge base of related objects), which are used to organize knowledge "chunks" and their related user-interfaces into digital education-related items that can be reused in different contexts. The game logic is also made stable by architecting the game engine as a set of agents with local decision-making capability and locally provided services. The data analysis component of the game is made stable through what we term "interaction data virtualization". The actual placement is enabled (as in the examples in the previous section) through a configuration file and through rules that are interpreted by the agents. We discuss the details below.

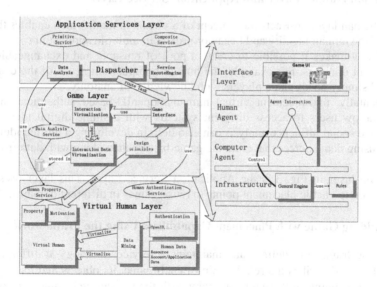

Fig. 3. Details of the "Reuse by Placement" framework

3.1 Game Layer

- Interaction and User Interface Virtualization

The idea used here is based on declarative computational models that describe games as state transition systems[6, 10]. Essentially, a game can be looked at as agents that interact with each other. Each agent receives events and executes state transitions in response to these events, based on a set of configured rules. We use this technique to implement placement points by extending the concept of an agent to include its domain knowledge as well as its user-interface. A general engine can now be developed – that simply initiates the agents and drives their state transitions. We call the use of these techniques – that make it possible to place new user interfaces and interactions into existing games - "interaction virtualization".

- Interaction Data Virtualization

Agent interactions produce interaction data that are then processed using patterns that are common in a given domain. We abstract these as "Interaction Data Virtualization". For example, [5] categorizes (a subset of) games as output-agreement, input-agreement and inversion-problem games. We therefore argue that common data management processes can be developed for games within each category. These common processes make it possible to abstract the details of the game and reuse the interaction data of another application.

Finally, since interaction data is human-driven, it is necessary to provide a unified human identity and profile service across different games. This leads to another layer of the framework, namely, the Virtual Human Layer.

3.2 Virtual Human Layer and Application Service Layer

Virtual human layer abstracts the concept of a virtual human, which enables the unification of the human identity and behavior profile in multiple applications.

This now makes it possible to create a pool of reusable and exchangeable games for different domains. For example, the human computation needs of the example in section 2 simply needs game players with knowledge of anatomy.

Incidentally, to implement virtual humans, openID-based authentication can be used to allow users to access different systems with a single digital identity. Data mining and social influence analysis can also help in developing a unified identity and profile, using data sources that combine game history data along with data from social networks.

The top layer in Fig. 3 is the Application Service Layer. This layer uses service composition to enable placement points to reuse games in different domains.

3.3 Building Game with Placement Capabilities Using the Framework

Finally, the framework defines and maintains a services ontology at different levels. This ontology describes the relationship of each game, its objects and its services, as well as the mapping of the game ontology with the pre-defined framework ontology. This configuration is stored in files that we term the "Scape API".

Thus, the construction of game using the framework can be divided into 4 steps. 1) Describe storyline and scenario. 2) Identify game objects and build domain ontology (users, interactions, goals and events). 3) Map the game ontology on the predefined ontology in the framework. 4) Develop the user-interface, and (5) Develop the application logic using the services provided in framework.

To place a new requirement, the game storyline or scenario will be revised to incorporate the new requirement, and the Scape API will be revised for the new interaction and user-interface.

4 Implementation Case Study

Within the Center for Experimental Research in Computing Systems (an NSF-funded Industry University Collaborative Research Center) we have developed a knowledge-based cyber-infrastructure we call Mirror [11, 12] and refactored it based on the framework concepts described in this paper. It uses well-known design and software architecture patterns to provide game services, which may be reused to address requirements across domains.

4.1 A Health Game with Placement Points

To begin with, an interactive "Health Game" has been developed. In this game, one of the scenarios is one that interacts with the user to determine whether he or she is drunk. In this scenario, a view with an embedded image and data is sent to the player (the view is defined through configuration). The players interact with the user-interface of the view, the system gets the response, records it and publishes it to Facebook. By invoking the transition rule according to player's response, the game identifies the supposed alcohol level of the user and then transitions to the next state depending on this alcohol level (a sequencer drives the state transitions - essentially the Interaction Virtualization and Rules Engine shown in Figure 3.) It loads the scenario specification from the configuration file that contains the necessary information about the interaction, and then sends the proper user interface (the Game User Interface component in Figure 3.) to the player. This process is repeated until the goal state is reached. Finally, this application uses a Facebook service, as the virtual human layer in Fig. 3. Interaction data is also collected in Facebook for analysis.

4.2 Placement-Based Reuse of the Health Game

We illustrate the placement-based reuse implementation of an "intelligent" application that determines whether two sentences have the same meaning. This application essentially implants the comparison task as a human computation task into the drunk driving scenario above. A policeman (played by Player B) tests Player A to determine whether he is drunk by essentially asking, "Can you tell me whether the following two sentences have the same meaning?" Player A has to give correct answers to all the questions to demonstrate that he is not drunk. In the game, if policeman finds player A has all correct answers, a blood test will be conducted to make sure that he is not drunk. Otherwise, player A will be judged (by Player B) as drunk directly based on the wrong answers to the question.

Thus, by analyzing answers of Player A and the judgment of Player B in multiple sessions, we will get the answer to the sentence comparison.

To implant this interaction, we simply add to the configuration file a human user whose goal is to answer certain questions, an initial state that initiates the interaction with the police, a user-interface for the presentation of the comparison questions, and rules that drive this interaction. Thus the Health Game now becomes a human-computation-based application that answers sentence comparison questions.

Note that although the game has been configured for a different purpose, the data-management process is the same. However, the interaction data may be different.

5 Related Work

There is a fair amount of existing work that describes placement-based reuse in different forms. But this concept has not been methodically approached from a purely reuse perspective. Also, no paradigm has so far been presented regarding the design of a placement-based framework and tools that facilitate such reuse.

One related practice is public resource computing, which reuses screen savers for crowdsourcing purposes, such as GIMPS [13], the Distributed.net project[14] and the SETI@home project[15]. BOINC[16] and XtremWeb [17] are two examples of a framework and tools developed to assist the creation of public resource computing projects. Human computation reuse has been described in reCAPTCHA [4], and GWAPs(Games With A Purpose) [5], both projects being designed to solve large-scale human-computation problems. The practices above prove the effectiveness and value of our proposed paradigm. Also, point-and-click game engines already exist, such as the Adventure *Game* Studio[18] and the Wintermute Engine[19]. They provide editors to help create adventure games, and provide runtime engines to play the game. [6] describes an education game based on a specially designed educational game engine: e-Adventure. These engines use script languages to facilitate the development of the game. However, all these focus on their specific domain – by providing reusable components that specifically facilitate the development of adventure games, while our work focuses on imposing new requirements on an existing game in order to reuse it in a different domain or context. These requirements are incorporated into placement points that determine the behavior of the game in a *different* context. Thus, the unique feature of our framework is that it facilitates reuse of multiple games in multiple domains for multiple purposes.

6 Conclusions and Future Work

Our paradigm of placement-based-reuse facilitates reuse of existing software at a high level of granularity in different domains, as exemplified in the prototypes described in Section 4.

The new paradigm identifies several potential areas for further study. Some of them are: How to improve the framework for more complex scenarios in support of more domains? Are there any new forms of placement points identifiable when extending this concept to other domains? How do we quantify game attributes for appropriate game selection during task routing? In general, how may we improve the choice of games in the game pool for reuse? What attributes of the game would affect learning and human computation the most, and how would this affect the reuse? How may we reason about the existing functionality of the game that has been influenced by placement? We seek to study these issues in our future work.

Acknowledgements

We wish to acknowledge the support of the National Science Foundation's IUCRC program for CERCS and the industry sponsors and graduate students for generating interesting ideas and discussion.

References

1. Krueger, C.W.: Software reuse. ACM Comput. Surv. 24, 131–183 (1992)
2. Vidani, A.C., Chittaro, L.: Using a Task Modeling Formalism in the Design of Serious Games for Emergency Medical Procedures. In: Proceedings of the 2009 Conference in Games and Virtual Worlds for Serious Applications, pp. 95–102. IEEE Computer Society, Los Alamitos (2009)
3. von Ahn, L.: Human computation. In: 2008 IEEE 24th International Conference on Data Engineering, vol. 1-3 1-2 (2008)
4. von Ahn, L., Maurer, B., McMillen, C., Abraham, D., Blum, M.: reCAPTCHA: Human-based character recognition via web security measures. Science 321, 1465–1468 (2008)
5. von Ahn, L., Dabbish, L.: Designing games with a purpose. Communications of the ACM 51, 58–67 (2008)
6. Moreno-Ger, P., Burgos, D., Martinez-Ortiz, I., Sierra, J.L., Fernandez-Manjon, B.: Educational game design for online education. Computers in Human Behavior 24, 2530–2540 (2008)
7. Russell, C.A.: Toward a framework of product placement: Theoretical propositions. In: Alba, J.W., Hutchinson, J.W. (eds.) Advances in Consumer Research, vol. 25, pp. 357–362. Assoc. Consumer Research, Provo, (1998)
8. Xu, C.S., Wan, K.W., Bui, S.H., Tian, Q.: Implanting virtual advertisement into broadcast soccer video. In: Aizawa, K., Nakamura, Y., Satoh, S. (eds.) PCM 2004. LNCS, vol. 3332, pp. 264–271. Springer, Heidelberg (2004)
9. Vorvilas, G., Karalis, T., Ravani, K.: Applying Multimodal Discourse Analysis to Learning Objects user interface. Contemporary Educational Technology 1(3), 255–266 (2010)
10. Winskel, G.: The formal semantics of programming languages: an introduction. MIT Press, Cambridge (1993)
11. Singh, N.: Sense Respond Environment for Adaptive Participatory Services. Computer Science and Engineering, vol. Master. The Ohio State University (2010)
12. Deshpande, S.: Knowledge-based Cyberinfrastructures for Decision Making in Real World Domains. Computer Science and Engineering, vol. Master. The Ohio State University (2011)
13. Great Internet Mersenne Prime Search:GIMPS, http://www.mersenne.org/
14. Distributed.net Project, http://distributed.net
15. Anderson, D.P., Cobb, J., Korpela, E., Lebofsky, M., Werthimer, D.: SETI@home: An experiment in public resource computing. Communications of the ACM 45, 56–61 (2002)
16. BONIC:Open-source software for volunteer computing and grid computing, http://boinc.berkeley.edu
17. XtremWeb: the Open Source Platform for Desktop Grids, http://www.xtremweb.net/
18. AGS: Adventure Game Studio, http://www.adventuregamestudio.co.uk/
19. Wintermute Engine, http://dead-code.org/

A Semi-supervised Approach for Component Recommendation Based on Citations

Sibo Cai[1,2], Yanzhen Zou[1,2,*], Lijie Wang[1,2], Bing Xie[1,2], and Weizhong Shao[1,2]

[1] Software Institute, School of Electronics Engineering and Computer Science,
Peking University, Beijing 100871, P.R. China
[2] Key Laboratory of High Confidence Software Technologies, Ministry of Education,
Beijing 100871, P.R. China
{caisb06,zouyz,wanglj07,xiebing}@sei.pku.edu.cn,
wzshao@pku.edu.cn

Abstract. Reusing existing components can help developers improve the development productivity as well as reduce the cost. Reuse repositories in this scenario act as a fundamental facility for acquiring needed components. While retrieving components in reuse repositories, developers often face the problem of choosing components from candidates which provide similar functionalities. To address the problem, this paper proposes a semi-supervised method to recommend developers components in reuse repositories. With a random walk algorithm, our approach calculates the recommendation probability of components based on their citations on the Internet to identify recommendable components. We implemented our approach with a prototyping system and conducted an experimental study to evaluate the effectiveness of the approach.

1 Introduction

It is widely believed that reusing existing components can help developers create applications with less effect and improved quality [1]. In a typical process of reuse-based software development, developers first need to work out a reuse plan and then search reuse repositories to find proper components according to the reuse plan [2]. In detail, the component retrieval process can be divided into two steps: Firstly, developers search reuse repositories to find component candidates that provide needed functionalities. Secondly, developers select proper ones from the candidates and integrate them together to build the target system.

Selecting components from candidates is very crucial for system integration. Before the adaption and integration of the components, developers often have to prototype a testing environment to validate the selected components to make sure that the selected components could satisfy the detailed requirements [3]. A casual selection of components may put developers into the risk of wasting a lot of time and effort. Therefore, some user rating/review mechanisms have been developed to help developers make informed component selection decision in real world reuse repositories, such as SourceForge [5] and ComponentSource [6]. User rating/review mechanisms

---

* Corresponding author

K. Schmid (Ed.): ICSR 2011, LNCS 6727, pp. 78–86, 2011.

can provide information to assist developers in making selection decision; however, such mechanisms are always blamed for their shortage of rating/review due to the user motivation problem [7]. In most cases, developers have to spend extra effort collecting related information or try the retrieved candidates one by one to decide which component to use. The selection process becomes inefficient.

To resolve the problem, we propose a novel component recommendation method based on the citations of the components appearing on the Internet. With the development of Internet, especially the emergence of Web 2.0, more and more reusable components are likely to be involved on the Internet [8]. The appearance of components on the Internet can be components for download (such as the components in Download.com [12]), components at runtime (like Java Applet [9]) or component-centric description or discussion (such as the appearance in Ohloh [13]). In general, the more times a component appears on the Internet, the more probable it should be recommended to developers since developers usually tend to choose components cited by more websites (called *host* in this paper). Furthermore, when a host is known to involve amounts of recommended components, then the components cited on this host can be considered more probable to be recommendable ones.

In this paper, we propose a semi-supervised approach for component recommendation in reuse repositories based on their citations on the Internet and implement the approach in a prototyping system. In our approach, a crawler is designed to obtain hosts which involve the components and build the associations between the components and the hosts. Through exploring the associations with a random walk algorithm, we work out the recommendation probabilities for all components. In order to provide access to the components, a free-text based component retrieval mechanism is also implemented. We evaluate our approach through an experimental study based on real data. The results show that our approach can accurately identify recommendable components.

The rest of this paper is organized as follows: Section 2 describes our proposed approach for recommending components. Section 3 presents our experimental study on the proposed approach with the results analyzed. Section 4 presents some discussions about our approach and the future work. Then in the last section, we conclude this paper.

2 Our Approach

As presented in Fig. 1, our approach consists of three functional parts: the *retriever*, the *crawler* and the *recommend engine*. The retriever obtains relevant component candidates from the reuse repository according to the query submitted by developers for further recommendation. The crawler obtains the hosts which involve the components in the reuse repository from the Internet and builds associations between the components and the hosts. The recommend engine calculates recommendation probability for each component utilizing the associations generated by the crawler and produces the recommendable components based on the retrieved candidates to developers.

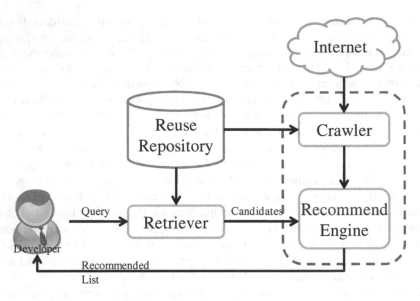

Fig. 1. The architecture of our approach

2.1 The Retriever

In the retriever, we simply adopt free-text based approach [10] for component re-trieval where components are indexed by name and descriptions. Note that although we use free-text approach to acquire relevant components from the reuse repository, our method for recommending components is not limited by the component retrieval mechanisms. The retrieved component candidates will be further analyzed in the recommend engine to get their recommendation probability.

2.2 The Crawler

The crawler is used to obtain the hosts which involve the components in the reuse repository from the Internet and build the associations between the components and the hosts. We use the web search engine Google[1] to accomplish the hosts crawling task. We search the components with component name as the query and extract URLs from the returned result list. Since the most relevant results are usually distributed at the top position, we only keep the top 30 URLs for each component (returned list less than 30 URLs will all be kept). Then the list of hosts related to the component is iden-tified using the URLs (we use the domain part of URL to represent a host. URLs with the same domain part will be merged).

Since the returned results by Google do not always refer to the exact component if we directly use the component name as the query, some strategies are adopted to obtain the hosts and build the associations more accurately. Firstly, we validate the returned results by using full match of the component name in both the title and the

---

[1] http://www.google.com/

snippet returned by Google. Secondly, we append the keyword "Software" to the query to refine the returned results.

Formally, the associations between components and their hosts can be described as a weighted bipartite graph $G = <COMP, HOST, EDGE>$. The component set $COMP$ and the host set $HOST$ constitute the partitions of the graph. Components and hosts are nodes in the graph whose edges represent the associations between components and hosts. Every association is a non-directional weighted edge $(comp, host) \in EDGE$ where $comp \in COMP$ and $host \in HOST$. The association weight between a component and a host denotes the relevance degree of the component to the host.

$$w_{comp-host} = w_{host-comp} = \frac{N_{comp-host}}{\sum_{c,h:(c,h) \in EDGE} N_{c-h}} \tag{1}$$

In our approach, the association weight of a component related to a host is firstly set as the number of URLs related to the component which are merged into the host. Then, the weights of all associations are normalized using formula (1) where $N_{comp-host}$ is the number of URLs related to the component $comp$ and merged into the $host$. Since the association is non-directional, the weight of a component related to a host equals to the one in reverse order.

2.3 The Recommend Engine

The recommend engine calculates the recommendation probability for each component using the associations and produces the recommendable components based on the retrieved candidates to developers. Every component has a recommendation probability (called "component recommendation probability" in this paper), which means the degree of the component to be recommended. We also set a weight (called "host recommendation probability" in this paper) to every host. The host recommendation probability denotes the degree of the host involving recommended components.

Based on the idea that the component recommendation probability and the host recommendation probability will affect each other, we propose a propagation algorithm to calculate the recommendation probability by adopting a random walk algorithm with absorbing states [11]. The starting point of the propagation is some components which are assigned high recommendation probability. We call this group of components "seeds". The algorithm is described in Fig. 2.

The input of the algorithm contains the seed set S, COMP-HOST bipartite graph G and two parameters α and β. The transition probability α denotes that both the components and the hosts have the probability to transfer to the absorbing state ω [11]. The vanishing threshold β is used as the threshold to distinguish the recommendable components. The output of the algorithm is the component recommendation probability $P(comp)$ for each component except for the seeds.

Initially, the component recommendation probability of the seeds is set to 1 (Line 1). Then the algorithm iteratively calculates the probability for both the components and the hosts (Line 3 to Line 10). In each iteration, the host recommendation probability

---

Input: the seed set S, COMP-HOST bipartite graph G, the vanishing threshold β, the transition probability α to ω

Output: $P(comp)$, for every component except for the seeds

1:    **for each** *comp* **in** S **do** $P(comp) = 1$

2:    **repeat**

3:     **for each** *host* **in** HOST **do**

4:        $P(host) = (1-\alpha)\sum_{comp:comp \in C(host)} w_{host-comp} P(comp)$

5:        **if**($P(host) < \beta$) **then** $P(host) = 0$

6:     **end for**

7:     **for each** *comp* **in** COMP \ S **do**

8:        $P(comp) = (1-\alpha)\sum_{host:host \in H(comp)} w_{comp-host} P(host)$

9:        **if**($P(comp) < \beta$) **then** $P(comp) = 0$

10:    **end for**

11:    **until** convergence

12:    output $P(comp)$, for every component except for the seeds

---

Fig. 2. The propagation algorithm

(denoted as $P(host)$) for each host is calculated by aggregating the weighted component recommendation probability of the components which have associations with the host. *C(host)* in Line 4 denotes the components which are related to the *host*. The probability then will be weakened by $(1-\alpha)$. If the calculated probability is less than β, the probability will be set to 0. The calculation of the component recommendation probability of the components is similar to the one of the hosts where *H(comp)* denotes the hosts which involve the component (Line 8). The iteration will continue until the recommendation probability of both the components and the hosts is convergent. Components with the recommendation probability greater than 0 then will be regarded as recommendable ones.

3   Experimental Study

3.1   Experimental Organization

To evaluate our approach, we applied it to the data collected from a real world reuse repository, i.e. SourceForge, which now provides more than 370,000 open source software projects. We selected the category "Software Development" as our evaluation base, which contains 35,602 software projects at the time we carried out the evaluation. We acquired the project information including project name, description, user positive rating and negative rating etc. The 35,602 software projects constituted the reuse repository in our approach. We used Lucene[2] to index the software projects

---

[2] http:// lucene.apache.org/

and provide retrieval interface. In our experiment, each software project was viewed as a component.

Based on the built reuse repository, we used Google to search for the hosts which involve the components in the reuse repository and extracted associations between the components and the hosts. We totally fetched 251,873 hosts as well as 937,016 associations between the components and the hosts. We sorted the 35,602 projects according to the user ratings provided by SourceForge and selected the top 100 projects as the seed set (less than 0.3% of the component set). Finally, we set α to an empirically small value 0.01 [11] and tune β to 5E-5 using the algorithm described in Fig. 3.

Step 1: Randomly select 80 seeds from the seed set.
Step 2: Conduct the propagation algorithm with the parameter α set to 0.01 and β set to 0.
Step 3: Store the minimum value of the calculated probability of the remaining 20 seeds.
Step 4: Repeat Step1, Step 2 and Step 3 in 5 runs and set β as the average of the stored minimum values.

Fig. 3. Parameter tuning algorithm for β

3.2 Experimental Results

We evaluated the recommendation effectiveness of our approach by using developer queries. We identified 11 queries based on the interviews with 7 graduate students in Peking University and submitted the 11 queries to our prototyping system to retrieve relevant components and more importantly the recommended ones. To validate the recommended components, we adopted the user ratings provided by SourceForge. In the experiment, components are regarded as recommended ones if their number of positive ratings in SourceForge is more than the one of negative ratings.

To show the effectiveness of our approach, we first identified the recommended components by SourceForge from the retrieved ones for each query and found out whether our approach could also produce the recommended components identified by SourceForge. The results are presented in Table 1. The queries are listed in the "Query" column. Column "Retrieved" indicates the number of retrieved components according to the query while the "Recommended" column represents the number of recommended components by our approach contained in the recommended list of SourceForge. The number of components recommended by SourceForge is also indicated (in the bracket).

Through the comparison (exhibited in Table 1) with the recommended components by SourceForge which are based on the user ratings, we preliminarily drew to the conclusion that our approach possesses the ability to identify the recommended components suggested by SourceForge. In order to show the effectiveness of our approach in a better fashion, seeds (if retrieved) were excluded in the retrieval results.

Table 1. Recommended components by SourceForge compared to the ones by our approach

Query	Recommended	Retrieved
XML Parser	3(5)	14
Data Encryption	1(1)	7
Logging	9(11)	12
Math	5(5)	12
Statistics	5(5)	7
Data Compression	1(1)	10
Email	1(1)	6
File Upload	2(4)	14
Configuration File	3(3)	11
Network Utility	1(1)	11
IO Utility	2(2)	14

Table 2. Our recommended components compared to the ones by SourceForge

Query	Recommended	Retrieved
XML Parser	3(7)	14
Data Encryption	1(3)	7
Logging	9(9)	12
Math	5(8)	12
Statistics	5(6)	7
Data Compression	1(3)	10
Email	1(5)	6
File Upload	2(7)	14
Configuration File	3(7)	11
Network Utility	1(8)	11
IO Utility	2(6)	14

We also discussed the precision of the recommended components by our approach. Precision here means the ratio of actual recommended components compared to the ones suggested by our approach. We compared the number of recommended components by our approach to the ones suggested by SourceForge. The 11 queries were still used. Table 2 shows the results. In the column "Recommended", the number of recommended components of our approach is indicated in the bracket. In the recommended list of our approach, the number of components which are also suggested by SourceForge is indicated outside the bracket. In half cases, our approach performs well and produces recommended components similar to the ones by SourceForge, such as "Logging", "Statistics". While in the other half, our approach recommended more components than SourceForge does, especially in the case "Network Utility".

To explore the reason of this phenomenon, we investigated the recommended components by our approach while not suggested by SourceForge. We found that almost all these components received 0 positive rating and 0 negative rating in

SourceForge. "GSA Simple XML Parser[3]" is one of the examples. However, through our investigation of "GSA Simple XML Parser" on the Internet by hand, we finally judged that this component should also be recommended.

4 Discussion and Future Work

4.1 Issues about the Association Refinement

In our approach, we refine the association between components and hosts using the strategies described in section 2, but there are still some problems in building the associations. The most extrusive case is that the name of a component is too general. For example, an xml parser named "xml parser". To search such keywords in Google, the returned results are often irrelevant to the component. Such cases will reduce the effectiveness of our approach and provide problematic recommended list to the developers. Nevertheless, we find that such examples only occupy a very small fraction of the components in real world reuse repositories since people who develop components are mostly intended to pick up a more meaningful name for their components.

4.2 How to Obtain the Seed Set

In our approach, one of the inputs to calculate the recommendation probability of the components is the seed set. The effectiveness of our approach will be greatly reduced if the seed set is hard to obtain. However, the seed set seems not so difficult to identify in real world reuse repositories. Firstly, just like our experimental study, components which have already received high user positive ratings can be considered. Secondly, famous software projects are another option. Thirdly, components that developed by famous companies or organizations, such as Apache, can also be taken into consideration.

Another issue about the seed set is how to select a better seed set. The selection of the seed set may influence the performance of our approach since it is the starting point. Selecting seeds as divergent as possible may be one of the possible strategies that can be used to enhance the performance of our approach. For instance, seeds can be selected considering their application domains. Further study will be conducted in our future work.

5 Conclusion

In this paper, we proposed a semi-supervised approach to produce recommendable components to the developers to assist their selection of components in reuse repositories. The approach utilizes the associations between the components and the involved hosts. With a group of components which are supposed to be recommended and a propagation algorithm, the recommendation probability for each component is calculated. We also implemented a prototyping system to validate our approach using

---

[3] http://sourceforge.net/projects/gsa-simple-xml/

real world data. The results show that our approach can accurately recommend components to the developers comparing to the data from SourceForge.

Acknowledgement

We would like to thank Jing Jin for the experimental data collection. This research was sponsored by the National Natural Science Foundation of China under Grant No. 60821003, the National Basic Research Program of China (973) under Grant No. 2009CB320703 and the National High-Tech Research and Development Plan of China under Grant No.2007AA010301-01.

References

1. Basili, V., Briand, L., Melo, W.: How reuse influences productivity in object-oriented systems. Communications of the ACM 39(10), 104–116 (1996)
2. Mili, H., Mili, A., Yacoub, S., Addy, E.: Reuse based software engineering: techniques, organizations, and measurement. Wiley-Interscience Press, Chichester (2001)
3. Land, R., Alvaro, A., Crnkovic, I.: Towards efficient software component evaluation: an examination of component selection and certification. In: 34th Euromicro Conference Software Engineering and Advanced Applications, pp. 274–281 (2008)
4. Land, R., Blankers, L., Chaudron, M., Crnkovic, I.: COTS selection best practices in literature and in industry. In: Proceedings of the 10th International Conference on Software Reuse: High Confidence Software Reuse in Large Systems, pp. 100–111 (2008)
5. SourceForge (2010), http://sourceforge.net/
6. ComponentSource (2010), http://www.componentsource.com/
7. Jøsang, A., Ismail, R., Boyd, C.: A survey of trust and reputation systems for online service provision. Decision Support Systems 43(2), 618–644 (2007)
8. Hummel, O., Atkinson, C.: Using the web as a reuse repository. In: Proceedings of the International Conference on Software Reuse, pp. 298–311 (2006)
9. Seacord, R.C., Hissam, S.A., Wallnau, K.C.: AGORA: a search engine for software components. IEEE Internet Computing 2(6), 62–70 (1998)
10. Maarek, Y.S., Berry, D.M., Kaiser, G.E.: An information retrieval approach for automatically constructing software libraries. IEEE Transactions on Software Engineering 17(8), 800–813 (1991)
11. Fuxman, A., Tsaparas, P., Achan, K., Agrawal, R.: Using the wisdom of the crowds for keyword generation. In: Proceeding of the 17th International Conference on World Wide Web, pp. 61–70 (2008)
12. Download.com (2010), http://download.cnet.com/
13. Ohloh (2010), http://www.ohloh.net/

Capability Assessment for Introducing Component Reuse

Hugo Rehesaar

Griffith University
Brisbane, Queensland, Australia
+61 414 597 171
hugo.rehesaar@griffithuni.edu.au

Abstract. Despite initial technical barriers having been overcome, organizational wide component reuse has not enjoyed universal acceptance. Research has identified social and organizational factors as probable causes. This paper describes the Social Factors for Reuse Model (SFR Model), a predictive capability model based on Keidel's triadic model of the organization. It determines an organization's readiness for the introduction of Component Based Software Engineering (CBSE); describing the social and organizational conditions that should be met to maximize the chances of successful implementation. A sample application of the Model is described.

Keywords: Component reuse, reuse capability assessment, component based software engineering.

1 Introduction

The reuse of interchangeable components for software systems development was first publicly discussed in 1968 at the NATO Science Committee Conference on Software Engineering: Concepts and Techniques, at Garmisch, Germany [1]. McIlroy argued that a "components industry could be immensely useful" and described the benefits of the reuse of components. Since then, Component Based Software Engineering (CBSE) has been shown to have benefits which include improvement of quality, faster development, and reduction in costs of development and maintenance [2].

Initially, technical factors prevented its successful implementation. Over time, the technical barriers have been all but overcome, and individuals have enthusiastically embraced the reuse of components. Yet, the organization-wide implementation of component reuse has yet to be adopted universally. [3],[4],[5],[6],[7],[8].

Research suggests that the reasons are related to socio-organizational barriers [4],[9],[10]. In order to better understand these, there is a need for a model that formalizes the socio-organizational factors influencing the successful implementation of component reuse. The model described in this paper, The Social Factors for Reuse Model, is inspired by Keidel's Triadic Model of organizations [11] and consists of factors that influence the organization-wide implementation of component reuse in the software engineering environment. It is intended that it will serve as a capability model for assessing an organization's readiness for the implementation of CBSE. By applying this Model, the organization can better decide what must be done to prepare

K. Schmid (Ed.): ICSR 2011, LNCS 6727, pp. 87–101, 2011.

itself for Reuse. The results of the assessment can be entered into an appropriate model to determine the economic and practical feasibility of making the required changes. Thus a Go/No Go decision can be made with greater confidence than otherwise would be possible.

For the purposes of this Model, component based software engineering (CBSE) is defined as the development of a system by the reuse, wholly or partially, of existing components. These components are not restricted to software artifacts or programs. They may include all products of the software development process ranging from requirement specifications and designs through to test data and implantation plans. Processes are also included, for example the elicitation of users' requirements and training of users. The following terms are held to be synonymous with CBSE: organization-wide component reuse, systematic (component) reuse, and component based software development [12]. Object Oriented Development and the use of Commercial off the Shelf (COTS) components are specific implementations of CBSE.

2 Background

2.1 Benefits of CBSE

The expected benefits of the implementation of organization-wide component reuse are well documented and tend to highlight savings in time and cost to develop [13],[14],[15],[16],[17]. IEEE1517-1999(Rev. 2004) [2] lists the following: increase in productivity; shorten software development time; move personnel, tools, and methods more easily from project to project; reduce software development and maintenance costs; produce higher quality software products; improve software product interoperability; provide a competitive advantage to an organization that practices reuse.

It is not suggested that an organization would enjoy all of these benefits, however any one of these would provide a sufficient reason to implement CBSE.

2.2 Non-technical Obstacles to Implementation

Initially, researchers and practitioners identified the technical obstacles to the successful adoption of CBSE, requiring enhancements to existing technology as well as the development and introduction of new technology.

Through the elimination of many of the technical issues in the 1980's and 1990's, component based development gained favour with developers and, in the early 1990's became of growing interest to researchers in the field of software engineering [18], [19],[20],[21],[22],[23]. Brown and Wallnau [24] offer two reasons for this, stating "several underlying technologies have matured that permit building components and assembling applications from sets of those components [and] the business and organizational context within which applications are developed, deployed and maintained has changed" in favour of component reuse.

More recently, 2009, it has been suggested [25] that the organization may have cultures that are not conducive to systematic reuse and may lack the means to change its infrastructure to support the processes of systematic reuse without major disruption to its business. "Producing original software is sometimes more well-regarded than reusing existing software. Changing attitudes and associated non-reuse behaviors can be difficult. Policy changes and capital investments, which require senior management to be firmly committed to the achievement of systematic reuse, may be necessary" [25].

Indeed, the MIT Center for Information Systems Research [26] held a special session during its Summer Session, June 2010, and determined that companies do not reuse for reasons relating to behavior, politics and corporate culture.

Hence, the cause for the continuing lack of successful adoption of organizational wide reuse appears to lie most likely in the areas of organization and culture.

2.3 Reuse Models

Many models for reuse have been proposed, but not necessarily developed, for example [27] in 1993 and more recently [28] in 2007 and [29] in 2009, as well as many more in between. Several models have been developed as far back as 1992 [30] and as recently as 2010 [31]. However, all of these propose or provide for analyses of existing reuse programs and are not intended as predictors of implementation success.

In the late 80's and early 90's, reuse economics gained favour. A review of 17 reuse economic models [32] observed that all the models described and analyzed post-implementation reuse. It recommended that further research should be undertaken into models that would enable not just the evaluation of, but more importantly, the prediction of the costs, return-on-investments and other indicators. The Social Factors for Reuse Model is one such predictive model.

3 The Social Factors for Reuse Model

3.1 Evolution of the SFR Model

The SFR Model was inspired by the Triadic Model of the Organization by Robert Keidel [11]. The triadic shape "counterposes the three critical organizational variables: autonomy, control and co-operation" [11]. These correspond to the ways people interact.

1.   Autonomy relates to working on your own.
2.   Control relates to a hierarchical structure.
3.   Co-operation relates to working together towards a common goal.

This structure is well established in management literature and practice [11].

The influence on the implementation of CBSE of the 36 factors that comprise the Model was obtained from literature and in-depth interviews with experienced software engineers.

The Triadic Model is used to analyze the current state of an organization and also describe the ideal state it needs to be in to successfully implement CBSE, as described in 3.4. By comparing the two states, a determination can be made as to what must be changed in order for the organization to best prepare itself for CBSE implementation.

3.2 Structure of the Model

In the Social Factors for Reuse Model, the Organization is represented by a three tiered structure – see Table 1.

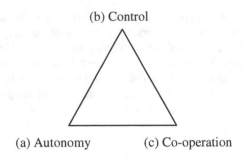

Fig. 1. The Attribute Triad

Tier 1: The Organization is firstly broken down into 2 Dimensions.
(A) Organizational Strategy is concerned with planning and describes the proposed future state of the organization. (B) Organizational Implementation is concerned with processes and describes how the organization expects to achieve the future state.
Tier 2: Each of the Dimensions is further broken down into 6 Attributes: a total of 12. The Attributes for the SFR Model are based on the Keidel Model [11] and been adapted to align them with the domain of software engineering.
Tier 3: Each Attribute comprises of 3 Factors, for a total of 36 factors. The three factors in each Attribute correspond to

a) Autonomy,
b) Control, and
c) Co-operation.

The position of an organization on the triangle, Figure 1, describes its organizational behavior. To effectively manage an organization, a balance must be stuck among these three variables. For any given situation, the decision must be made as to which of these three is the most important. At best, two can share importance, but not all three. The triangular representation of the factors illustrates that you cannot fulfill all three factors at the same time.

An organization that can be described by one of the corners, is said to exhibit 100% of that factor.

An organization that can be described by a point along one of the sides, will exhibit a combination of the two factors at the corners of that side.

The centre area represents an organization that exhibits equal amounts of each of the three factors. Porter describes such an organization as one that "engages in each generic strategy, but fails to achieve any of them" [33].

3.3 Attribute Co-relations

The Attributes are not independent of each other and therefore cannot be assessed independently. Table 1 shows the co-relations. They are

1) Meeting System, Decision System
2) Social Values, Organization's Expectations, Employee's Expectations, Reward System

3) Employee's Expectations, Developmental Plan
4) Reporting Lines, Physical Layout, Information Flow

3.4 The 'Ideal' Candidate for Reuse Implementation

The SFR Model, summarized in Table 1, can be used to describe a generic ideal state for an organization that is about to embark on the implementation of organizational component reuse. The exact definition of 'ideal' is dependent on a number of factors. For any particular organization, this ideal state is called the 'goal state'.

The SFR Model is not all-inclusive. This is not a failure of the model, but rather it is intentional. No two organisations are alike. This applies to how they behave now and in the future. Each organization that embarks on change will do it from a different base and for different reasons. This was part of Keidel's original design for his model, and this philosophy has been adopted for the SFR Model. Some organizations have a need for extra attributes that are peculiar to their products, process, or environment, while others do not have the need for all of the attributes. An organization that enjoys a monopoly, for example an internal IT department and sole supplier to the organization as a whole, would not usually consider its Competitive Strategies. In like manner, if an organization does not have a mature training function, it may need to consider that as an additional attribute. One of the strong points of the SFR Model is that it allows for tailoring to the particular needs of the subject organization, resulting in an organization specific goal state.

As a minimum, the following should be considered when developing an organization's goal state: the size of the organization and subject I.T. division, company ownership (government, listed, or private), the industry sector it is in, the effect of the market, the country of origin and location (culture and socio-economics), and single or multi location. Any one of these will affect the choice of factors, their influence and consequent mitigation strategies. The following is presented as a generic Ideal.

With respect to the Organizational Strategy Dimension, such an organization can be expected to have empowered its managers and developers with the ability to exert an influence on the manner in which the implementation is to take place. It should promote a culture of complementarity where all components are produced with the expectation of possible future reuse. Adherence to standards and procedures should be promoted, as too the acceptance that its employees are valuable and should be cared for. Promotion is best done from inside and partnerships with other organizations should only be done if that organization already has a culture of reuse. It would benefit from promoting it products' unique characteristics and exercising cost control.

With respect to the Organizational Implementation Dimension, the organization should promote formal and informal communications between all employees and provide a physical environment that promotes ad hoc communications, resulting in sharing of ideas and solutions. Its reward system should encourage co-operation amongst employees in achieving the common goal of reuse. Its meetings should not be simply talk-fests, but result in meaningful and practical solutions to problems as well as promoting the formation of like-minded teams to implement the solutions. Rather than mandating, the organization should have a delegatory style of decision making based on the consensus of all those involved in the implementation.

Table 1. The Social Factors for Reuse Model (Breakdown of the Organization Showing the Influence of Factors)

Attribute co-relations are shown thus: (99). Like numbers connect the attributes that are co-related.

A. ORGANIZATIONAL STRATEGY DIMENSION		
ATTRIBUTES	**FACTORS**	**INFLUENCE**
1 Stakeholders (1) For whose benefit does the Organization exist?	1a Customers/ End users	Zero
	1b Managers	positive
	1c Developers	positive
2 Social Values (2) What behavior does the organization reward?	2a Diversity of Approach	Negative
	2b Uniformity of Identity	Negative
	2c Complementarity	positive
3 Organization's Expectations (2) - from its employees.	3a Self-reliance	Negative
	3b Compliance	positive
	3c Collaboration	positive
4 Employee's Expectations (2) (3) - from the organization.	4a Opportunity	Negative
	4b Security	positive
	4c Community	positive
5 Developmental Plan (3) How does the organization grow?	5a From Outside	Negative
	5b From Inside	positive
	5c In Partnership	positive
6 Competitive Strategies How does the organization compete?	6a Differentiation	positive
	6b Cost	positive
	6c Flexibility	Negative
B. ORGANIZATIONAL IMPLEMENTATION DIMENSION		
7 Reporting Lines (4) What is the form of our Reporting and Communications relations?	7a Flat/clear Lines	Zero
	7b Steep/clear Lines	Negative
	7c Flat/amorphous Lines	positive
8 Physical Layout (4) What interaction does our physical design encourage?	8a Independent Action	Negative
	8b Programmed Action	Negative
	8c Spontaneous Action	positive
9 Information Flow (4) How does our work/information Flow?	9a Pooled	Negative
	9b Sequential	Negative
	9c Reciprocal	positive
10 Reward System (2) What behaviors are reinforced financially and non-financially?	10a Individualistic	Negative
	10b Hierarchical	Zero
	10c Mutual	positive
11 Meeting System (1) For what reason do people get together?	11a Forum	Negative
	11b Decision-making	positive
	11c Team-building	positive
12 Decision System (1) How does the organization exercise authority?	12a Delegatory	positive
	12b Mandatory	Negative
	12c Collaboratory	positive

4 Application of the SFR Model

For a model to be more than just a theory, it must be shown to be of practical use. This section describes its application to an organization that has had a history of failed CBSE implementations.

4.1 Steps in the Application of the Model

The following are the steps in the application of the SFR Model to assess the capability of an organization and better prepare it for the implementation of component reuse. Figure 2 shows the steps as a flowchart.

1. Use the SFR Model to assess the initial organizational state prior to the consideration of CBSE implementation – OS_I.
2. Use the SFR Model to develop the model of the goal state of the organization – OS_G. This model represents the state in which the organization should be in order to maximize its likelihood of successful implementation.
3. Compare the results from Steps 1 and 2 to determine the difference between the initial and goal states. This is an assessment of the organization's initial capability to successfully implement a reuse program - OC_I. It will describe the changes required to increase the likelihood of success in implementing CBSE.
4. Implement the changes required to better prepare the organization for CBSE implementation, resulting in a prepared organization. As an option, an economic model can be applied prior to implementing the changes.
5. Use the SFR Model to assess the prepared organization's state – OS_P.
6. Assess the prepared organization's capability by comparing the prepared state with the goal state, resulting in the Prepared Organization's Capability – OC_P.

A major part of the predictive nature of the SFR Model is the feasibility assessment of the organizational change required to increase the likelihood of implementation success. There are many economic models for reuse, but they all relate to an organization that is already practicing reuse [32]. What is required is a model that is designed to be used pre-implementation. One such model that appears to be suitable is Benefit Cost Analysis [34]. The unique feature of this method is that it focuses on the benefits first and then the cost to achieve them. Jules Dupuit, an eighteenth century French economist, was the first to propose the concept central to benefit cost analysis of identifying the correct project benefits, and then the cost measurement criteria through demand and supply price mechanism. Applied to the introduction of reuse, it forces the quantification of the benefits of implementing reuse and so facilitates the decision to spend, or not to spend, the time and money needed for the required organizational change. A description of the Benefit Cost Model as it can be applied to IT projects is provided in [34].

4.2 A Case Study

This section presents a summary of an application of the SFR Model, describing the data collection method, results and recommendations for improving the subject organization's position with respect to the implementation of organization wide component reuse.

The data collection methods are based on those suggested by Keidel [11] and are presented as examples only. Both the date collection methods and the recommendations will vary for each individual application of the SFR Model. Other methods may prove to be more successful, depending on the subject organization. The recommendations also may vary depending again on the subject organization and of course on the particular results obtained.

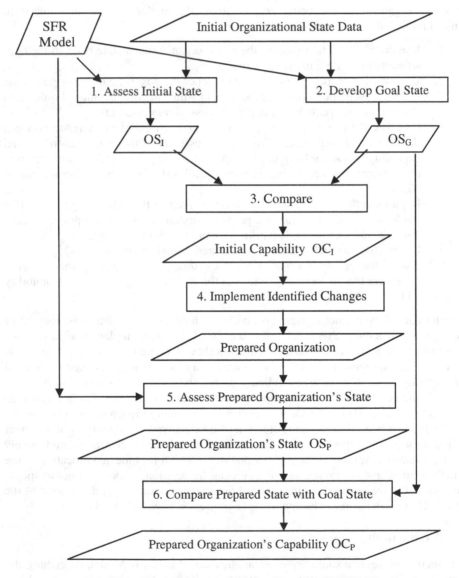

Fig. 2. Flowchart of the Application of the SFR Model

The subject organization is a large multi-national company, which develops embedded software for companies world-wide in a number of industries, as well for its own products. The implementation of CBSE has had mixed results, ranging from successes to outright failures. The successes have not been as a result of well thought out plans.

The subject division, since its failed attempt, has implemented a number of changes, which it believes will improve its implementation capability – OC_P. The following is a summary report of the subsequent application of the SFR Model to this division to assess its new state. The assessment commenced at Step 5 and used the generic ideal state as the goal state.

Organizational Strategy Dimension

4.2.1 Attribute 1: Stakeholders

Data Collection Method: Analysis of various archival documents, providing information on the relative actual importance of the various stakeholders. In-depth interviews with staff, both managers and developers.

Results: Documentation stated that staff at all levels have been given the necessary delegation and authority appropriate to their jobs. This however was not supported by many of the managers and developers, who reported that their managers often mandated actions that should have been the decision of the sub-ordinate. They felt that they did not have the influence that they were meant, and consider that they deserve, to have.

Recommendations: It is necessary for the organization to realize that there is difference between statement and action. Their current attitude has resulted in dissatisfaction among employees and is seen as one of the reasons for the previous failure. A review of the Decision System is recommended. Refer to Attribute 12: Decision System.

4.2.2 Attribute 2: Social Values

Data Collection Method: In-depth interviews with managers representing all levels.

Results: There was unanimous agreement at (almost) all levels that working together was the key to success both for the individual and the company. There was disagreement amongst those in the highest of management, with some supporting co-operation. A small majority felt that the company could not advance if it did not have some individual 'high flyers'. These people were felt to ward off risks of complacency.

Recommendations: It is felt that there is no threat to CBSE implementation and so there is no recommendation to change.

4.2.3 Attribute 3: Organization's Expectations

Data Collection Method: In-depth interviews with managers representing all levels.

Results: Apart high flyers (described in Attribute 2: Social Values), the management expressed an expectation of compliance and promoted an environment of collaboration.

Recommendations: Organization Expectations are satisfactory and no recommendations are offered.

4.2.4   Attribute 4: Employees' Expectations

Data Collection Method: In-depth interviews with managers and developers.

Results: All but a few (and these corresponded with the individual's identified by management as being 'high flyers' - see Attribute 2: Social Values) were in alignment, to varying degrees, to the factors of 'security' and 'community'.

Recommendations: Employee Expectations are satisfactory and no recommendations are offered.

4.2.5   Attribute 5: Developmental Plan

Data Collection Method: Analysis of archival documents, providing historical information on what plans, events and reasons for recruitment and partnerships/mergers. In-depth interviews with staff.

Results: Staff at all levels admitted that promotion did occur from within. This was confirmed by the documents. However, they were resentful when an outsider was brought in at a managerial level and was not aware of the existing culture (social values). Management stated that this was sometimes done in order "to change the way things were done. To shake things up". They were not concerned that some staff did not like it as they were often the reason for the required change. The company very rarely participated in mergers or takeovers, preferring to start a new division from within.

Recommendations: Generally, the plan is satisfactory. However, care must be taken that the engineered change is necessary as a whole and not simply to facilitate the removal of undesired personnel. There are less disruptive ways to do this.

4.2.6   Attribute 6: Competitive Strategies

Data Collection Method: Analysis of archival documents. In-depth interviews with management. Discussions with customers/clients to provide the 'other' view, that is, the success or not of these strategies.

Results: The division had an established culture of producing 'differentiated and quality' products. This was supported by the majority of the customers/clients. All staff recognized that a cheaper product was beneficial and were willing to do what was needed to achieve this, without sacrificing quality.

Recommendations: Organization Strategies are satisfactory and no recommendations are offered.

Organizational Implementation Dimension

4.2.7   Attribute 7: Reporting Lines
Data Collection Method: Analysis of the organizational chart and in-depth interviews with manager and developers.

Results: Although the company as a whole exhibits all three styles of Reporting Lines, this division has flat/amorphous reporting. The formation of individual teams is flexible, dependent on specific project needs and availability of appropriates experienced staff.

Recommendations: Reporting Lines are satisfactory and no recommendations are offered.

4.2.8 Attribute 8: Physical Layout

Data Collection Method: Determination of who should be talking to whom by reference to project records and organizational chart. Comparison with locations of these personnel.

Results: As this is a multi-national company, it was found that many projects spanned countries and time zones. Small groups of developers were co-located (and there was evidence of successful reuse within these groups), but many who would be expected to have face-to-face communication were in fact in different time zones and countries. Staff said that this did not present a problem because of excellent electronic communications being in place. Some found that the use of such facilities was preferred, because it allowed for the other party to respond after thought had been given to the problem. A small number found that these did not fully replace face-to-face.

Recommendations: While the physical layout is not ideal, communications seem to be as good as they can be given the international nature of the company and its customers. No recommendations are offered.

4.2.9 Attribute 9: Information Flow

Data Collection Method: Network analysis of staff working on similar projects to determine actual flow to compare with expected communication patterns based on the needs of the projects.

Results: The expected patterns of communication co-related well with the actual information flows.

Recommendations: Information Flow is satisfactory and no recommendations are offered.

4.2.10 Attribute 10: Reward System

Data Collection Method: In-depth interviews with staff (managers and developers) and analysis of archival documents relative to pay scales and bonuses over the previous three years.

Results: Bonus schemes do not exist in this division and employee's are accepting of this. Pays are reviewed annually and set commensurate with the employee's job description and their past performance. Employee's are satisfied with this.

Recommendations: Management could consider a rewards system for reuse implementation, but considering that employee's appear satisfied with current arrangements, this is a suggestion only and no recommendations are offered.

4.2.11 Attribute 11: Meeting System

Data Collection Method: Ratios of the number of meetings and total time (man-hours) spent on each type of meeting over the previous month. In-depth interviews with staff, both managers and developers.

Results: While the mangers saw the meetings as positive decision-making and team-building in nature (an opinion supported by documentation), this was not the opinion of the developers and lower managers. The decisions from the meetings were often subsequently over-ruled by the manager, for reasons that were seen by the manager as practical, and by the sub-ordinates as taking away their influence. They were in agreement, that despite the claimed best intentions of the management, the reality was that the majority of meetings ultimately resulted in being only "talk-fests" or forums. They also believed that the managers did not have the authority to over-ride meetings' decisions, but felt powerless to act.

Recommendations: The disparity between the apparent meeting style and the implementation is a real concern. If it is not possible to stop managers over-riding meeting decisions, then the façade of co-operation should be discontinued. Meetings should be openly announced as forums and managers authority made clear. This is not a good solution. Although it clarifies an anomalous situation for the staff, it promotes a mandatory style of management, which usually has a negative influence. Enforcing the finality of decision made at meetings is the better alternative, though in practice more difficult to enforce.

4.2.12   Attribute 12: Decision System

Data Collection Method: Analysis of archival documents over the previous three months (meeting records, authorization and delegation lists, project plans and memos) to determine the decisions made, how they were made and by whom. In-depth interviews with staff.

Results: The majority of decisions were made collaboratorially. However, there was a tendency to mandate major decisions, including that of implementing reuse. Delegation, although practiced widely, also tended to use a mandatory style and often the delegation was not welcomed by the recipient, often being interpreted as a test of ability and in a few instances as 'traps' to facilitate the dismissal of the employee. It was found that managers often over-rode decisions made by a team and their immediate subordinates.

Recommendations: At the very least, the next decision to implement reuse should involve all divisional personnel. The details of the implementation must be agreed to in a collaboratory way. Delegation should be seen as a reward and have the agreement of the recipient. Refer to Attribute1: Stakeholders.

Concluding Remarks

The Division seems to have improved its Implementation Capability, although the extent of this could not be determined with any precision owing to a lack of reliable records of the changes that had already been made. There remain a number of areas that require attention, which relate to the Attributes of Stakeholders, Development Plan, Meeting System and Decision System. These centre on a disparity between the organization's stated intentions and the implementation of them, leaving staff "on edge" and with a decreasing openness to change. It is recommended that an assessment be done to determine the economic and social/organizational viability of implementing these changes prior to the next attempt to implement division wide component reuse.

5 Further Development

As it should be with any such model, the SFR Model is under regular review and a number of developments and enhancements are described here.

The current Model also considers only the influence that the presence of a Factor exerts on the implementation of CBSE. While it can be generalized that the absence of a Factor equates to the absence of an influence, this is not always the case. A Factor can also exert an influence by its absence, for example the absence of a Development Plan (Attribute 5) can have a negative influence on the Employee's Expectations (Attribute 4). Work is continuing to determine the influence of the absence of the Attributes and Factors.

A similar situation arises when, for example, the result of a Collaboratory Decision (Factor 12c) is to not implement component reuse, even though management is in favour of it. While normally the Collaboratory Decision System would exert a positive influence, in this case the influence would be negative. Such instances need to be incorporated into the Model.

As the SFR Model is a predictive model, it lends itself to being coupled with an appropriate costing model for the changes that are identified as necessary for successful implementation. The Benefit Cost Model [46] appears to be well suited to this task. Further work is required to determine whether this or another cost model is most suitable.

6 Conclusions

Systematic component reuse has yet to be successfully adopted by the vast majority of organizations, even though individuals have embraced it enthusiastically for decades. The initial technical barriers have been all but overcome and tThe current barriers appear to be based on socio-organizational factors.

The Social Factors for Reuse Model was developed from a perceived need for a model for Component Based Software Engineering implementation that considered the social and organizational factors. The SFR Model comprises 36 factors that provide a structure to describe an ideal state for an organization, against which it can be assessed to determine its capability to embark on the implementation of CBSE. Such an ideal state describes an organization that is not only sympathetic to the concept of reuse, but also actively promotes its organization wide implementation.

When coupled with a suitable costing model, the organization can make an informed decision whether or not to proceed with CBSE implementation. This then has the potential to greatly reduce the number and cost of unsuccessful CBSE implementations.

References

[1] McIlroy, M.D.: Mass-produced software components. In: Buxton, J.M., Naur, P., Randell, B. (eds.) Software Engineering Concepts and Techniques, 1968 Nato Conference on Software Engineering, Garmisch, Germany, pp. 88–98 (1976)

[2] IEEE1517-1999(Rev. 2004). IEEE1517 Standard for Information Technology - Software Life Cycle Processes - Reuse Processes: 1999, reaffirmed 2004. Software Engineering Standards Committee of the IEEE Computer Society, USA (2004)

[3] Garcia, V.C., Lucrédio, D., Alvaro, A., de Almeida, E.S., de Mattos Fortes, R.P., de Lemos Meira, S.R.: Towards a maturity model for a reuse incremental adoption. In: The 1st Brazilian Symposium on Software Components, Architecture and Reuse, Campinas, Sâo Paulo, Brazil, pp. 61–74 (2007)

[4] Chroust, G.: Motivation in component-based software development. In: Ghaoui, C. (ed.) Encyclopedia of Human Computer Interaction. Idea Group Reference, Hershey (2006)

[5] Sherif, K., Vinze, A.S.: Barriers to adoption of software reuse: a qualitative study. Information and Management 41(2), 159–175 (2003)

[6] Ravichandran, T.: Software reuseability as synchronous innovation: a test of four theoretical models. European Journal of Information Systems 8, 83–199 (1999)

[7] Allen, P.: Using CBD to improve your business. In: Component Strategies, vol. 2(1), SIGS Publications, New York (1999)

[8] Kim, Y., Stohr, E.A.: Software reuse: Survey and Research Directions. Princeton University Press, Princeton (1998)

[9] Crooks, M.: Capitalizing on component reuse. In: Component Strategies, New York, p. 44 (July 1999) ISSN: 10993673

[10] Kunda, D., Brooks, L.: Human, social and organizational influences on component-based software engineering. In: Proceedings of the 21st International Conference on Software Engineering, Los Angeles. IEEE Computer Society, Los Alamitos (1999)

[11] Keidel, R.: Seeing Organizational Patterns, 2nd edn. Beard Books, Washington (2005)

[12] Haines, C.G., Carney, D., Foreman, J.: Component-based Software Development/COTS Integration, Software Engineering Institute, Carnegie Mellon University (1997)

[13] Waguespack, L., Schiano, W.T.: Component-based IS architecture. Information Systems Management 21(3), 53–60 (2004)

[14] Vitharana, P.: Risks and challenges of component-based software development. Communications of the ACM 46(8), 67–72 (2003)

[15] Dué, R.T.: The economics of Component-based Development. Information Systems Management 17(1), 92–95

[16] Kunda, D., Brooks, L.: Assessing organizational obstacles to component-based development: a case study approach. Information and Software Technology 42(10), 715–725 (2000)

[17] Pour, G.: Moving toward component-based software development approach. In: Proceedings of the 27th International Conference on Technology of Object-Oriented Languages and Systems, Beijing, China, pp. 296–300. IEEE Computer Society Press, Los Alamitos (1998)

[18] Hall, P.A.V.: Architecture driven software reuse. Information and Software Technology 41 (1999)

[19] Kiely, D.: Are components the future of software? IEEE Computer 31(2), 10–11 (1998)

[20] Szyperski, C.: Component Software: Beyond Object-oriented Programming. Addison-Wesley Longman, Reading (1998)

[21] Sametinger, J.: Software Engineering with Reusable Components. Springer, Heidelberg (1997)

[22] Aoyama, M.: Componentware: building applications with software components. Journal of the International Process Society of Japan 37(1), 71–79 (1996)

[23] Brown, A.W.: Component Based Software Engineering. IEEE Computer Press, Los Alamitos (1996)

[24] Brown, A.W., Wallnau, K.C.: The current state of CBSE. IEEE Software 15(5), 37–46 (1998)

[25] IEEE1517-2009 D2. IEEE1517 Standard for Information Technology - Software Life Cycle Processes - Reuse Processes: 2009 D2. Software Engineering Standards Committee of the IEEE Computer Society, USA (2009)

[26] MIT. 2010 Summer Session, Barriers to design, process and code reuse. MIT Center for Information Systems Research (June 2010), http://www.ciodashboard.com/it-strategy/13-barriers-to-reuse/ (Downloaded July 12, 2010)

[27] Davis, T.: The reuse capability model: a basis for improving an organization's reuse capability. In: The Proceedings of Advances in Software Reuse, Lucca, Italy, March 24-26. IEEE, Los Alamitos (1993)

[28] Alvaro, A., de Almeida, E.S., Meira, S.L.: A software component maturity model. In: Proceedings of the 33rd EUROMICRO Conference on Software Engineering and Advanced Applications, SEAA 2007, Lübeck, Germany, pp. 83–90. IEEE, Los Alamitos (2007)

[29] Tripathi, A.K., Ratneshwer: Some observations on a maturity model for CBSE. In: 14th IEEE International Conference on Engineering Complex Computer Systems, ICECCS 2009, Potsdam, Germany, June 02-04, pp. 274–282. IEEE, New York (2009)

[30] Creps, R.E., Simos, M.A., Prieo-Diaz, R.: The STARS conceptual framework for reuse processes. In: The Proceedings of the Fifth Annual Workshop on Software Reuse, WISR 1992, Palo Alto, California, USA (October 1992)

[31] Jasmine, K.S., Vasantha, R.: A new capability maturity model for reuse based software development process. IACSIT International Journal of Engineering and Technology 2(1), 112–116 (2010) ISSN 1793-8236

[32] Lim, W.C.: Reuse economics: a comparison of seventeen models and directions for future research. In: Proceedings of the 4th International Conference on Software Reuse, pp. 41–50. IEEE Computer Society, DC, USA (1996)

[33] Porter, M.: Competitive Advantage: Creating and Sustaining Superior Performance, p. 16. Free Press, New York (1985)

[34] Rehesaar, H., Mead, A.: An extension of Benefit Cost Analysis to IT Investments. Business Review 4(1), 89–93 (2005) ISSN 1553-5827

Software Product Line Evolution with Cardinality-Based Feature Models

Nadia Gamez and Lidia Fuentes

Dpto de Lenguajes y Ciencias de la Comunicación, Universidad de Málaga
{nadia,lff}@lcc.uma.es

Abstract. Feature models are widely used for modelling variability present in a Software Product Line family. We propose using cardinality-based feature models and clonable features to model and manage the evolution of the structural variability present in pervasive systems, composed by a large variety of heterogeneous devices. The use of clonable features increases the expressiveness of feature models, but also greatly increases the complexity of the resulting configurations. So, supporting the evolution of product configurations becomes an intractable task to do it manually. In this paper, we propose a model driven development process to propagate changes made in an evolved feature model, into existing configurations. Furthermore, our process allows us to calculate the effort needed to perform the evolution changes in the customized products. To do this, we have defined two operators, one to calculate the differences between two configurations and another to create a new configuration from a previous one. Finally, we validate our approach, showing that by using our tool support we can generate new configurations for a family of products with thousands of cloned features.

Keywords: Software Product Lines, Feature Models, Evolution.

1 Introduction

Recently, pervasive systems and Ambient Intelligence environments are gaining popularity to support people's daily tasks. These systems are composed by a large variety of networked heterogeneous devices with embedded software. For instance, Ambient Assisted Living systems or Intelligent Transportation Systems (ITS) can be formed by a large number of sensor nodes (grouped in Wireless Sensors Networks, WSNs), smart phones, vehicles onboard computers or other devices with RFIDs or cameras. Application domains like pervasive systems, where heterogeneity is present at any level, can greatly benefit from Software Product Line (SPL) engineering [1], which is specifically focused on variability modelling. SPLs aim to provide techniques for creating infrastructures that allow the rapid and systematic production of similar software systems, promoting the reuse of common core assets.

Feature Models (FM) [2] have been widely adopted by the SPL community to specify which elements, or *features*, of the family of products are common, which are variable and the reasons why they are variable, i.e. if they are alternative elements or optional elements. Then, a feature model permits specifying where the variability is,

K. Schmid (Ed.): ICSR 2011, LNCS 6727, pp. 102–118, 2011.

independently of the core asset, and enables reasoning about all the different possible configurations of a family of products.

Specifically in heterogeneous pervasive environments, the most common variability is the *structural variability*, defined as variations in type, cardinality or naming of elements [3]. We propose using cardinality-based features models and *clonable features* [4] to model the structural variability present in the new generation of pervasive systems. The use of clonable features increases the expressiveness of FMs since they allow the creation of different configurations for the same kind of device using only one feature model. Using clonable features we can model so that a system has a variable number of different kinds of devices (e.g. *s* sensors, *c* cameras, *a* alarms, or *sm* smartphones). The cloning of these device features leads to the cloning of the related structure (e.g. for 3 sensors, the configuration will contain *s1*, *s2* and *s3* clones of the sensor feature, joint with its sub-tree), increasing the complexity of the resulting configurations, and moreover the number of possible configurations increases a lot. Then, as the FM evolves, the impact of propagating changes made in the FM to the possible configurations is much higher in a cardinality-based FM.

Evolving a FM may imply adding or removing a feature (e.g. adding a new encryption algorithm as a mandatory feature), which in a cardinality-based feature model may cause many changes in all the clones. Specifically in pervasive systems, configurations could have hundred of clones composing a single product configuration. So, considering the evolution of a concrete SPL, it would be useful to automatically obtain the evolved configurations according to the changes introduced to the FM. From the point of view of the SPL engineer, it would be useful to know the necessary effort to evolve a previous existing product configuration to a new valid configuration after a FM modification was performed. This effort could be calculated by comparing the previous and the list of new possible configurations; which is not trivial to do at first glance due to the high number of cloned features.

In this paper, we present how we manage automatically the evolution of an pervasive system software product lines using cardinality-based FM and clonable features. To do this, we have defined two operators between FM configurations that are not trivial for cardinality-based FM. The *create_configuration* operator allows the creation of a new configuration from a previous configuration and the features that must be added or removed in the new configuration. The *differences* operator calculates the differences between two configurations of a feature model. We use the *create_configuration* operator to create evolved configurations from the previous configuration and the evolved feature model. Furthermore, we use the *differences* operator to calculate the effort of evolving the product configurations of a SPL, reusing and preserving the elements of the previous configuration. Finally, we validate our approach showing that by using our tool support we can easily evolve FMs with clonable features, automatically generating new configurations, for configurations with a high number of clones.

The remainder of the paper is organized as follows. In Section 2, we present our motivation example and the challenges for evolving pervasive systems SPLs and how we achieve them. In Section 3, we show our approach and Section 4 details the *differences* and *create_configuration* operators. The validation and the tool support of our approach are presented in Section 5. In Section 6, we compare our approach with related work. Finally, in Section 7 we outline some conclusions.

2 Motivation

In this section we present a motivating example and we will discuss the special challenges of pervasive systems that make them good candidates to take advantage of the evolution process using SPL and cardinality-based FMs.

2.1 Motivation Example

One of the most popular pervasive systems are smart homes with a lot of appliances that helps the occupants of the house in their daily life. When the purpose of a smart home is to enhance the quality of life of dependant people, then we are talking about Ambient Assisted Living (AAL). In this paper our motivating example is a SPL of AAL homes, equipped with sensors, smartphones, alarms, and cameras as shows the FM of Fig. 1.a.

Fig. 1.a represents a FM in Hydra[1] (all the FM and configurations presented throughout this paper are modelled using our featuring modelling tool, Hydra). In a FM every feature has one parent except the *root feature* (as *AALHome* in Fig.1). The features can be *mandatory* (as *Encryption*), *optional* (as *VideoSurveillance*), or *clonable* (as *Sensor* that has a 0 to infinite cardinality). Apart from the features, Hydra also defines two groups of features: *xor*-group (as the group composed by the operating systems of the *Smartphone*: *Android* or *iPhone*) and *or*-group (as the one composed for the sensing units of the *Sensor*: *Accelerometer*, *Light*, *Humidity,* or *Temperature*). So in Hydra, we can distinguish two kinds of relations: between a feature and its children features (*and*-relationship, as in the relation between the *AALHome* and its *Services*) and between a feature and one group (as in the relation between the *Sensor* and its *xor*-group).

Fig. 1.b shows a valid configuration for the AAL home family. A configuration of a feature model is the selection of a set of features belonging to the feature model. A configuration is valid if all features contained in the configuration and the deselection of all other specific features contained is allowed by the feature model [5, 6]. So, a valid configuration must satisfy the *tree-constraints* and the dependencies or interactions between features (*cross-tree constraints*). In Hydra, the cross-tree constraints are expressed in a textual way using the combination of regular expressions, as for example, *VideoSurveillance implies any Camera*.

The home of the configuration shown in Fig. 1.b has video surveillance facilities to transmit periodically video to the health centre. Also an automatic control of the lights and heat is provided. Furthermore all the data transmitted must be encrypted. This configuration has 10 sensors: the sensor S1 has a temperature sensing unit and offers temperature monitoring, the sensor S2 has in addition a humidity sensing unit and the sensors from S3 to S10 are identical and are equipped with accelerometers and light sensing units and offer light monitoring facilities. In this configuration there are also 2 smartphones and 8 cameras. Note that the figure does not show all these devices for the sake of simplicity. The Phone 2 is an Android smartphone and provides an application to transmit the video received from the camera to the health centre. Similarly, the cameras must transmit the video to the smartphones. Finally, all the devices have an encryption algorithm installed since this feature is mandatory.

---

[1] http://caosd.lcc.uma.es/spl/hydra

Normally, only a subset of the family products are developed and marketed. Later, these products are mainly subject to two evolution scenarios: (1) one AAL home may focus on dependant people with movement difficulties. However, some of the dependant people may not have special movement problems, but problems due to diabetes, or both. So, this AAL home family of products must evolve in order to incorporate a glucose sensor device, specific for diabetic people. This means that the customers demand a new functionality to the family of products, so each product already developed, and even deployed in some houses, must be evolved in order to incorporate the new requirements; (2) the hardware and software technology for pervasive systems is continuously evolving. New operating systems (e.g. Android for mobile phones) or special sensors (e.g. new accelerometers) are frequently appearing. So, vendors must incorporate these new devices or facilities into their products already derived, in order to be competitive in the market.

2.2 Challenges

The heterogeneity present in pervasive systems is easily manageable with cardinality-based feature models. Furthermore, these kinds of systems are continually evolving, as new devices, application facilities or requirements appear, and as a consequence of this some obsolete features disappear. So, the evolution of these systems must be properly supported by advanced tools. Now, we enumerate and detail the specific **challenges** to manage the evolution of pervasive systems using SPLs.

- **C1 Structural Variability Evolution:** A special characteristic of pervasive systems is that many instances of the same device may compose the same product, but each device, although being of the same type may have a different configuration. In the AAL home presented, the device infrastructure would be similar for all products, but must be customized to the physical structure of each house or to the necessities of the dependant person. Such structural variability must be explicitly modelled in the SPL, but also its evolution must be part of a SPL engineering process. Achieving C1: We model such structural variability with clonable features, and manage its evolution, not at the feature, but at the clone level (see Section 3). So, it is possible to modify the configuration of sensor S1, but not of the other sensors.

- **C2 Automatic Change Propagation:** When a SPL evolves, the changes must be propagated to the customized products of the family. Nevertheless in these kinds of systems with a high number of devices, each one with very specific characteristics

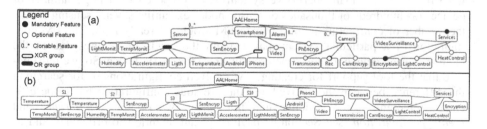

Fig. 1. AAL Home Family Feature Model (a) and Configuration (b)

(Fig.1.a) the propagation of changes is very complex. So, we need an automatic process that supports the evolution changes made in some characteristics of the SPL to all the derived products of this family. <u>Achieving C2</u>: We provide a tool support to automatically propagate the changes made at FM level into all customized configurations (Section 3.1). Note that representing configurations graphically with many cloned features will complicate the management of configurations evolution. This is important, since some pervasive systems may be composed of hundreds of devices of the same type, so it would be impossible to handle changes one by one manually.

- **C3 Evolution Effort:** Since most pervasive systems are composed of several or many different clones of each device, this implies that evolution changes must be performed in every clone in a different way. Let's imagine that we want to remove the encryption algorithm of the sensors in our AAL home family. But the application architecture may be different for every sensor, so, the way to remove the encryption is also different. So, it is necessary to automatically evaluate the required effort to make the changes in the products of the family when the family evolves, since when we have several instances of similar devices, but with different architectures, this is a very complex task. <u>Achieving C3</u>: We automatically calculate the differences between a previous configuration and the new evolved configuration for all the existing configurations (see Section 3.2). We use this difference, the FM and a mapping between every feature and the corresponding architecture to obtain which components of the architecture must be added or removed in every device. In this way, we can quantify the effort of evolving a product and the impact of change when the FM evolves. This may also help the SPL engineer to assess the persons per month required to produce upgraded versions of previous products.

- **C4 Preserve Compatibility:** In pervasive systems, the applications installed in all devices normally interact and collaborate between them. This means that the SPL process must guarantee that the configurations running in every device of a certain pervasive system are compatible with each other. An example of compatibility in the context of sensor nodes is that all of them have to use the same routing protocol, otherwise the communication is impossible. The SPL evolution process must ensure that new configurations of different kinds of devices are compatible. <u>Achieving C4</u>: We also use the cross-tree constraints to guarantee that the configurations of all the devices (i.e. *clones*) of a certain system are compatible with each other (see Section 3.1). This novel use of the constraints specified between clones makes it possible to specify which architectural elements must be present in all devices that interact.

- **C5 Efficiency:** As many pervasive systems are composed of a large number of devices (as hundreds or thousands of sensor nodes executing several sensing tasks), the number of configurations of a simple FM would be really high. The FM configuration of a particular system may contain thousands of features due to the cloning of each device related structure (sub-tree) for every device. So, we must ensure that the tool support for creating new evolved configurations or for searching the difference between the evolved and the previous configuration has to be efficient. <u>Achieving C5</u>: We define and implement two operators *difference* and *create_configuration* (see Section 4) paying special attention to efficiency and as we will show in the evaluation (see Section 5), the execution time is efficient, being appropriate for thousands of features, typical of pervasive systems.

3 Evolution of Feature Models with Clonable Features

We have proposed an automatic process to derive different system configurations depending on the input constraints, determined by mainly hardware and software requirements [7]. We apply model-driven and SPL engineering techniques to automate this configuration process. The first step when creating a SPL is to analyze the variability inherent in the application domain and create the FM. In the next step the global architecture of the system (named *product line architecture* or PLA), which contains both the commonalities and the variabilities specified by the FM is defined. A *Feature Mapping* between the FM and the PLA defines the correspondence between features and architectural components. We propose the use of the variability language VML [8], which was defined specifically to do this mapping. The customization of the architecture is determined by a set of high-level parameters (e.g. number and type of sensors or the necessary services). Using this set of parameters as input features, Hydra is able to automatically infer the rest of the features needed for each product making use of tree and cross-tree constraints (i.e. feature interaction), defined as part of the FM. So the output of Hydra is then a configuration of a product. This product configuration and the mapping between the FM and the PLA specified in VML are the inputs of a model transformation that automatically generates a customised architectural model. Finally, the architectural model of a product is the input of a model-to-text transformation, which produces the code for deploying the specific application inside the devices. We detail how our process automatically propagates the changes made in a FM into current configurations, and also we evaluate the necessary effort to propagate those changes to the final architecture.

3.1 Feature Model Evolution

As we have mentioned previously, the SPLs need to evolve in order to satisfy new user or application requirement or to incorporate new technological advances as for instance, devices with new operating systems or new facilities to achieve energy efficiency or the security of the system. These evolution scenarios must be modelled as modifications in the FM. We have identified what elements of the FM may change as a consequence of an evolution scenario: (i) adding or removing features, (ii) adding or removing groups of features ('or' or 'xor' groups), (iii) adding or removing constraints between features and (iv) modifying the variability of a feature (e.g. a mandatory feature is transformed in optional). Note that the modification of a feature can be defined by means of removing a previous feature and adding a new one. The same happens with the modification of groups of features and with the constrains.

Let's imagine that we want to evolve the AAL home family with new services: glucose control for diabetic people and fall detection for people with movement problems or other illnesses that may provoke falls. Furthermore, due to the rapid loss of energy of the sensors, the removal of the encryption algorithm in those sensors where it is not strictly required is recommended. Fig. 2.a shows the FM of the AAL home with these evolution changes. The two new services are added as new optional features (*GlucoseControl* and *FallDetection*) and since they can be used in any device, they are also added as children optional features of every device (as the glucose and fall monitoring in sensors or the diabetes application in the smartphones). Also the glucose sensing unit is added as a child of the sensor 'or' group. Furthermore, the *Encryption* mandatory feature is now an optional feature and we have added a new constraint for this feature: *Encryption implies (PhEncryp and CamEncryp)* to force both camera and mobile phone to transmit secure data. Finally, we have added other constraints related with the new services, for example, *GlucoseControl implies Diabetes* or *FallMonit implies Accelerometer*.

After evolving the FM we have to propagate the changes in all the previous configurations, as the one shown in Fig.1.b. Our process automatically obtains the new configuration from the previous one, the new FM and the requirements with respect the evolved features for this specific product. Consider as these requirements, that for the configuration shown in Fig. 1.b either the customers or the vendor needs the fall detection and glucose control services. The output of our process after this evolution will be the configuration shown in Fig. 2.b. The modifications are: (1) two new features are added as children of the *Services* feature; (2) the *Encryption* feature is removed; (3) in all the sensors the *SenEncryp* feature has been deleted; (4) a new sensor *S11* with a glucose sensing unit and with a glucose monitoring service is added; (5) in all the sensors equipped with accelerometers the fall monitoring feature is added; (6) the fall recording task is added to the cameras (7) and finally, the facility for controlling the diabetes and for transmitting the fall is added to the smartphones.

We can observe that with this small example we have to manage many changes in several features, so in systems with hundreds of nodes the number of changes increases exponentially. Therefore, we need a tool support that creates this new configuration in an efficient way, considering that the number of features of these kinds of systems may be really large. As is shown in Fig. 3.a, in order to automatically obtain this new configuration the **Create Configuration** facility of Hydra takes as input the evolved feature model, the previous configuration and the constraints with the requirements of this configuration for the evolved features, and it returns a set of constraints with all the features that we have to select in the new configuration. These constraints are used together with the new feature model by the Hydra facility to automatically generate a **Minimal Valid Configuration.** To implement the **Create Configuration** we use the *create_configuration* operator, defined in the Section 4, that obtains the features that must be selected in the new configuration for cardinality-based feature models. Also, how Hydra gets the **Minimal Valid Configuration** is explained in Section 4.

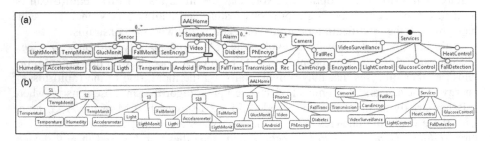

Fig. 2. AAL Home Family Evolved Feature Model (a) and Evolved Configuration (b)

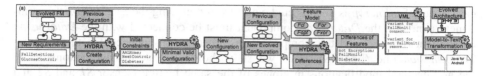

Fig. 3. (a) Evolving FM Configurations and (b) Obtaining Architectural Differences

3.2 Evolution of Existing Configurations

In order to evaluate the impact of change when a FM is evolved, we need to know the specific differences between the previous configuration and the new evolved configuration. To do this, as Fig. 3.b shows, the **Differences** facility of Hydra takes as inputs the previous, the new configurations and the four sets of variable features of a FM (clonable, optional, '*or*' and '*xor*' group) and it returns the difference between configurations by means of a set of features that must be selected and unselected in the new configuration. Obtaining the differences of FM configurations with clonable features is not a trivial task, since it cannot be calculated as a simple difference of sets as can be done for normal FMs. So, in the next section we have defined a *difference* operator for the special case of FM configurations with clonable features. Our process then uses this *differences set of features* and the mapping between FM and the PLA in VML to automatically produce the evolved architecture. Thanks to VML it is possible to automate the customization of the family architecture in an SPL context. Using VML, we specify which actions must be performed on the architectural model when a certain feature is selected or unselected. These mechanisms are basically adding and removing components, and connecting component interfaces. The family architecture is specified using the components model of UML 2.0.

Figure 4.a shows an extract of the mapping between our AAL home FM and the UML components of the family architecture, including all the variants of the FM (i.e. mainly devices and services). We only include in Figure 4.a the mapping for the features involved in the evolution changes, but in a full version of this VML file all the features which have an influence in the architecture are included. Lines 01-09 show the architectural modifications that must be performed when the *SenEncryp* feature is not selected, that is, the encryption-related components must be removed from all the applications installed in the sensor devices. Nevertheless, as we have explained previously, because the architecture in some sensors is different, how to remove the encryption-related components is also different for each sensor. We illustrate this for sensors *S1* and *S2* and sensors *S3-S10*. Lines 01-04 show the architectural mapping when *SenEncryp* and *LightMonit* features are not selected, which is the case of sensors *S1* and *S2*. In this case, the *elliptic curve cryptography* algorithm component must be removed (line 02) and also the component that composes output messages with the data collected by the sensor (*DataReady*) must be connected through *IData* interface with the component that transmits the data through the network (*DataTransmission*, line 03). We can see at the top of Fig.4.b the evolution of the architecture corresponding to these features. Nevertheless, as is shown at the bottom of Fig. 4.b., in sensors *S3-S10* where the *LightMonit* feature is selected, we also have a component that is responsible for fusing the data using an aggregation function, with the goal of reducing the number of messages that are sent through the network. In the case, where *SenEncryp* is not selected, apart from removing the *ECCALgorithm* component (line 06), the *DataReady* component must be connected with the *DataFusion* component (line 07) and this component in turn must be connected with the *Data-Transmission* one (line 08). Here we show how we can manage automatically the architectural modifications in clones of the same feature (sensor *S1* and *S2* and sensors *S3-S10*) that have different architectures. In this figure we highlight only the components or architectural parts that are previously implemented so they can be reused in the new architecture.

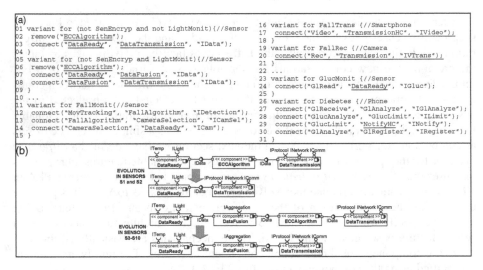

Fig. 4. (a) Mapping between Features and Architecture and (b) Removing the Encryption

Now, we need to implement the new functionality. Firstly, an algorithm to detect possible falls and also that switches to the nearest camera when a fall is detected. This new component must be deployed in the 7 sensors equipped with an accelerometer. Also, the video captured by the camera has to be transmitted through the smartphone to the health centre. But, the components that implement this functionality were previously used for the video surveillance, so we simply reuse them. Lines 11-15 show the architecture corresponding with the selection of the *FallMonit* in sensor devices, lines 16-18 specify that in the smartphone we have to connect the *Video* with the component that transmits it to the health centre only if the *FallTrans* feature of the smartphone is selected. But all this functionality was already in the architecture, so we reuse the corresponding components. The same happens when the *FallRec* feature is selected in the camera (lines 19-21). Finally, a new sensor with glucose monitoring facilities must be incorporated (lines 23-25). Also, the components that analyze and register the glucose measures and that notify the health centre if any measure exceeds the limits is added in the smartphone (lines 26-31). These components are new, so the effort of adding this new sensor must take into account the effort of implementing all of them. In total, 9 components were added and the rest were reused. Our process is able to infer the list of these components automatically, helping the architect to assess the effort of evolving each existing product when the FM evolves.

4 Differences and Create Configuration Operators

Differences Operator. The *differences* operator obtains the set of different features between two configurations of a FM. This set of difference contains the features that were selected in the Previous Configuration (PC) and are not selected in the New Configuration (NC) and the features selected in the NC but were not selected in the PC. When considering FM without cardinality the problem for getting the differences can be simplified to the differences between two sets. Likewise, if we rename all the cloned features with a unique name, a first approach could be to also reduce the problem of the difference of cardinality-based FM configurations, to a simple difference between sets. In order to have a unique name for every feature, we can prefix the name of all the clones with the original name of the feature (e.g. *Sensor_S10*) and all the features of the cloned structures with the name of the clone (e.g. *S10_Accelerometer*). So, to obtain the differences firstly we have to cover all the features of the NC in order to know which ones are not in the PC and secondly, we have to cover all the features of the PC in order to know which ones are not in the NC. This would be correct since all the differences are returned but it is not efficient. Firstly, we have to rename all the features. Then, we have to navigate through all the features of the PC and find them in the NC. After that, we have to do the same with all the features in the NC by navigating through the PC to find them. So, the main disadvantage of this approach is that all the features selected in the two configurations have to be searched twice. Furthermore, we know in advance that mandatory features are selected in both configurations so we do not need to search for them in order to obtain the differences. Apart from the mandatory features, other features will be selected in both configurations, so the effort of searching the configuration tree twice is not justified. This approach would work well in small FMs and small configurations, i.e. configurations with a few cloned features, but this is not happening in real pervasive systems that may have hundreds of devices. Also, a FM representing a real SPL system usually has a big core asset, so they have many mandatory features. Finally, we may want to obtain the differences between two similar configurations, where only some of the features in a few clones are different, as is mainly happen with evolved configurations. To summarise, this approach for calculating the difference is extremely inefficient for real SPL of pervasive systems. And, as we will show in the evaluation section the time needed to find the differences between two configurations increases greatly when the number of clones increases. So, we have defined a more efficient algorithm in order to make our approach scalable to configurations with several thousands of total features.

Syntactic Definition. $differences: PC, NC, Fcl, Fopt, For, Fxor \rightarrow SEL, UNS$ It takes six sets of features as input arguments. The features selected in the PC and in the NC, the clonable and optional features and the features belonging to an 'or' and a 'xor' group. Also, it returns two sets of features. SEL is the set of the features that are selected in the NC but were not selected in the PC. Similarly, UNS is the set of the features that are not selected in the NC but were selected in the PC.

For the evolved FM shown Fig. 2.a the sets of features are:

$Fcl = \{Sensor, Smartphone, Alarm, Camera\}$
$Fopt = \{GlucoseControl, FallDetection, Encryption, ...\}$

$For = \{Accelerometer, Ligth, Temperature, Glucose, Humidity\}$
$Fxor = \{Android, iPhone\}$

For the configurations presented in Fig. 1.b and Fig 2.b, we have:

$PC = \{AALHome, VideoSurveillance, Sensor\ Sensor10:\{SenEncryp, Ligth, ...\},$
$Smartphone\ Phone2:\{Video, ...\}, Camera\ Camera4:\{Transmission, ...\} ...\}$
$NC = \{AALHome, GlucoseControl, FallDetection, VideoSurveillance,$
$Sensor\ Sensor10:\{FallMonit, Light, ...\}, Smartphone\ Phone2:\{Video, Diabetes, ...\},$
$Camera\ Camera4:\{Transmision, FallRecord, ...\}, ...\}$

And as result of the *differences* operator, we will have to obtain:

$SEL = \{GlucoseControl, FallDetection,$
$Sensor\ Sensor10:\{FallMonit\}, Sensor\ Sensor11:\{Glucose, GlucoseMonit\},$
$Smartphone\ Phone2:\{Diabetes,\ FallTrans\}, Camera\ Camera4:\{\ FallRecord\}\} ...\}$
$UNS = \{Encryption, Sensor\ Sensor10:\{SenEncryp\} ...\}$

Semantics. It is represented by the relationship that exists between the PC and the NC and the selected and unselected features. Intuitively, the NC minus the PC is equal to the selected set of features. And in the same way, the PC minus the NC is the unselected features set. Then, $SEL = NC \setminus PC$ and $UNS = PC \setminus NC$.

Algorithm 1. *Differences*
returns two sets of features: one (SEL) with the features that are selected in the NC and not selected in the PC and other set (UNS) with the features that were selected in the PC not selected in the NC.
inputs six sets of features $PC, NC, Fcl, Fopt, For, Fxor$
output a tuple of two sets of features $diff = (SEL, UNS)$

```
1: SimplePC := remove_clones(PC)
2: SimpleNC := remove_clones(NC)
3: (SEL, UNS):= diff_simple (SimplePC , SimpleNC , Fopt, For, Fxor)
4: foreach f ∈ Fcl do
5:     (ClPC, StPC) := extract_clones (PC, f)
6:     (ClNC, StNC) := extract_clones (NC, f)
7:     for i := 1..length(ClPC) do
8:         c := ClPC(i) //clone of the i position
9:         if (c ∈ ClNC) then
10:            j := pos(c, ClNC) //search for the position of the clone c
11:            (CSEL, CUNS):= diff_simple (StPC(i), StNC(j), Fopt, For, Fxor)
12:               SEL := SEL ∪ precede_clones(c, CSEL)
13:               UNS := UNS ∪ precede_clones(c, CUNS)
14:         else
15:               UNS := UNS ∪ precede_clones(c, StPC(i))
16:         end if
17:     end for
18:     for i := 1..length(ClNC) do
19:         c := ClNC(i)
20:         if (c ∉ ClPC) then
21:             SEL:= SEL ∪ precede_clones(c, StNC(i))
22:         end if
23:     end for
24: end for
25: diff := (SEL, UNS)
26:return diff
```

Algorithm. This algorithm firstly obtains the differences of the non clonable features. To do so, it uses the *diff_simple* algorithm (Algorithm 2) that obtains the difference between two configurations with non clonable features. *diff_simple* covers all the optional, '*or*' and '*xor*' features in order to know which ones are in the NC but were not in the PC to construct the *SEL* set, and which ones were in the PC but are not in the NC to construct the *UNS* set. Note that we avoid looking for the mandatory features, since they will be selected in both configurations. Also, using this algorithm we avoid covering all the features for the PC and the NC twice.

The *differences* algorithm uses *diff_simple* algorithm giving as input the PC minus the cloned structures, the NC minus the cloned structures and the optional, '*or*' and '*xor*' features (Algorithm 2, lines 1-3). Then, for each clonable feature, the algorithm extracts the clones of the PC and NC (lines 5-6). The *extract_clones* function returns a tuple with the names of the clones and with the cloned structures. The cloned structures are the features under a clone but only those that are not clonable again, since they will be considered later in the algorithm. Then, for each clone of the PC, if they appear in the NC, the *diff_simple* algorithm calculates the differences between both corresponding cloned structures (line 11). If the clone it is not present in the NC, all the structure (preceding the feature with name of the clone) must be added to the *UNS* set (line 15). Following on, for each clone of the NC, if it does not appear in the PC, all the structure must be added to the *SEL* set (lines 18-21).

Finally, we have to consider the possibility that some descendant features of a clonable feature will also be clonable (nested clones). Our algorithm takes into account this possibility since, as we mentioned before, the *extract_clones* function return all features in the cloned structure minus the clonable ones. And, as the algorithm covers all the clonable features, when the turn of a clone that belongs to a cloned structure comes, the *extract_clones* function obtain again the substructure of this clone features (without clonable features).

Algorithm 2. *diff_simple*
returns two set of features: one (SEL) with the features that are selected in the NC and not selected in the PC and other set (UNS) with the features that were selected in the PC and not selected in the NC.
inputs five sets of features $PC, NC, Fopt, For, Fxor$
output a tuple of two sets of features $diff = (SEL, UNS)$

```
 1: SEL := ∅
 2: UNS := ∅
 3: foreach f ∈ (Fopt ∪ For ∪ Fxor) do
 4:       if (f ∈ NC) ∧ (f ∉ PC) then
 5:             SEL := SEL ∪ {f}
 6:       elseif (f ∈ PC) ∧ (f ∉ NC) then
 7:             UNS := UNS ∪ {f}
 8:       end if
 9: end for
10: diff := (SEL, UNS)
11: return diff
```

Create Configuration Operator. The *create_configuration* operator creates a NC from a PC and the two sets of differences: the features that must be selected in a NC (*SEL*), and ones that must be unselected (*UNS*). To generate the NC, firstly, we have to remove the unselected features from the PC set. After, with this set plus the set of selected features we use the facility of Hydra to create a minimal valid configuration.

Syntactic Definition. $create\_configuration: PC, SEL, UNS, FM \rightarrow NC, Valid$ It takes three sets of features and the FM as input arguments: the features selected in the PC, the set of features that has to be selected in the NC but they were not selected in the PC, and the set of features that must not be selected in the NC but they were selected in the PC. The FM is given as input, represented by a propositional formula [6]. It returns the set features that must be selected in the NC and a Boolean that indicates if it is possible to create a valid configuration with those inputs.

Semantics. It is represented by the relationship that exists between the PC and the NC. Similarly to the *difference* operator, the NC is equal to the PC minus the unselected features plus the new selected features: $NC = (PC \backslash UNS) \cup SEL$.

Algorithm. This algorithm firstly assigns to the NC the features of the PC (line 1). Then, for each feature of the *UNS* set checks if it is a clone, to remove it using the *remove_clone* function (lines 3-4). This function has two inputs, the clone and the features of the configuration. If the feature is not a clone, i.e. it is simple feature, the algorithm removes it directly (lines 5-6). Similarly, for each feature of the *SEL* set, checks if it is a clone, to add it using the *add_clone* function (lines 10-11). This function has two inputs, the clone and the set of features of the configuration. Finally, if the feature is not a clone, the algorithm adds it directly (lines 12-13).

Algorithm 3. *create_configuration*
returns a tuple of a set of features of the new configuration and a Boolean value that indicates if for the inputs a valid configuration must be generated
inputs three sets of features PC, SEL, UNS and a feature model as a propositional formula FM
output a tuple with the set of features of the new configuration NC and a Boolean value $Valid$

```
1: NC := PC
2: foreach f ∈ UNS do
3:    if (is_clone(f) ) then
4:        NC := remove_clone(f, NC)
5:    else
6:        NC := NC \{f};
7:    endif
8: end for
9: foreach f ∈ SEL do
10:   if (is_clone(f) ) then
11:       NC := add_clone(f, NC)
12:   else
13:       NC := NC ∪ {f};
14:   endif
15: end for
16: (NC, Valid) := minimal_valid_conf (NC, FM) // implemented by Hydra
17: return (NC, Valid)
```

After all the features in *UNS* and in *SEL* sets are covered, we have all the features that we want that will be selected in a NC. Then, this NC set is given as input together with the propositional formula of the FM to the Hydra minimal valid configuration function (*minimal_valid_conf*, line 16). This function returns *true* if a valid configuration can be generated (i.e. the NC given as initial constraints satisfy the tree and cross-tree constraints) or *false* in the other case. Also, this function returns the definitive NC. Maybe other features must be added to satisfy some constraints.

In order to check if a configuration is valid, Hydra uses a java library for Constraint Satisfaction Problems (CSP) [9], called Choco [10]. A CSP is defined by a triplet (X, D, C), where X is a set of **Variables**, D is a set of **Domains** for the variables and C is a set of **Constraints**. Hydra models the configurations by a CSP where the **Variables** are the features of the FM, the **Domain** is {0,1} that corresponds with the semantic of the unselected feature or selected feature, and the **Constraints** include the implicit and the explicit cross-tree constraints. Furthermore, Hydra permits the automatic generation of the minimal valid configuration given a set of **initial constraints**. This is the valid configuration with less numbers of features that satisfy these initial constraints that are formulated in the same way that the explicit cross-tree constraints. This time, the **Constraints** include also these initial constraints and to get a minimal configuration Hydra uses the CSP **Objective Function**. For our purpose the function to **minimize** is the number of features selected, i.e. the number of variables with 1 value. So the objective function to minimize is $\sum_{i=1}^{n} v_i$.

5 Evaluation

Hydra, was first implemented as an Ecore-based Eclipse plugin [13, 14], to provide support for the modelling of cardinality-based feature models in an intuitive and graphical way. Hydra also provides support for the configuration, validation and automatic generation of minimal configurations of this kind of FM with clonable features. Within the scope of the present work, we extended the tool to implement the *differences* and the *create_configuration* operators to help the evolution of FMs. In this section, we present the experimental results of using the evolution support of our feature modelling tool, Hydra. We will show that Hydra works well with FM with a large number of cloned features, as required by challenge C5.

The time needed to create a configuration depends on the number of features selected for the configurations. So, for our small example, it depends very much on the number of clones, as is shown in Fig. 5.a. The experiments were done in a PC Intel Core 2 Quad, 2,5GHz, 2 GB of memory and with 1.6 JVM. In our evolved FM (Fig. 2.a), if we consider 30 sensors, 3 smartphones, 10 alarms and 10 cameras, the time needed to create a configuration is 1,7 seconds. It is a very reasonable time, since configurations of our feature model with 100 devices may have around 400 features.

So, if we clone 500 devices (we have 4000 features) the time is around 2 minutes. Instead, the time required to know the differences between two configurations is reduced (Fig. 5.b). Concretely, for 500 clones it takes 49 seconds. This happens because when Hydra creates a new configuration, executing the *create_configuration* algorithm it also has to paint the model of the configuration, which is the most time consuming task. By contrast, the *difference* only produces a file with the constraints. But both times are more than acceptable for huge configurations, so our approach is also scalable to configurations with around 4000 features.

Although the results presented here can be applied to any SPL, we specifically have applied them to a family of middleware for pervasive systems (FamiWare [7]). With FamiWare we have developed many case studies from the domain of pervasive systems. Specifically, we have implemented several versions of smart homes, AAL

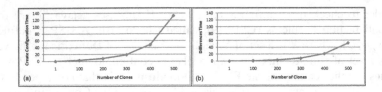

Fig. 5. Create Configuration (a) and Difference (b) operators time in seconds

homes and ITSs, with good results, although the number of clonable features, specifically in the ITS, was in the hundreds. For the ITSs, with a variable (without an upper limit) number of devices, an undetermined large number of different configurations were obtained. For this and for case studies similar in size, is not possible to manage the configuration evolution manually due to the high number of possible configurations and features per configuration. Since the ITS are novel, is very important that the SPL engineer can manage automatically the configuration evolution as proposed in our process, reducing the time to market for producing upgraded versions of this products. Although our process helps in the quantification of the effort required to produce the upgraded versions of previous products, it cannot calculate it in terms of the number of people per month. The output of our process for this is simply the list of components reused (those that were found in the component repository), and those which have to be implemented from scratch. So, the SPL engineer will have to assess the person per month per each new component and then make a final calculation of the estimated cost of evolving each product asset.

One desirable situation is that running products must continue their execution after evolution, so the initial requirements imposed by both the physical infrastructure (e.g. number of rooms) and the customer, which continue to be valid, must be preserved in the upgraded versions. Our process preserves the requirements and architecture, introducing the architectural modifications in the least intrusive way possible.

6   Related Works

Previous works [4,13,14] proposed some operations with cardinality-based FM. In [4] a cardinality-based notation for FM, on which Hydra is based, is presented. Also, the concept of staged configuration based on the specialization of FM is defined, where in each stage the products described by the specialized models is a subset of the products described by the FM. In [13] a verification of FM with clonable features using binary decision diagrams is presented. Both approaches are focused on cardinality-based FM but they do not deal with the evolution of this kind of FM. In [14] a synchronizing operation in cardinality-based FM is presented. They consider the possibility of propagating the changes produced in a FM to a existing specialization of this FM. So, in some way, they deal with the evolution of the FM and the corresponding changes to the specific products. Nevertheless, they do not provide a solution to the problem of propagating these changes at architecture level, as we do. Our model-driven process to evolve SPLs is one of the most important contributions of our work, since it allows the creation of new products and the evaluation of the effort of the evolution.

A classification of the evolution of a FM via modifications as refactoring, specializations, generalizations or arbitrary edits is presented in [6, 15]. So, an algorithm for classifying feature models with differences is defined. Similarly, in [16] an insert operator (to add a feature to a FM) and a merge operator (to compose two FM) were proposed. With these operators, the development of large feature models by composing smaller feature models is enabled. These proposals tackle the evolution of FM but they do not address how to propagate the changes made at FM level into the configuration level, as is the focus of our approach.

At configuration level, in [17] the work presented has similar motivations as our approach, since the authors propose the necessity of automated diagnosis of configurations in large FM. Also, they deal with the automatic configuration evolution. Nevertheless, they do not take into account the FM with clonable features, which are the main motivation of our work.

7 Concluding Remarks

We have presented an model-driven process for managing the evolution of SPL pervasive systems using a cardinality-based FM. Our process automatically propagates the evolution changes of the FMs into the existing configurations and also allows us to calculate the effort in performing the changes in every configuration. To do this, our tool Hydra creates new configurations from previous ones and the evolved FM. Furthermore, having the previous and the new configuration and using the variability language VML we can identify which parts of the architecture must be changed to evaluate the impact of the changes. We have defined the *differences* and the *create_configuration* operators and we have developed efficient algorithms to show their functioning. We have shown that Hydra is able to create new configurations and to see differences for configurations with a large number of clones.

References

1. Pohl, K., Böckle, G., Linden, F.: Software Product Line Engineering – Foundations, Principles, and Technique. Springer, Heidelberg (2005)
2. Lee, K., Kang, K., Lee, J.: Concepts and guidelines of feature modeling for product line software engineering. In: Gacek, C. (ed.) ICSR 2002. LNCS, vol. 2319, pp. 62–77. Springer, Heidelberg (2002)
3. Sánchez, P., Gámez, N., Fuentes, L., Loughran, N., Garcia, A.: A Metamodel for Designing Software Architectures of Aspect-Oriented Software Product Lines. Technical Report D2.2, AMPLE Project (2007)
4. Czarnecki, K., Helsen, S., Eisenecker, U.W.: Staged Configuration through Specialization and Multilevel Configuration of Feature Models. Software Process: Improvement and Practice 10, 143–169 (2005)
5. Batory, D.S.: Feature models, grammars, and propositional formulas. In: Obbink, J.H., Pohl, K. (eds.) SPLC 2005. LNCS, vol. 3714, pp. 7–20. Springer, Heidelberg (2005)
6. Thüm, T., Batory, D., Kästner, C.: Reasoning about edits to feature models. In: Proceedings of the 31st International Conference on Software Engineering (2009)

7. Fuentes, L., Gámez, N.: Configuration Process of a Software Product Line for AmI Middleware. Journal of Universal Computer 16(12), 1592–1611 (2010)
8. Loughran, N., Sanchez, P., Garcia, A., Fuentes, L.: Language Support for Managing Variability in Architectural Models. LNCS, vol. 49, pp. 36–51 (2008)
9. Tsang, E.: Foundations of Constraint Satisfaction. Academic Press, London (1933)
10. Choco Solver Home Page (December 2010), http://www.emn.fr/z-info/choco-solver/index.html
11. Stephan, M., Antkiewicz, M.: Ecore.fmp: A Tool for Editing and Instantiating Class Models as Feature Models. Technical Report 2008-08, University of Waterloo (2008)
12. Budinsky, F., Steinberg, D., Merks, E., Ellersick, R., Grose, T.J.: Eclipse Modeling Framework. Addison-Wesley Professional, Reading (2003)
13. Zhang, W., Yan, H., Zhao, H., Jin, Z.: A BDD-based approach to verifying clone-enabled feature models' constraints and customization. In: Mei, H. (ed.) ICSR 2008. LNCS, vol. 5030, pp. 186–199. Springer, Heidelberg (2008)
14. Kim, C.H.P., Czarnecki, K.: Synchronizing cardinality-based feature models and their specializations. In: Hartman, A., Kreische, D. (eds.) ECMDA-FA 2005. LNCS, vol. 3748, pp. 331–348. Springer, Heidelberg (2005)
15. Kuhlemann, M., Batory, D., Apel, S.: Refactoring feature modules. In: Edwards, S.H., Kulczycki, G. (eds.) ICSR 2009. LNCS, vol. 5791, pp. 106–115. Springer, Heidelberg (2009)
16. Acher, M., Collet, P., Lahire, P., France, R.: Composing feature models. In: van den Brand, M., Gašević, D., Gray, J. (eds.) SLE 2009. LNCS, vol. 5969, pp. 62–81. Springer, Heidelberg (2010)
17. White, J., et al.: Automated diagnosis of feature model configurations. Journal of Systems and Software 83(7), 1094–1107 (2010)

Recovering Object-Oriented Framework for Software Product Line Reengineering

Yijian Wu, Yiming Yang, Xin Peng, Cheng Qiu, and Wenyun Zhao

School of Computer Science, Fudan University, Shanghai 201203, China
{wuyijian,051021056,pengxin,10212010021,wyzhao}@fudan.edu.cn

Abstract. A large number of software product lines (SPL) in practice are not constructed from scratch, but reengineered from legacy variant products. In order to transfer legacy products to SPL core assets, reverse variability analysis should be involved to find commonality and differences among variant artifacts. In this paper we concentrate on the recovery of SPL framework which can be represented by an object-oriented design model with variation points. We propose a semi-automatic SPL framework recovery approach with the assumption that involved legacy products have similar designs and implementations. In this approach, we adopt a bottom-up process based on clone detection and context analysis to identify corresponding mappings among design elements in different products. Then we use a top-down process from class level to method level with some heuristic rules to determine the commonality/variability classification and the variability type for each design element. In order to evaluate the effectiveness of our approach, we conduct a case study on an industrial product line and present comprehensive analysis and discussions on the results.

1 Introduction

Software Product Line (SPL) has been recognized as an emerging and effective paradigm for domain-specific software development with remarkable improvements on productivity, time to market and quality. In real-world SPL practice, development of a software product line rarely starts from scratch as product line engineering requires sophisticated domain experience [1]. A more popular situation for SPL adoption is that a company has already several variant products successfully developed in the domain, usually by ad-hoc copy-paste code reuse. In order to reduce risk of SPL adoption, the company usually chooses to reengineer those legacy variant products into a product line rather than to build one from scratch.

Reengineering for SPL transferring usually involves a series of similar legacy products in the same domain. Therefore, SPL reengineering should involve differencing and variability identifying for artifacts from different legacy products besides extracting them from source code, documents or execution traces. Although there have been some research on SPL reengineering and case studies [2-7], automatic or semi-automatic approaches for artifact differencing and variability analysis are seldom considered.

What we concentrate on in this paper is the recovery of SPL framework from legacy products. A framework is a reusable, "semi-complete" application that can be

K. Schmid (Ed.): ICSR 2011, LNCS 6727, pp. 119–134, 2011.

specialized to produce custom applications, and usually targeted for particular business units and application domains [8]. By SPL framework, we mean an object-oriented design model with variation points and extension points for application product customization. For the purpose of SPL transferring, we try to recover an SPL framework from multiple similar legacy products by recovering a common design model (e.g. in UML class diagram) with variability. To that end, the following research problems must be addressed: how to identify the corresponding mappings of the design elements (e.g. classes, methods) among different legacy products; how to determine a design element to be common or different; how to further evaluate the variability type (optional, alternative or extensible) for each difference.

In this paper, we propose a semi-automatic SPL framework recovery approach which includes two stages: 1) a *mapping stage*, in which corresponding mappings among design elements from different products are established automatically; and 2) a *variability evaluation stage*, in which the variability type for each design element is identified. In the mapping stage, we adopt a bottom-up process based on clone detection and context analysis, first on method level and then class level. In the variability evaluation stage, we employ a top-down process from class level to method level, and use some heuristic rules to determine the commonality/variability classification and variability types for design elements. The recovered SPL framework is ultimately represented by an extended class diagram supporting variation point representation.

In order to evaluate the proposed approach, we conducted an experimental study on an industrial product line **DirectBank**, which had several variant products developed in different periods before they were reengineered into a product line. Our experiment has confirmed the feasibility of semi-automatic SPL framework recovery from multiple similar variant products by clone detection and context analysis. We also evaluate the effectiveness of our approach from two aspects: precision and recall of reverse variability analysis; the significance of the recovered SPL framework for further SPL understanding and transferring.

The remainder of this paper is organized as follows. Section 2 presents an overview of our approach, including the background, rationale and process. Section 3 and Section 4 describe the two stages of our approach respectively, i.e. mapping corresponding design elements among different variant products and evaluating variability types for all the mapped or unmapped elements. Section 5 evaluates the approach with an experimental study and presents some discussion. Finally, Section 6 discusses related work before Section 7 draws our conclusions.

2 Overview

In this section, we start with a general picture of our reverse variability analysis, showing the rationale behind. We then introduce the main process of our approach.

2.1 Reverse Variability Analysis

In forward SPL engineering, core assets with variations are created to support product-specific configuration and customization. In SPL reengineering, however, we expect to recover these core assets (also variability) from existing similar legacy products using a reverse engineering process.

A general picture of our reverse variability analysis is shown in Figure 1. The input is a set of legacy artifacts (including models) extracted from different variant products. The output is an object-oriented framework with abstract variations. The two stages (i.e. establishing element mappings and deciding types of variability) are explicitly labeled. The mapping stage considers the correspondence between elements. The mappings usually can be computed based on the similarity (either literally or structurally) between design elements. Specifically, two mapped elements do not necessarily have the same implementation, but possibly a very similar topological position in the design model. The variability evaluation stage is usually conducted according to the mapping results. Intuitively, for example, two mapped elements with completely different implementation are possibly *variant* elements.

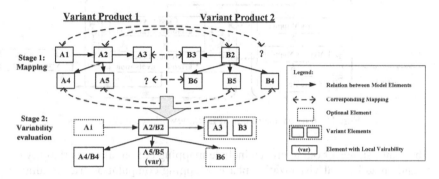

Fig. 1. A general picture of reverse variability analysis

In this paper, our ultimate goal is to recover an object-oriented design framework, especially a static class-based framework with variation points. A variation point here means a group of design elements that can be customized in application engineering, e.g. an optional element to be bound, an alternative element to be replaced by one of its variants. Based on our observations, we identify five variability types of design elements (see Table 1).

Table 1. Element variability in legacy products

Element variability	Description
Identical	mapped design elements that are exactly the same in different variant products
Variant	mapped design elements that have different implementations
Similar	mapped design elements that have some slight internal differences
Optional	a non-mapped design element that exists in some of the variant products
Product-specific	a non-mapped design element that exists in only one legacy product

The first three types (identical, variant and similar) are for *mapped* design elements which can be mapped with corresponding design elements in other variant products. The last two types (optional and product-specific) are for *non-mapped* design elements which cannot be mapped in all variant products. An optional element is not necessary for all products, while a product-specific element exists in only one legacy product. These different types indicate different variability intent in the recovered

SPL framework. For example, identical design elements usually belong to a common part of the framework; similar elements are usually common designs with local variations; and variant elements imply alternatives in the framework.

2.2 Recovery Process

The recovery process of our approach is presented in Figure 2. In our approach, each round of analysis takes two legacy variant products as inputs and tries to align design elements to recover an SPL framework with variability. More variant products can be incrementally compared and merged into the SPL framework.

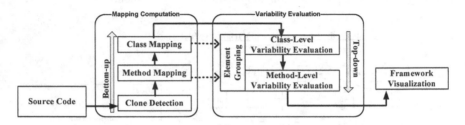

Fig. 2. An overview of our SPL framework recovery process

The major stages of our approach include mapping computation, variability evaluation, and an additional visualization phase. Mapping computation tries to align corresponding design elements for different legacy products. The mapping process follows a bottom-up process that conducts method-level mapping first and then class-level mapping (see Mapping Computation part in Figure 2). On method level, initial mappings are detected by clone analysis, and then internal similarity and external (context) similarity are considered to iteratively discover more mapping pairs. Similarly, class-level mapping first uses method-level mappings to directly establish some mapping pairs, and then employs design context to identify more mapping pairs.

After mapping computation, variability evaluation is conducted with a top-down process from class-level to method-level (see Variability Evaluation part in Figure 2). In class-level variability evaluation, each non-mapped class is evaluated to be optional or product-specific, and each mapped class is evaluated to be identical, similar or variant. For each similar class, method-level variability evaluation is conducted to determine more detailed variability similarly. The element variability decision result is then used for framework variability decision with design element groups.

Finally the recovered SPL framework is represented by framework visualization, using variability-extended UML class diagram.

3 Mapping Computation

In this section, we first describe the rationale of our mapping computation process with an illustrating example. Then we define a combined similarity measurement for similarity computation, and introduce the sub-processes of method and class mapping respectively.

3.1 Rationale

An illustrating example of mapping computation between two variant products is shown in Figure 3. Intuitively, corresponding mappings can be identified by computing the similarity between two elements in a candidate pair. Some **internal similarity** measurements can be computed directly on a candidate pair. For example, elements Payment in both products (in Figure 3) are corresponding because they have the same name; elements Auditing and Audit are also very likely corresponding because their names are similar and (if we investigate their source code and find that) their source codes are similar. Besides, we also need some **external similarity** measurements to reflect similar roles that corresponding elements play in the design model. Usually, this external similarity can be measured by their structural contexts.

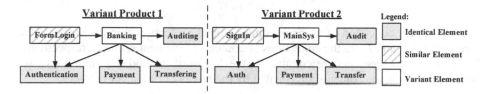

Fig. 3. An illustrating example of mapping computation

In the example in Figure 3, elements Banking and MainSys do not share name and (we assume that) their source code are not similar. Thus Banking and MainSys are not internally similar enough to be declared as a mapping. We then consider their context and find most of the context elements are *mapped*, which may lead us to believe that they actually form up a mapping pair.

It should be noted that structural contexts for mapping are based on other element pairs previously mapped. For example, if Banking and MainSys are mapped first, they can provide usable contexts when considering the mapping between FormLogin and SignIn, and vice versa.

3.2 Similarity Measurement

In this subsection, we formally define internal, external similarity and the combined overall similarity between two design elements from different variant products.

3.2.1 Internal Similarity
Currently, we consider name similarity and content similarity as internal similarity.

Name similarity measures the similarity between the names of two design elements (methods or classes). The name of an element includes the name of the package that the design element resides in. If the element is a class, we also consider the class name. If the element is a method, the class name, the method name and the names of the parameters (if exist) are also included.

Given two design elements e_i, e_j, their name similarity is defined as the following:

$$SIM_{name}(e_i, e_j) = \sum_{type} w_{type} \frac{|W_i \cap W_j|}{(|W_i| + |W_j|)/2}, (0 < w < 1, \sum w = 1) \qquad (1)$$

where W is the set of split words of the element e's full name and w is the weight of each type of name string. We believe that different parts of the name contribute differently to the name similarity. For example, the method names and the parameters play a more important role than package names when we decide whether two methods are similar or not.

Content similarity measures the commonality of the content of two design elements. On the method level, the content means the source code, and thus the content similarity can be measured by code clones. On the class level, we take methods as the content. Thus the content similarity for classes is measured based on the number of corresponding method pairs. Content similarity between two elements is generally defined as the following:

$$SIM_{content}(e_i, e_j) = \frac{|T_c|}{(|T_i| + |T_j|)/2} \tag{2}$$

where T_c is the collection of corresponding mapped contents within the scope of the element, and T_i and T_j are the collections of contents of element e_i and e_j, respectively. For methods, the contents are counted by the length of method (e.g. number of tokens); for classes, the contents are counted by the number of member methods.

3.2.2 External Similarity

We now consider **context similarity**[9] as external similarity. Context similarity here presents structural similarity between two products. The context similarity of two elements is computed based on topological structure. For a method, the structure is the call graph, with a set of caller methods and another set of callee methods. We also consider the method signature and the class it resides in. All these elements are context of the method. For a class, the structure is a set of classes that have associations with the class under consideration.

We denote the context of an element e as $CT(e)$. To avoid considering all element pairs from $CT(e_i) \times CT(e_j)$, we consider only those pairs in the *DMS* (Determined Mapping Set, see 3.3 for detail) which involve elements in $CT(e_i)$ or $CT(e_j)$. We define Determined Context Mapping Set (*DCMS*) as a set of mapping pairs (e_{ci}, e_{cj}) where $(e_{ci}, e_{cj}) \in DMS$, $e_{ci} \in CT(e_i)$, and $e_{cj} \in CT(e_j)$. Then context similarity of two elements e_i and e_j is defined as the following:

$$SIM_{context}(e_i, e_j) = \begin{cases} \dfrac{|DCMS| * 2}{|CT(e_i)| + |CT(e_j)|}, & \text{if } |CT(e_i)| + |CT(e_j)| > 0 \\ 0, & \text{if } |CT(e_i)| + |CT(e_j)| = 0 \end{cases} \tag{3}$$

Particularly, if the context of both elements are not null and all elements in the context of both elements are in the DMS, the contextual similarity is 1; if neither element has a non-null context, the contextual similarity is 0.

In formula (3), a problem arise when the number of $|CT(e_i)| + |CT(e_j)|$ is small, meaning that the context of the element is not rich enough for analysis. Intuitively, we believe that rich context will increase the *confidence* of the result of context similarity analysis. Otherwise, context similarity will contribute less than internal similarity. Therefore, we adopt the confidence as a weight balancing between external and internal similarity when calculating the combined similarity.

The **confidence** of context similarity is an additional, experimental value between 0 and 1 determined by the number of contextual elements. The richer the context is, the higher value is the confidence. Particularly, if no caller/callee methods exist (thus the contextual similarity is zero according to formula (3)), the confidence is not applicable; if the number of caller/callee methods is over a certain value (for example, five), the confidence can be one(1).

3.2.3 Combined Similarity

Each of the above similarity measures a specific aspect of combined similarity. We believe that each aspect may contribute quite differently in different cases. Therefore, we define a combined similarity as the following:

$$SIM(e_i,e_j) = conf * SIM_{context}(e_i,e_j) + (1-conf)(w_{name}SIM_{name}(e_i,e_j) + w_{content}SIM_{content}(e_i,e_j)) \quad (4)$$

where w_{name} and $w_{content}$ are weight for name and content similarity, respectively, $\sum w = 1$, and *conf* is the confidence of context similarity.

In our approach, content similarity is covered by clone detection. Therefore, we simplify formula (4) into the following:

$$SIM(e_i,e_j) = conf * SIM_{context}(e_i,e_j) + (1-conf) * SIM_{name}(e_i,e_j) \quad (4')$$

Formula (4') implies that, if confidence of context similarity is high, we may not take name similarity into account when deciding a mapping between two elements. Also, we will have to consider in the process to include the elements that are not discovered by clone detection.

3.3 Clone Detection and Method Mapping

Theoretically, the mapping between any two methods can be decided by only calculating the values of combined similarities. But a practical problem is that calculating the context similarities of *all* pairs of methods from two products is difficult. Therefore, we perform clone detection before calculating name and context similarity to limit the initial set of method pairs.

Our method mapping process is started with source code clone detection. Methods are mapped based on the similarity value for each pair of methods. We define a **candidate mapping set** (CMS) to store possible corresponding method pairs and a **determined mapping set** (DMS) to store the mapping result. Basically, whether a pair of methods is determined as a mapping (i.e. added to the DMS) is based on the combined similarity value. The process is shown in Figure 4.

First, clone detection is applied to find method mappings across the (two) products under investigation based on *content similarity*. We use a clone detection tool, Clone Miner, provided by Basit and Jarzabek, to find both simple clone class (SCC) and method clone class (MCC) [10]. The clone detection process provides a reduced result set of method pairs so that methods with the most similarity can be found first while less similar methods are filtered out, reducing unnecessary analysis work. Clone instances of MCCs (cloned method pairs from different products) are taken as the initial

CMS. With all clone instances, we will calculate name similarity and context similarity to find proper correspondences in the following steps.

The second step is to calculate *name similarity* for each method pair in the CMS. For each pair of methods in the CMS, if the name similarity value is above a given threshold, the method pair is moved to the DMS.

The third step is to add more method pairs to the DMS using *context similarity*. For each method pair in the CMS, if the contextual similarity of a method pair exceeds a certain threshold, the method pair is moved to the DMS. Once a method pair is moved to the DMS, their context methods are paired up for internal similarity filtering; if their internal similarity is not very low, they are added to the CMS as a candidate pair. This operation is repeated until no method pairs are added to the DMS anymore.

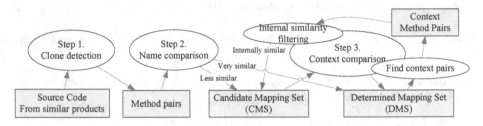

Fig. 4. The process for method mapping

The result mapping across products could be one-to-one, one-to-many or many-to-many. This cardinality will be used later when analyzing variability of the framework by **grouping** (see 4.2). In this step, however, all method pairs are just stored as-is.

3.4 Class Mapping

Similarity between classes for establishing a mapping is calculated based on the similarities between the two classes. The *name similarity* of classes is calculated with the text string of the class' full names, similar to that of methods. The *content similarity* of two classes is defined by the number of corresponding mapped member methods and the total number of member methods. The implementation of each class (thus implementation of the methods) is not concerned. The *context similarity* of two classes is defined by the overlapping context of the two classes. The context of a class C includes three parts: the classes that C declares as a member, the classes that C declares in its member methods as a parameter type, return type or a local variable type, and the sub-/super-classes of C.

A class mapping is identified if the combined similarity of two classes is above a threshold. Class mapping pairs also have to be **grouped** for framework variability decision (see 4.2).

4 Variability Evaluation

In this section, we present the top-down variability evaluation process. We first identify element variability for each element pair in the mappings with some heuristic rules, and then try to group elements in the mappings to decide framework variability.

4.1 Element Variability Decision

After element mapping, we have a collection of non-mapped elements and mapped element pairs. We now try to decide variability for each non-mapped element and for each mapped element pair. The decision process is shown in Figure 5, which is based on the mapping result and follows some heuristic rules. The variability decision process is top-down, from a class level to a detailed method level. It is also mentioned in Figure 5 that identical classes/methods and similar classes need to be further investigated for framework variability, as will be discussed in Subsection 4.2.

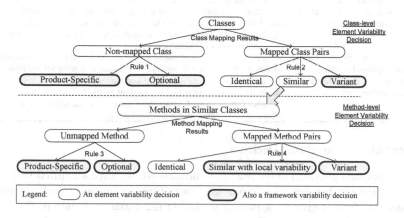

Fig. 5. Decision tree for element variability evaluation

In class-level variability decision, we check whether a class is mapped or not, according to class mapping computation. A non-mapped class can be either optional or product-specific according to Rule 1. For a mapped class pair, we evaluate the two classes in the pair to be identical, similar or variant according to Rule 2. As identical/variant classes represent exactly the same/different design elements, there is no need to further analyze method-level variability for them. For similar class pairs, further method-level evaluation is needed.

In method-level variability evaluation, we first check whether a method is mapped according to the results of mapping computation. Non-mapped methods are determined to be either optional or product-specific according to Rule 3. Mapped methods are evaluated to be identical, similar with local variability, or variant according to Rule 4.

Details of all the four heuristic rules are listed in Table 2. A difficult part of the rules is to distinguish product-specific and optional elements with Rules 1 and 3. In fact, we can only expect an approximate rule in most cases: product-specific elements only appear in one product, but optional elements usually appear in several but not all products. Therefore, when considering only two variant products, we simply expect the appearance of an optional element in other potential variant products.

Rule 2 and Rule 4 are used to distinguish among identical, similar and variant elements based on content similarity. Identical elements have nearly the same content. Variant elements usually have quite different content, and they are mapped by their external (context) similarity. Similar elements are those between identical elements and variant elements, having considerable content and embody local differences at the same time. Therefore, Rule 2 and Rule 4 use two content similarity thresholds respectively to distinguish among identical, similar and variant elements.

Table 2. Heuristic rules for variability evaluation

Rule	Description
Rule 1: distinguish between **product-specific** and **optional** classes	If the corresponding classes of a class can be found in at least one other variant product, then it is **optional**; otherwise, it is **product-specific**.
Rule 2: distinguish among **identical**, **similar** and **variant** classes	If the content similarity among the corresponding classes is lower than $threshold_{c1}$, then the class is a **variant** class; if the content similarity is higher than $threshold_{c2}$ ($threshold_{c2} > threshold_{c1}$), then it is an **identical** class; otherwise it is a **similar** class.
Rule 3: distinguish between **product-specific** and **optional** methods	If the corresponding methods of a class can be found in at least one other variant product, then it is **optional**; otherwise, it is **product-specific**.
Rule 4: distinguish among **identical**, **similar** and **variant** methods	If the content similarity among the corresponding methods is lower than $threshold_{m1}$, then the method is a **variant** method; if the content similarity is higher than $threshold_{m2}$ ($threshold_{m2} > threshold_{m1}$), then it is an **identical** class; otherwise it is a **similar** class.

4.2 Framework Variability Decision

With the approach provided in the previous subsections, we have identified variability for design *elements* but there is still one step away from a *framework* with variability. Therefore, we further give an approach to decide the variation points in the framework based on *element groups*. That is, we try to group a set of mapped elements to form up an element group as a variation point of the recovered framework.

An element group is a closure of all elements in a set of element mappings. For example, we have two element mappings (e_1, e_2) and (e_1, e_3), where e_1 is from product A and e_2 and e_3 are from product B. We then infer instinctively that it is possibly the case that e_1, e_2 and e_3 are all variants in the recovered framework at a variation point. Therefore, we group e_1, e_2 and e_3 into an element group $\{e_1, e_2, e_3\}$ as a variation point. An element group could be a class group (CG) or a method group (MG).

In the recovered framework, each class group presents a class-level variation point and each class in the class group acts as a variant. Similarly, a method group presents a method-level variation point.

In Figure 6, we have determined element variability. Here are some simple rules for determine framework variability on class level.

Given a class group $\{Ci\}$, where Ci is a class from a certain legacy product. If any two classes in the class group are identical, the class group can be converted to a common class in the recovered framework. Otherwise, if at least one pair of classes in the class group is similar and other classes are identical, the class group can also be converted to a common class by accommodating some local differences. If at least one pair of classes is variant, the class group should be converted to a variant class. In any cases, if a *null* element is contained in the class group (i.e. there is a class not mapped in a product), the framework class should be marked as optional.

For those variant classes, a detailed method level decision will be carried out. The method-level process is similar and will not be discussed in detail in this paper.

5 Evaluation and Discussion

5.1 The DirectBank Project

We applied our approach in recovering a framework for two similar web-based legacy products in the **DirectBank** project, namely DBankV1 and DBankV2. They were developed for different customers, but the development of DBankV2 was based on DBankV1. The overall structure remained untouched, while developers made some modifications to DBankV1 to create DBankV2. The sizes of the two products are quite similar, as shown in Table 3.

Table 3. Size comparison of the two **DirectBank** products

Product	LOC	#Class	#Method	#Method (excluding getter and setter)
DBankV1	10615	42	437	168
DBankV2	10517	41	424	160

5.2 Experiment Results

5.2.1 Mapping Results

In the mapping stage, we found 965 method mappings. Among them, 32 were one-to-one method mappings with high content similarity, which were directly added to DMS; 105 were added to CMS in the first iteration. The rest of mappings were established by analyzing name similarity and context similarity.

For class mappings, only 2 classes in DBankV1 and 1 class in DBankV2 are not mapped to classes in the other product. DBankV1 provides a class named `DownFTPFile` for file transfer protocol (FTP) support and another class named `DBankUtils` for specific byte-level operations. We cannot find correspondences for these two classes in DBankV2. Meanwhile, DBankV2 has a class named `BOCWeb` to extend functionality of class `BOCDirectBank`, but DBankV1 does not have the class `BOCDirectBank`, thus `BocWeb` is not mapped to any classes in DBankV1.

All identified class-level mappings are meaningful. Only one potential mapping is not discovered: the mapping between class `framework.NcSockConnection` in DBankdV1 and class `framework.NetworkSockConnection` in DBankV2. The reason is that the implementations of the two classes are too different and the context is not rich enough. More evaluations will be discussed in Subsection 5.3.

5.2.2 Variability Analysis and Framework Recovery

After corresponding mappings are established, we try to harmonize all these mappings into element groups.

In our case, 33 class groups are created. Among them, there are 30 groups that each contains only 2 classes (one from DBankV1, the other from DBankV2). This implies that these classes are very likely common classes in the recovered framework. Although there are possibly some differences between the two classes in the group, the differences can be easily eliminated. For example, differences in class `framework.DateUtils` in both products, which are caused by an upgrading, can be easily merged into one class.

The other 3 groups contain more correspondingly mapped classes. For example, a collection of business classes for bank payment (named after the name of the bank, such as `ICBCDirectBank`, `ABCDirectBank`, `BOCDirectBank`, etc.). Such classes usually present a variation point in the recovered framework, because different products may support one or more banks. The other two groups are `NetworkConnection` related classes and `PaymentInfoTransfer` related classes. Either group shows a variation point.

There are 248 method groups containing 763 methods (~3.1 methods per group on average). These method groups are later used for method-level variability decision for variant classes, which will not be discussed in detail in this paper due to page limit.

Based on the class/method groups, we successfully recovered a framework with variability. Figure 6 shows a partial framework at class level (a) with a zoomed-in view (b). The "CG 15" stands for Class Group 15 created by our automatic tool, which is a mapped class group consisting of banking payment classes in our experiment products. If more semantics are provided, the "CG 15" can be replaced by some meaningful name that helps a better understanding of the recovered framework.

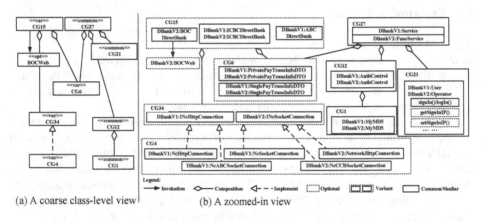

(a) A coarse class-level view   (b) A zoomed-in view

Fig. 6. Recovered (partial) framework at class-level

5.3 Evaluation

We have evaluated the precision and recall of the mappings at both class level and method level. The statistical result is shown in Table 4.

Table 4. Mapping results (class-level and method-level)

Mapping	All	All found	True-Pos	Precision	Recall
class-level	52	51	51	1.00(51/51)	0.98(51/52)
method-level	787	957	770	0.80(770/957)	0.98(770/787)

In Table 4, we can see that for class-level mappings both the precision and recall are quite high. For method-level mappings, we have checked all method mappings manually and find 770 method mappings out of 957 are meaningful, making a precision of

80%. The recall is a little bit difficult to calculate because the reference set of all potential method mappings is too large to identify manually. So we only checked all method pairs with high literal similarity (i.e. methods with similar names), and used those pairs confirmed by the developers as the reference mapping set. After analysis, we found only 17 method mapping pairs are not involved in the 770 true-positive mapping pairs (787 in total), making a recall of 98%.

After analysis, we find that an important contributor for the high precision and recall is the high similarity of our sample products. This implies that, if legacy variant products are architecturally similar enough, it is likely that our approach can recover precise mappings among classes and methods from different variant products.

On the other hand, we also confirmed that structural contexts help a lot in both class-level and method-level mapping computation. Intuitively, considering more structural contexts in mapping computation benefits the improvement of the precision and recall. Currently, we try to make more use of method context information (such as caller/callee methods) to identify potential mapping methods that have not so much direct similarity. In the result, we find 181 mappings established primarily due to high context similarity. These mappings were not detected by clone detection tool because they were not similarly implemented or their similar clone segments were too small to be detected. After applied the radical strategy, these contextually similar methods were finally mapped and added to the DMS, bringing great improvement of recall.

5.4 Discussion

5.4.1 Prerequisites and Limitations to Our Approach

We adopt clone detection at the first step to process the source code to re-construct a common structure of the potential SPL. Thus, similarity of source code and design is necessary. Our approach will only apply to projects that satisfy the following prerequisites: 1) the legacy systems under investigation are developed in the same object-oriented language; 2) the legacy systems are similarly designed and coded, usually developed by the same team or person(s).

Different OO languages or incompatible architectural designs will require other approaches to identify mappings between systems under investigation. The framework recovery process is not able to identify the differences across various languages or design decisions.

Another limitation is the experiment settings. We tried several settings on Clone Segment Length, similarity thresholds, and the context confidence value. We find these values experimental and sometimes difficult to decide when applying our approach in real SPL reengineering. Therefore, we suggest that the parameters of the approach be set according to the code style, domain type and product characteristics and be used only within an organization or development team.

5.4.2 How Precise Are the Mappings?

In our experiment, we also find some flaws of our approach. There are some specious mappings of methods that are really difficult for us to decide what variability they carry in the recovered framework.

Methods with antonyms. There are several mappings containing methods with antonymous names, such as (DBankV1:`MessageCenter.getSuccessXML()`,

DBankV2:Message-Center.getErrorXML()). These antonymous methods usually have similar names, implementation codes and invoking context. Usually, if such mappings exist, methods with the same name also form up mappings, such as (DBankV1:Message-Center.getErrorXML(), DBankV2: MessageCenter.getErrorXML()). These two mapping cases will not be distinguishable unless more semantics are introduced. Fortunately, these method-level false mappings do not affect the mappings at class level. In our experiment, the classes named MessageCenter in both products are identical, and thus form up a common class in the recovered framework.

Getter & Setter methods and other small methods. There are more than 300 Getter&Setter methods in each of our experiment products. Usually these methods are too small to be detected by clone analysis due to clone detection settings. But as we begin to consider the Getter&Setters, we find they are quite useful for deciding class mappings. Also, there are many (> 400) small methods with the same name additionally added to our method mapping set when two classes are mapped, which contributes a lot in enriching the context.

Variability identification vs variability implementation. There are methods in a single product with very similar names. These methods, such as BOCDirectBankpayTo-Private(), CommDirectBankpayTo-PublicSingle(), ICBCDirectBank-payToPrivateSingle(), are easily mapped to each other for their high similarity in both name and context. Thus the variability is identified correctly. But as we look into these cases, we find that how to implement the variability in the recovered framework is arbitrary. We do not try to propose a guideline for refactoring existing implementation, but provide with a high-level object-oriented framework as the beginning of further engineering process.

5.4.3 Optional Elements vs. Product-Specific Elements

In our experiment, we do not identify any product-specific element. The reason is that the designers believe most non-mapped elements are applicable to other (or future) products. The decision of whether a non-mapped element is optional or product-specific is experiential, as is also briefly discussed in Section 4.1.

Our sample products are comparatively small in size, and are similar enough. There are not many non-mapped elements, especially few non-mapped classes. Taking a few non-mapped elements in the recovered framework as optional is not a big threat for the complexity of the framework. In other cases where legacy products are not so similar that much more non-mapped elements are found, it would not be feasible to include all these elements in the framework. To solve this problem, a product plan or an SPL scope plan is needed for the project managers or architects to decide whether to include a non-mapped element in the recovered SPL framework.

6 Related Work

Researchers and practitioners seek efficient approaches for integrating a family of legacy systems into a consistent architecture with controllable variations. SEI proposed Mining Architectures for Product line evaluation (MAP) [11] and Options

Analysis for Reengineering (OAR) [12] for architecture recovery and variants identification. While a road map and practice guidelines are brought out, detailed techniques are not provided. Kolb [2] presents a case study in Ricoh company where a legacy component is to be refactored to accommodate Fraunhofer's PuLSE™-DSSA approach when creating a new product line from legacy products. The approach applied clone detection and variability analysis to refactor the component, rather than to recover a framework. Frenzel [4] provided a valuable extension to the reflexion model[13] to support software variants comparison on architecture level, but they did not "outline the technical details on how to reconstruct the architecture of the variants". John [5] focused on reusing legacy documents when establishing an SPL from legacy products. He argued a knowledge-rich approach for the process, but acquiring accurate and rich documentation is only too difficult. Knodel [6] presented a quality-driven approach to recover assets from existing systems and incorporate them in the SPL. His approach applied static, dynamic and historic analysis and was comparatively high-level, while ours is based on object-oriented source code to find commonality and variability of multiple products. Bianchi[14] proposed an iterative approach to reengineering legacy systems without interfering normal business operation and minimized the risk of refactoring. Although with different purposes from our recovery process, his process showed a feasible way to gradually reconstruct a new product line based on legacy systems. There are also some other reengineering work focusing on model recovery[15] and quality assurance[16].

The first stage (mapping stage) of our recovery process is closely related to research work in model differencing. Several differencing approaches and tools[17-19] could also be useful for establishing element mappings across products. In fact, any mechanisms that can efficiently establish corresponding mappings between design elements are applicable in our approach.

7   Conclusion and Future Work

Reengineering legacy products into software product lines is a practical choice for many companies to transfer their product development to SPL platforms. In this paper, we propose a semi-automatic method to support the recovery of SPL frameworks. The method is based on clone analysis and involves a two-stage recovery process, i.e. a bottom-up process for design element mapping and a top-down process for variability evaluation. In order to evaluate the effectiveness of our method, we conduct a case study on an industrial product line and the results have confirmed the effectiveness of our method.

In our future work, we will try to extend our approach to efficiently handle more complex mappings in reverse variability analysis, e.g. legacy variant products with structural refactoring, to provide more practical techniques and tools for SPL reengineering.

Acknowledgments. The work presented is supported by National Natural Science Foundation of China (NSFC) under grants 60903013, 90818009 and 60703092.

References

1. Pohl, K., Metzger, A.: Variability management in software product line engineering. In: ICSE 2006, pp. 1049–1050. ACM, New York (2006)
2. Kolb, R., Muthig, D., Patzke, T., Yamauchi, K.: A case study in refactoring a legacy component for reuse in a product line. In: ICSM 2005, pp. 369–378. IEEE, Los Alamitos (2005)
3. Lee, H., Choi, H., Kang, K.C., Kim, D., Lee, Z.: Experience report on using a domain model-based extractive approach to software product line asset development. In: Edwards, S.H., Kulczycki, G. (eds.) ICSR 2009. LNCS, vol. 5791, pp. 137–149. Springer, Heidelberg (2009)
4. Frenzel, P., Koschke, R., Breu, A.P.J., Angstmann, K.: Extending the reflexion method for consolidating software variants into product lines. In: WCRE 2007, pp. 160–169. IEEE, Los Alamitos (2007)
5. John, I.: Integrating legacy documentation assets into a product line. In: van der Linden, F.J. (ed.) PFE 2002. LNCS, vol. 2290, pp. 78–101. Springer, Heidelberg (2002)
6. Knodel, J., John, I., Ganesan, D., Pinzger, M., Usero, F., Arciniegas, J.L., Riva, C.: Asset recovery and their incorporation into product lines. In: WCRE 2005, pp. 120–132. IEEE, Los Alamitos (2005)
7. Duszynski, S., Knodel, J., Naab, M., Hein, D., Schitter, C.: Variant comparison - A technique for visualizing software variants. In: WCRE 2008, pp. 229–233. IEEE, Los Alamitos (2008)
8. Fayad, M.E., Schmidt, D.C.: Object-oriented application frameworks. Communications of the ACM 40(10), 32–38 (1997)
9. Yang, Y.: A Software Product Line Oriented Development Model and Reverse Eliciting Domain Components. Doctoral Dissertation. Fudan University (2010) (in Chinese)
10. Basit, H.A., Jarzabek, S.: A Data Mining Approach for Detecting Higher-Level Clones in Software. IEEE Transactions on Software Engineering 35(4), 497–514 (2009)
11. Stoermer, C., O'Brien, L.: MAP - Mining Architectures for Product Line Evaluations. In: WICSA 2001, p. 35. IEEE, Los Alamitos (2001)
12. Smith, D.B., Brien, L.O., Bergey, J.: Using the Options Analysis for Reengineering (OAR) Method for Mining Components for a Product Line. In: Chastek, G.J. (ed.) SPLC 2002. LNCS, vol. 2379, pp. 316–327. Springer, Heidelberg (2002)
13. Murphy, G.C., Notkin, D., Sullivan, K.J.: Software Reflexion Models: Bridging the Gap between Design and Implementation. IEEE Trans. Softw. Eng. 27(4), 364–380 (2001)
14. Bianchi, A., Caivano, D., Marengo, V., Visaggio, G.: Iterative reengineering of legacy systems. IEEE Trans. Softw. Eng. 29(3), 225–241 (2003)
15. Nierstrasz, O., Kobel, M., Girba, T., Lanza, M., Bunke, H.: Example-driven reconstruction of software models. In: CSMR 2007, pp. 275–284. IEEE, Los Alamitos (2007)
16. Tahvildari, L.: Quality-driven object-oriented re-engineering framework. In: ICSM 2004, pp. 479–483. IEEE, Los Alamitos (2004)
17. Collard, M.L.: An infrastructure to support meta-differencing and refactoring of source code. In: ASE 2003, pp. 377–380. IEEE, Los Alamitos (2003)
18. Maletic, J.I., Collard, M.L.: Supporting source code difference analysis. In: 20th IEEE International Conference on Software Maintenance, pp. 210–219. IEEE, Los Alamitos (2004)
19. Canfora, G., Cerulo, L., Penta, M.D.: Ldiff: An enhanced line differencing tool. In: 31st International Conference on Software Engineering, pp. 595–598. IEEE, Los Alamitos (2009)

Architecture Evolution in Software Product Line: An Industrial Case Study

Yijian Wu, Xin Peng, and Wenyun Zhao

School of Computer Science, Fudan University, Shanghai 201203, China
{wuyijian,pengxin,wyzhao}@fudan.edu.cn

Abstract. A software product line (SPL) usually involves a shared set of core assets and a series of application products. To ensure consistency, the evolution of the core assets and all the application products should be coordinated and synchronized under a unified evolution process. Therefore, SPL evolution often involves cross-product propagation and synchronization besides application derivation based on core assets, presenting quite different characteristic from the evolution of individual software products. As software architectures, including the product line architecture (PLA) and application architectures, play a central role in SPL engineering and evolution, architecture-based evolution analysis is a natural way for analyzing and managing SPL evolution. In this paper, we explore common practices of architecture evolution and the rationale behind in industrial SPL development. To this end, we conduct a case study with Wingsoft examination system product line (WES-PL), an industrial product line with an evolution history of eight years and more than 10 application products. In the case study, we reviewed the evolution history of WES-PL architecture and analyzed several typical evolution cases. Based on the historical analysis, we identify some special problems in industrial SPL practice from the aspect of architecture evolution and summarize some useful experiences about SPL evolution decisions to complement classical SPL methodology. On the other hand, we also propose some possible improvements for the evolution management in WES-PL.

1 Introduction

Reuse of unmodified components has not produced the promised rewards because the reusable components are seldom a precise fit to the reuse needs. One method of mitigating this shortcoming is to narrow the field of applicability to a software product line (SPL). An SPL is a group of products that share a common, managed set of features and that are developed from a common set of core assets in a prescribed way [1]. In the past decade, SPL is proven to be an efficient approach for both architecture- and component-level reuse.

Similar to individual software products, an SPL evolves continuously with requirement changes, scope extension and design refactoring. SPL evolution is usually more complex than the evolution of individual software products because both the core assets and a series of application products are involved. Successful SPL engineering requires management and coordination of the development of core assets and application products to meet the organization's overall business goals [1]. To ensure

K. Schmid (Ed.): ICSR 2011, LNCS 6727, pp. 135–150, 2011.

the consistency and unity of the SPL, the evolution of the core assets and all the application products should be coordinated and synchronized under a unified evolution process. Therefore, SPL evolution often presents quite different characteristics from the evolution of individual software products.

The product line architecture (PLA) in an SPL specifies the common structure of all member products and centers in the development and evolution of both core assets and application products [2]. Therefore, an architecture-based approach is a natural way for analyzing and managing SPL evolution.

In order to explore SPL evolution practices, we conduct a case study on architecture evolution in the Wingsoft examination system product line (WES-PL), an industrial product line with an evolution history of eight years and more than 10 application products. In the case study, we reviewed the evolution history of WES-PL and revealed that real SPL evolution is usually much more complex than ideal due to practical difficulties. For example, ideal SPL practices suggest that all application products be derived from the PLA to keep consistency, but we find that some application products occasionally and purposefully deviate from the core assets for some reasons (such as market uncertainty). We categorize several common evolution types in SPL development and identify some special real problems in SPL evolution. We also gather useful experiences for evolution decisions from our historical study.

The rest of the paper is organized as follows. Section 2 introduces the business background of the WES project and shows an overview of the evolution history. Section 3 presents several evolution types discovered in the development history and discusses typical evolution scenarios in real development. Section 4 describes some high level findings and experiences in our study and proposes possible improvements to WES-PL development. Section 5 discusses related work in both industry and academia. Section 6 concludes our work.

2   Background

2.1   Overview of WES Product Family

WES is an industrial product family developed by Fudan Wingsoft Co. Ltd., a software company with about 50 employees in Shanghai, China. The WES project was started in late 2002 as a product development project for Shanghai Municipal Education and Examination Authority (SMEEA). It was first developed as a computer-aided oral examination software product [3]. In the following years, it gradually evolved into a complete WES product family, covering the whole business process of computer-aided educational examination as shown in Figure 1.

Each process in Figure 1 is supported by a product category (a set of WES products) for various kinds of examinations. These examinations include high-end ones, such as College Entrance Examination of the State, and low-end ones, such as final examinations in high schools. The examinations also have various educational purposes, such as oral exams, listening exams, debating exams, so on and so forth.

In the past eight years, the WES team has developed more than 16 application products to support different examinations. These products are listed in Table 1 with corresponding product category and a brief description. Each product has about 50~90K lines of Delphi code. Some products share more than 80% source code.

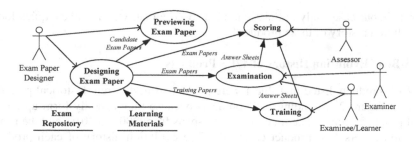

Fig. 1. Data flow chart of the computer-aided examination system

Table 1. A list of WES products developed

Product Category	No	Product	Description
Exam Paper Designing (EPD)	P0	EPDS: Exam Paper Design System	Various examinations are supported in several versions. The latest version covers all question types. This product provides complicated algorithms for making exam papers.
Examination	P1	SOLO	Each examinee orally answers questions played by the computer.
	P2	DISCUSS	Examinees are grouped in at most four and each group may discuss orally on a given topic via network.
	P3	DEBATE	Same as DISCUSS, except that the group is of two examinees.
	P4	LISTEN-SOLO:	Supports both listening comprehension (multiple choice questions) and oral examinations.
	P5	ONLINE	Supports internet-based listening and written examinations.
Exam Paper Preview	P6	PREVIEW	Gives a live preview of SOLO exam papers.
	P7	PREVIEW-LO	Same as PREVIEW but supports LISTEN-SOLO exam papers.
	P8	PREVIEW-ON	Same as PREVIEW but supports ONLINE exam papers.
Training	P9	TRAIN@home	Supports SOLO oral training. Training materials are delivered by compact disks (CDs). Learners typically use the product at home.
	P10	TRAIN@home2	Same as TRAIN@home but supports LISTEN-SOLO training.
	P11	TRAIN-ECLASS	Supports SOLO exams. Training materials are stored on a server. Typically used in classrooms with tutors' guidance.
Scoring	P12	ORALSCORE	Scoring for SOLO exams. Assessors listen to audio records of examinees and give a score anonymously.
	P13	DISCORE	Scoring for DISUSS and DEBATE exams. Preprocess is required to merge grouped examinees' audio into one stereo audio file. Assessors give scores to each examinee anonymously.
	P14	EClassSCORE	Scoring for TRAIN-ECLASS. Assessors listen to and score audio records of examinees, while name of each examinee is shown on screen. (i.e. not anonymously). Used in in-class guided learning.
	P15	GRAPHSCORE	Scoring for ONLINE exams. A graphical presentation of answers is shown to assessors.

The products are developed basically according to 1) supports of question types; 2) product category (e.g. examination, training, etc); and 3) how educational process will be brought out (such as self-learning or guided-learning). Among these products, EPD products shows most distinguishing features, since designing exam paper is quite different from showing them to the designers, examinees or assessors. Thus, the EPD category is not considered in the rest of our study. Also, Scoring product shows different features; thus not considered either. We will discuss the criteria for selecting products in our case study in Subsection 2.3. Before that, we first take a quick look at the evolution history of these products.

2.2   A Brief Evolution History of WES Products

The WES products listed in Table 1 were developed in different historical periods as shown in Figure 2 (excluding EPD products because they actually form up an individual product family). The time dimension spans from 2002 to 2010, and the product dimension covers four product categories. The evolution history of each product is denoted by a bar, whose left side showing the beginning of the product and right side fading out indicating the end of evolution. From Figure 2, it can be seen that some products like P2, P4, P7, P11 and P14 are no longer maintained (but may still in use with some customers).

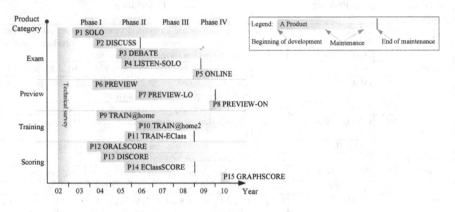

Fig. 2. Development history of WES-PL (Four phases)

The evolution history presented in Figure 2 can be distinctly divided into the following four phases.

Phase I: Startup (2003-2004)
Basic products of four product categories, i.e. P1, P6, P9, and P12, were developed, laying a foundation for future improvements. Moreover, products for group-discussion-exams (P2 and P13) were initiated due to market anticipation.

Phase II: Expanding (2005-2007)
Basic products were maturing. Meanwhile, new product series for group-discussion, debating and listening comprehension were released. In this period, the market of WES products kept expanding, and accordingly the WES team was often required to make quick responses to newly emerging or changing requirements. At the same time, some features became obsolete after delivery to market (e.g. P2 was not maintained since mid-2006) and was replace by some other products (e.g. P3).

Phase III: Maintenance and Refactoring (2008)
The theme of this phase was regular maintenance and refactoring. As traditional computer-aided examination market had been nearly carved up, no new products were

introduced in this phase. Therefore, the WES team had plenty of time to plan and conduct design refactoring on both the domain and application levels, providing better services or user experiences in existing products.

Phase IV: New Era of Development (2009-2010)
The WES team received new market opportunities, which is a driving force for deeper refactoring and future development. New WES products combining the features of listening and writing examinations were planned and developed by reusing existing software assets. The PLA was actually refactored and the products are gradually synchronized with the PLA to achieve higher development efficiency.

2.3 Scope of Our Case Study

Systematical architecture-based and comprehensive reuse-based product development is an essential characteristic of SPL engineering. Therefore, we confine our case study to Examination, Training and Preview products, because they share the essential common features of exam paper packaging, distribution, displaying and answering, and share a common PLA. EPD products and Scoring products, although mentioned together with the WES product family and sharing *some* commonalities with other products, are not included in the scope of our case study, since they do not share architecture-level commonality with other produces. Thus, eleven (11) products, i.e. P1~P11, are included in the scope of our case study. Among these products, Examination products (P1~P5) share almost the same architecture. The architecture of Preview products (P6~P8) is approximately a subset of corresponding Examination products (P1, P4 and P5). Training products P9 and P11 extend the architecture of P6 and are modified based on P1; P10 is built based on P7 and is modified based on P4.

In the following sections, WES-PL specifically denotes Examination, Training and Preview products.

3 Architecture Evolution in WES-PL

For better understanding of the architecture evolution history, we first give a brief introduction to the most recent PLA skeleton of WES-PL. Then we describe the architecture evolution types discovered in WES-PL evolution history. After that, we present an architecture evolution roadmap of WES-PL with detailed description of some typical evolution cases. Finally, we summarize architecture evolution in WES-PL with both qualitative and quantitative analysis.

3.1 The PLA Skeleton

The most recent PLA skeleton is presented in Figure 3, showing commonality and variability in all concerned products. The basic structure includes six variable components (i.e. Network, Server, GUI, Authentication, and PaperReader) with several variants each and other optional and variable accessory components (such as audio and video components). The major architectural variations are described as the following: 1) Network protocol: Some products work on TCP/IP protocols; some others work on HTTP protocol via Internet; even others do not need a network component (e.g. the

Preview products). 2) Server component: Examination and Preview products need EPC while Training products need LCM. There are also several variant for EPC and LCM. 3) GUI suite: Different products adopt various GUI suites for different examinations; also, user interactions provided by UI suites are different (e.g. Examination products typically provide only limited control for end users, while Training or Previewing products provide more freedom for end user interactions). 4) A/V processors: The PL has adopted several different audio/video components; some products need voice multicast; video playback support is an optional for certain examinations. 5) Other variants are trivial, such as Database, Authentication and Exam Paper Reader.

The PLA has been evolved for eight years, and is very likely to be evolving in the future. The skeleton is a quick snapshot of current PLA. In the following discussion, we actually address the problem that how *this* version of PLA is achieved.

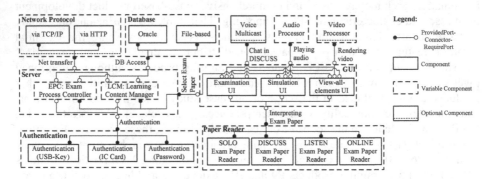

Fig. 3. The PLA skeleton of WES-PL

3.2   Typical Architectural Evolution Types

In our previous work [2], we have indicated that, besides application derivation, there are continuous interactions between application architectures and the PLA during the evolution of the PL. We now further categorize these architecture evolutions into six types, namely *linear evolution*, *derivation*, *merge*, *synchronization*, *clone* and *propagation*.

- **Linear evolution:** Linear evolution is driven by intrinsic factors of an application or the PLA.
- **Derivation:** Derivation is to create the initial architecture of a new application from the PLA by variability customization and extension.
- **Merge:** Architecture merge is a kind of periodic feedback from application architecture to the PLA. When merging, architects collect and analyze architectural differences within all current application architectures and resolve possible architectural conflicts before changes are integrated to the PLA. Note that the PLA may evolve after a merge to prepare for a synchronization to all products (see Synchronization below). Before such a follow-up linear evolution, all application architectures have to be frozen in order to prevent incompatibility or inconsistency. Such a "frozen" is also depicted in Figure 4.

- **Synchronization:** Synchronization is to reconcile application architectures with the PLA. Usually, architectural conflicts should have been resolved before synchronization.
- **Clone:** Architecture clone creates the initial architecture of a new application from an existing application architecture. Architecture clone allows application architectures to deviate from the PLA, although such deviations is ultimately to be resolved.
- **Propagation:** Architecture propagation is to propagate architectural modifications among application architectures. Modifications to an application architecture could be experimentally applied in sibling application architectures before merged into the PLA.

A typical architecture evolution trace in a PL with these types can be exemplified in Figure 4, followed by a short summary for each evolution type in Table 2.

With these types in mind, we further analyze the history of WES-PL architecture evolution and find out how these evolution types actually take effect in real development.

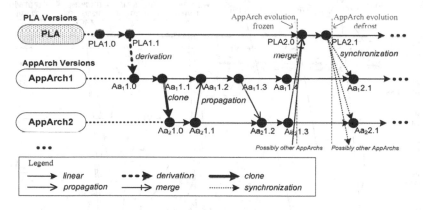

Fig. 4. Illustration of architecture evolution types

Table 2. A summary of evolution types

| Evolution type | Modification | | Comment |
	From	To	
Linear evolution	AppArch	**next version** of AppArch	Usually involves proactive reuse considerations to better feed future application development
	PLA	**next version** of PLA	Usually reflects a quick response to changes in requirements or environment
Derivation	PLA	**new AppArch**	A traditional way to create a new application from the PLA
Merge	AppArchs	**next version** of PLA	Modifications on AppArchs are collected in the PLA
Synchronization	PLA	**all** existing AppArchs	New design features are spread from the PLA to all applications
Clone	AppArch	**new AppArch**	An informal but useful way to create a new application from an existing application
Propagation	AppArch	**some** other existing AppArchs	Architectural changes to an application can be experimentally applied to another application

3.3   A Roadmap of WES-PL Architecture Evolution

In this subsection, we show a more detailed evolution history than that in Section 2.2. We do not investigate every revision in the evolution history, but focus on primary milestones of each product. Figure 5 shows such a history, with the eleven products in the scope, indicating the *overall* complexity of the evolution trace. The vertical axis represents concerned products, while the horizontal axis indicates time.

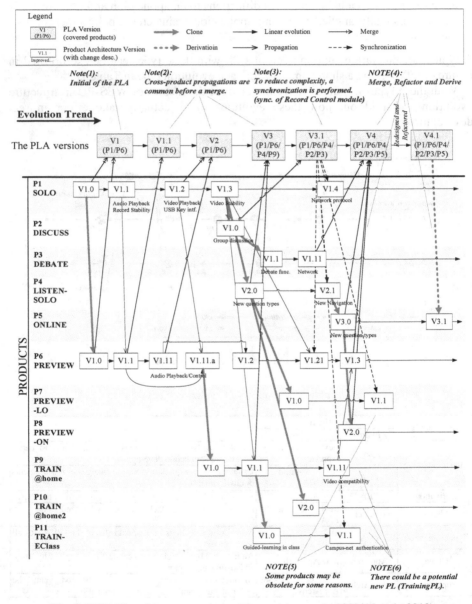

Fig. 5. WES-PL architecture evolution history (since early 2003 till early 2010)

Several special cases depicted in Figure 5 as *NOTE(n)* are worthy of mentioning. The rationales behind will be discussed in subsection 3.4.

- *NOTE(1): Initial of the PLA.* The PLA is created from the first merge. In our case, we find that the PLA is not designed purely in domain engineering processes, but merged from P1 and P6.
- *NOTE(2): Propagations before merges.* Architectural changes are usually propagated to at least one other product before being merged into the PLA. PLA versions 1.1, 2 and 3 take changes that have been made to at least two products.
- *NOTE(3): Synchronization for lower complexity.* At this point of time, developers maintain several versions of sound recording control in at least five products. In order to reduce the complexity, all related products are synchronized on the Sound Recording Control subsystem after the new mechanism is proved to be usable and effective in the previous versions of P2 and P9.
- *NOTE(4): Merge, Refactor and Derive.* Only a carefully designed architecture is suitable for derivation. A derivation happens on PLA Version 4.1, rather than on PLA Version 4 which is immediately after a merge. A careful redesign is made to PLA v4 to achieve better maintainability.
- *NOTE(5): Obsolete products.* P7 is obsolete at the point of time when no more customers are interested in its functionality. Most customers are interested either in more stable, old products, or in the next generation of a new product (P8). Also note that P8 is not cloned from P7, which is in the same product category, but from P5, the examination correspondence with more similarity. Also, P11 is temporarily obsolete for different reasons that potential users have not been inspired and that current products (P9 and P10) have already fulfilled most of current requirements.
- *NOTE(6): New product lines may be identified.* P9~P11 are getting more and more different than other products. While they are getting "too different", the architect is deciding to create a new PL for these products.

These practices give a quick glance at the industrial product line development reality. More detailed analysis will be shown in the following subsection.

3.4 Summary of Architecture Evolution in WES-PL

A quantitative and qualitative summary of the evolution practices is listed in Table 3.

Table 3. An analysis for evolution types

Evolution type	Count	Comment
Linear evolution	many	Linear evolution is trivial in the whole development process. We only consider major builds of products and versions of the PLA.
Clone	10	New products are typically cloned from similar products, rather than derived from PLA.
Synchronization	>5	Existing products may take part of the modifications from the PLA. Future products are not explicitly affected.
Derivation	1	In our case, "derivation" happens only when the new online examination system is developed.
Merge	>12	Architectural modifications are merged into the reference architecture. The reference architecture then covers several products.
Propagation	>5	There are at least 20 modifications propagated among products, but most of them are between small revisions. If products share similar modules, then a modification to that module will propagate to other products containing the same modules.

As we review this history, we can find the answers to the following questions: First, how a new product is created; second, how a new product line is created; third, how the PLA evolves; and finally, what tends to be typical evolution decisions in an industrial SPL development in the real world.

- Clone vs. Derivation

In real development, both derivation and architecture clone are ways of creating a new product. Derivation from the PLA is regarded as a good and standard practice in SPL development. But in our case, developers typically do not derive new products from the PLA. Rather, they tend to create products by cloning the architecture (usually also with source code) of an existing product. The reason is that cloning is usually cheaper in early development, especially when the team of developers is stable. Moreover, a complete domain engineering process is usually not available due to limited resources in the company. Thus, blindly deriving a product from the PLA is only too risky for most developers. Therefore, the reality is that most new products are built from older products, rather than derived from the PLA.

- Initiating a product line with actual products

The beginning of all these eleven products is not a design of the PLA, but actual working products P1/P6. In real development in a medium-small company, there are not enough time and resources to trade a working product for a PLA. It is only acceptable that, when there *are* several products working, the PLA can be tentatively built and incrementally evolve. The PLA is not necessarily the source of all products in the SPL, but provides a broader vision for all future products.

Meanwhile, new PLs may be created by "splitting" current PL when the application architecture shows too many differences. As is noted in Figure 5, a Training-PL may be created by considering all Training products in the future.

- The evolution of the PLA

There are two cases that drive PLA evolution: 1) merge and 2) redesign. We find that architectural changes in the PLA are primarily driven by merge from various products. In our case, the architect did not frequently directly modify/redesign the PLA actively. He believed that a modification to the architecture was risky; therefore, unless there was a significant reason (say, for improving performance or for a clear and splendid future), the architect was not willing to modify the PLA proactively[6].

If such a significant reason is present, architectural refactoring happens periodically and inevitably, which triggers a pure linear evolution of the PLA.

In practice, a relaxed approach is adopted: modifications are experimentally made to a single product. Such modifications are cheap and safe, because they are restricted within one single product. If the modifications are proven to be not useful or not acceptable to the market, the features are simply abandoned, and the PLA remains untouched.

- The PMS pattern: accepting new features in SPL

We find in our case that a typical path to add a new feature to all products follows the Propagating-Merging-Synchronizing (PMS) pattern, meaning that a feature should not be integrated in the SPL unless it is propagated to more than one product.

First, a linear evolution is carried out for the specified product (Product A). Then the modification is propagated to another product (Product B) sharing the same components relative to the modifications. If Product B shows the modification reasonable, then the modification is a candidate to be collected in the PLA. After the architect identifies the new feature as a common one, the modification is then merged in the PLA. Before the modification is synchronized to all other products, the architect should further evaluate the quality of the new architecture. Typically, a refactoring will be carried out, leading to a linear evolution of PLA. After that, the new features can be finally synchronized to all other products in the SPL.

4 Evaluation and Discussion

Before evaluation and discussion, we have to mention that, although the architecture evolution trace observed in our case study with the six evolution types faithfully reflects the actual development history, we still find some limitations in our study. One is that our case is with a medium-small software company developing products of its own. Therefore, our case may not be applicable to large, international software companies or outsourcing companies. Another is that our study is based on only one PL developed continuously by one team. Some complicated architectural evolution phenomena (such as those with collaboration issues) may not be observed.

The threats do exist and may provide some new perspectives for our future study. However, we can still elicit common practices valuable within the scope of our case study. In the following discussions, we highlight some special problems in industrial SPL practice from the aspect of architecture evolution and discover some useful experiences about SPL evolution decision to complement classic SPL methodology. On the other hand, we also realize that the current development practice in WES-PL is far from perfect, so we would like to propose some possible improvements for evolution management in WES-PL.

4.1 Proactive Evolution vs. Reactive Evolution

McGregor [7] describes two approaches in SPL engineering: the proactive approach, which leads to a risk of developing possible useless assets, and the reactive approach, which implies more effort in reactively prepare assets for later reuse. Our case confirms this conclusion. Moreover, we also find that, regardless future conformance with PLA, reactive approach may achieve short time-to-market because short-sighted modification may be more light-weighted and thus captures short-termed opportunities (such as in a bidding).

Proactive reuse-based strategy is the foundation of SPL development, promising benefits like improved quality and reduction of development costs and time to market. However, reactive strategy can significantly reduce the upfront investment, requiring closer coordination within the SPL project [1].

In fact, after an SPL is established, both proactive and reactive evolutions exist. In proactive evolution, feedbacks from application engineering to domain engineering are also allowed, but evolution decisions must be initiated on the PLA before applied to application architectures. In Figure 5, proactive architecture evolution only involves architecture derivation and synchronization besides PLA linear evolution. On the contrary, reactive architecture evolution allows application architectures to temporarily deviate from the PLA by clone or self evolution and then synchronize with the PLA by consequent merging and synchronization.

Apparently, proactive evolution is consistent with the SPL principle of proactive reuse, thus should benefit the SPL promises on quality, cost and time to market. However, we find reactive evolution has its rationality in SPL practice, especially in small or middle-sized SPL projects facing intense market competition. The SPL promise of reducing time to market by proactive reuse is on the premise of accurately predicting emerging and changing product requirements. However, in a competitive and rapidly changing market like computer-aided online examinations, such long-term predictions are not realistic. For example, when preparing for a bid, urgent new features may come from competing products and/or potential customers (usually the bid inviters). In such a situation, the SPL team is always under the pressure of rapid responses to the new features even if the new features are out of the scope of the PL. Thus, application engineers usually choose to clone from a most similar exiting product rather than start a proactive evolution process.

Besides response time, the risk of overdesign for uncertain features can also be reduced by reactive evolution. Due to immaturity of the market and uncertainty of requirements, newly planned features may finally be abandoned. Implementing such a feature in an experimental product would be much cheaper than incorporating it in the PLA as a variation point. If the uncertain new feature is validated in one or more products before incorporated into the PLA, unnecessary time and efforts would be saved.

Reactive evolution may make application architectures deviate from the PLA. In order to reconcile them, architecture merge and synchronization should be conducted, usually when the whole SPL is relatively stable. This means that new features have been fully validated by the market, and that the whole SPL team can focus more on refactoring the PLA and coordinating all application architectures with the PLA.

4.2 Business Strategy and Technical Decisions

SPL methodology is market-oriented, so technical decisions should undoubtedly support and serve the business strategy. The technical decision of proactive or reactive evolution discussed above actually reflects this principle. The experiences from WES-PL confirmed that the technical choice of whether adopting a proactive approach or a reactive approach largely depends on the market position of the SPL organization. If it has the leading position in the target market, the organization usually takes the initiative in SPL evolution and prefers a proactive strategy. On the contrary, if it is in the expanding stage struggling to earn a place in the market, the team often passively absorbs emerging ideas from competitors and customers. Therefore, the reactive evolution strategy is better for rapid responses to emerging features and reducing the risk of misestimating the evolution trends.

On the other hand, technical decisions can adversely affect the business strategy of the organization by providing feedbacks. The technical decisions have great influence on the cost aspect of business considerations, and the influences are usually hard to be evaluated at the business level. For example, the scoring products were initially included in the WES-PL from the business perspective, since they share some components in common with examination products. However, according to the feedback from reactive architecture merging (not shown in our case study), too many differences are found and too much complexity is included. Thus, scoring products were excluded from the WES-PL finally. A similar demerge chance can be found in the Training product category, which is mentioned as a "split" in subsection 3.4.

4.3 Possible Improvements

Proactive evolution and reactive evolution essentially reflect the tradeoff between unity and agility in SPL development. In WES-PL, reactive evolution decisions like architecture clone and propagation are adopted for agility. Architecture merge and synchronization should be continually enforced to keep balance between unity and agility.

However, we find the current development practice in WES-PL emphasizes agility over unity too much. Related problems include 1) loose control on reactive architecture evolution, 2) long synchronization cycle and 3) incomplete synchronization. Intense market competition and tight time arrangement make the SPL team overuse reactive evolution approaches, which partly causes these problems.

Loose control and long synchronization cycle are resolvable by adjusting team organization and development process. But such adjustments should be based on a stable profit of existing products to the company. The problem of incomplete synchronization can be resolved by PLA refactoring. As inconsistent designs exist across the application architectures, PLA refactoring involves adaptations to the variability design to accommodate the inconsistencies among application architectures and deviations away from the PLA. We find the PLA refactoring practices are not well established in WES-PL.

All these problems reflect the shortcomings of reactive evolution in WES-PL, i.e. the basic role of the PLA in reuse-based SPL engineering is crippled. If no effective measures taken, the product line may degenerate to a series of individual product projects with manual copy/paste-based code reuse. Based on the above analysis, we suggest possible improvements to the current WES-PL practice. From the aspect of management, we suggest strict control over reactive evolution. The synchronization cycle should be shortened and formulated in the organization or within the team. From the technical aspect, we suggest more effort on PLA-level refactoring to better reconcile application architectures and the PLA.

5   Related Work

There are several industrial case studies on SPLE, focusing on adopting SPL methodology in software development [8,10,13,14,15]. But there is not yet a widely adopted or general approach for industry to easily and efficiently transit from traditional single product development to software mass customization [9]. There are also challenges in contemporary industrial SPL development in managing continuous changing and emerging variabilities [10]. In a newly created product line, changes to the reused core assets and their customized instances also need to be efficiently propagated and managed [11]. Our case study actually shows such attempts that a medium-small company focusing on a particular market tried to adapt the SPL methodology in the past eight years to maximize the throughput of customized products.

Svahnberg and Bosch [12] conducted a detailed evolution analysis on two software product lines with a history of nearly 10 years since 1990. Among several generations and releases of products, they identified several categorizations of SPL evolutions on requirements, architectures and components, and provided some guidelines for software product line evolution. We have adopted a similar methodology with their work. Our case study, however, tries to find some special practices other than standard PL development. We explore deep into one particular product line, and focus specifically on the architecture evolution. We believe our findings in our case present more recent SPL engineering in medium-small companies, including both standard and agile practices.

There are also researches and case studies on interactions, integrations and feedbacks between single products and common assets in an SPL, including military development with US Navy [16] and commercial organizations [1,17,18,19]. Our case study further discusses what exactly these interactions and feedbacks are, and what other interactions exists between the core assets and instantiated applications.

More research and industrial groups reported their SPL engineering and reengineering practices, showing adoption SPL methodology in traditional development. These research and practices include adopting product line development without the use of a PLA [20], reusing legacy components in a product line [21], and migrate legacy systems into product lines [22,23]. There are also researches on incrementally introducing features in product line development with proactive scheduling and road mapping [24].

In these cases and researches, we find side effects when adopting non-standard SPLE process, but such practices also bring some effectiveness to industrial development.

Despite of all these non-standard SPLE practices, researchers pointed out that SPLE in commercial organizations is ultimately evolving towards high maturity, both technically and organizationally [25,26]. Our WES project is actually at a relatively low maturity level and evolves towards higher maturity, as the PLA gradually integrates all features and variability from other existing or potential products. The evolution direction of an SPL can be anticipated by long-term forecasting [27], contributing to SPL design decisions in current development. This is why we believe the possible improvements proposed in Subsection 4.3 are reasonable.

The SPL development in Wingsoft also shows something in common with agile software product line method [7]. A successful integration of SPL development practices and agile software development practices is described by M.A. Babar [28].

In our previous work, Peng [2] has outlined an architecture-based evolution management method, which illustrates several architecture evolution cases. In another product line with Wingsoft, we identified common implementation mechanisms for product variations [4]. We also tried to manage interleaved interactions between the core assets (including PLA) and application architectures (including instantiated artifacts) [5].

6 Conclusion and Future Work

In this paper, we report an industrial case study on architecture evolution in SPL engineering. We identify a series of architecture evolution types and several typical evolution paths. Some evolution types, such as propagation and clone between products, usually causing architectural deviations, are quite common in the evolution history, showing a typical reactive style. We find that such reactive evolution plays an important role in small or middle-sized SPL projects facing intense competitions and market uncertainty. Although not conforming to classical SPL methodology, reactive evolution has rationality in SPL practice due to its rapid responsibility to emerging features and low risk of overdesigning. To keep the unity across all products, periodical merges and synchronizations are performed. In particular, architectural unifications are reasonably derived from specific variant products, rather than totally designed proactively. Based on the industrial case, we also propose some possible improvements for the evolution management in similar industrial product lines. Although our experiences may not apply to large, international PL development, we believe our case represents the reality of PL practices in medium-small companies.

Our case study highlights some real industrial SPL practices on the perspective of architecture evolution and provides useful experiences about SPL evolution management to complement classical SPL methodology. In our follow-up study, we plan to introduce knowledge-based method to model SPL design decisions and explore knowledge-based SPL evolution analysis from the perspective of design decisions.

Acknowledgments. The work presented is supported by National Natural Science Foundation of China (NSFC) under grants 60903013, 90818009 and 60703092. The authors would also thank Xiaofeng Qian and Shunxiong Ma in Wingsoft for their help in the case study.

References

1. Clements, P.C., Jones, L.G., Northrop, L.M., McGregor, J.D.: Project Management in a Software Product Line Organization. IEEE Software 22(5), 54–62 (2005)
2. Peng, X., Shen, L., Zhao, W.: An Architecture-based Evolution Management Method for Software Product Line. In: SEKE 2009, pp. 135–140. KSI Graduate School, IL (2009)
3. Wu, Y., Zhao, W., Peng, X., Xue, Y.: A Concept Model for Computer-based Spoken Language Tests. In: AICT-ICIW 2006, pp. 19–24. IEEE Computer Society, Los Alamitos (2006)
4. Ye, P., Peng, X., Xue, Y., Jarzabek, S.: A Case Study of Variation Mechanism in an Industrial Product Line. In: Edwards, S.H., Kulczycki, G. (eds.) ICSR 2009. LNCS, vol. 5791, pp. 126–136. Springer, Heidelberg (2009)
5. Shen, L., Peng, X., Zhu, J., Zhao, W.: Synchronized Architecture Evolution in Software Product Line using Bidirectional Transformation. In: COMPSAC 2010, pp. 389–394 (2010)
6. McGregor, J.D.: The Evolution of Product Line Assets. Techinal report, CMU/SEI-2003-TR-005, ESC-TR-2003-005 (2003)
7. McGregor, J.D.: Agile Software Product Lines, Deconstructed. Journal of Object Technology 7(8), 7–19 (2008)
8. Jiang, M., Zhang, J.: Maintaining Software Product Lines – an Industrial Practice. In: ICSM 2008, pp. 444–447 (2008)
9. Krueger, C.W.: Easing the Transition to Software Mass Customization. In: van der Linden, F.J. (ed.) PFE 2002. LNCS, vol. 2290, pp. 282–293. Springer, Heidelberg (2002)
10. Chen, L., Babar, M.A.: Variability Management in Software Product Lines: An Investigation of Contemporary Industrial Challenges. In: Bosch, J., Lee, J. (eds.) SPLC 2010. LNCS, vol. 6287, pp. 166–180. Springer, Heidelberg (2010)

11. Anastasopoulos, M.: Increasing Efficiency and Effectiveness of Software Product Line Evolution–An Infrastructure on Top of Configuration Management. In: Joint International and Annual ERCIM Workshops on Principles of Software Evolution (IWPSE) and Software Evolution (Evol) Workshops, pp. 47–56. ACM, New York (2009)
12. Svahnberg, M., Bosch, J.: Evolution in Software Product Lines: Two cases. Journal of Software Maintenance 11(6), 391–422 (1999)
13. Bosch, J.: Product-line architectures in industry: a case study. In: ICSE 1999, pp. 544–554. ACM, New York (1999)
14. Maccari, A.: Experiences in assessing product family software architecture for evolution. In: ICSE 2002, pp. 585–592. ACM, New York (2002)
15. Axelsson, J.: Evolutionary Architecting of Embedded Automotive Product Lines: An Industrial Case Study. In: WICSA 2009, pp. 101–110. IEEE, Cambridge (2009)
16. Brownsword, L., Clements, P.: A Case Study in Successful Product Line Development. Technical report. CMU/SEI, CMU/SEI-96-TR-016 (2006)
17. Riva, C., Rosso, C.D.: Experiences with Software Product Family Evolution. In: 6th International Workshop on Principles of Software Evolution, pp. 161–169. IEEE, Los Alamitos (2003)
18. Takebe, Y., Fukaya, N., Chikahisa, M., Hanawa, T., Shirai, O.: Experiences with software product line engineering in product development oriented organization. In: SPLC 2009, pp. 275–283. CMU, Pittsburgh (2009)
19. Lee, H., Choi, H., Kang, K.C., Kim, D., Lee, Z.: Experience Report on Using a Domain Model-Based Extractive Approach to Software Product Line Asset Development. In: Edwards, S.H., Kulczycki, G. (eds.) ICSR 2009. LNCS, vol. 5791, pp. 137–149. Springer, Heidelberg (2009)
20. Staples, M., Hill, D.: Experiences Adopting Software Product Line Development without a Product Line Architecture. In: 11th Asia-Pacific Software Engineering Conference, pp. 176–183. IEEE, Los Alamitos (2004)
21. Kolb, R., Muthig, D., Patzke, T., Yamauchi, K.: A Case Study in Refactoring a Legacy Component for Reuse in a Product Line. In: ICSM 2005, pp. 369–378. IEEE Press, Los Alamitos (2005)
22. Breivold, H.P., Larsson, S., Land, R.: Migrating Industrial Systems towards Software Product Lines: Experiences and Observations through Case Studies. In: 34th Euromicro Conference Software Engineering and Advanced Applications, pp. 232–239. IEEE, Los Alamitos (2008)
23. Hanssen, G.K.: Opening Up Software Product Line Engineering. In: The 2010 ICSE Workshop on Product Line Approaches in Software Engineering, pp. 1–7. ACM, New York (2010)
24. Savolainen, J., Kuusela, J.: Scheduling Product Line Features for Effective Roadmapping. In: The 15th Asia-Pacific Software Engineering Conference, pp. 195–202. IEEE, Los Alamitos (2008)
25. Bosch, J.: Maturity and evolution in software product lines: Approaches, artefacts and organization. In: Chastek, G.J. (ed.) SPLC 2002. LNCS, vol. 2379, pp. 247–262. Springer, Heidelberg (2002)
26. Ahmed, F., Capretz, L.F.: An organizational maturity model of software product line engineering. Software Quality Journal 18(2), 195–225 (2010)
27. Chen, Y., Gannod, G.C., Collofello, J.S., Sarjoughian, H.S.: Using simulation to facilitate the study of software product line evolution. In: 7th International Workshop on Principles of Software Evolution, pp. 103–112. IEEE, Los Alamitos (2004)
28. Babar, M.A., Ihme, T., Pikkarainen, M.: An Industrial Case of Exploiting Product Line Architectures in Agile Software Development. In: SPLC 2009, pp. 171–179. CMU, Pittsburgh (2009)

Improving Product Line Architecture Design and Customization by Raising the Level of Variability Modeling

Jiayi Zhu[1,2], Xin Peng[1,2], Stan Jarzabek[3], Zhenchang Xing[3], Yinxing Xue[3], and Wenyun Zhao[1,2]

[1] Shanghai Key Laboratory of Intelligent Information Processing
[2] School of Computer Science, Fudan University, Shanghai, China
[3] School of Computing, National University of Singapore, Singapore
{072021130,pengxin,wyzhao}@fudan.edu.cn,
{stan,xingzc,yinxing}@comp.nus.edu.sg

Abstract. Product Line Architecture (PLA) plays a central role in software product line development. In order to support architecture-level variability modeling, most architecture description languages (ADLs) introduce architectural variation elements, such as optional component, connector and interface, which must be customized during product derivation. Variation elements are many, and design and customization of PLA at the level of individual variation elements are difficult and error-prone. We observed that developers usually perceive architecture variability from the perspective of variant features or variant design decisions that are mapped into groups of architecture variation elements. In the paper, we describe heuristics to identify configurations of variation elements that typically form such groups. We call them variation constructs. We developed an architecture variability management method and a tool that allow developers to work at the variation construct level rather than at the level of individual variation elements. We have applied and evaluated the proposed method in the development and maintenance of a medium-size financial product line. Our experience indicates that by raising variability modeling from variation element to construct level, architecture design and customizations become more intuitive. Not only does our method reduce the design and customization effort, but also better ensures consistent configuration of architectural variation elements, avoiding errors.

Keywords: software product line, architecture, variability, ADL.

1 Introduction

Product Line Architecture (PLA) plays a central role in software product line development. A PLA differs from traditional software architecture for a single product in that it must be customizable for different products. Therefore, product line architecture description languages (ADLs), e.g. xADL 2.0 [1], introduced architectural variation elements such as optional component, connector and interface.

K. Schmid (Ed.): ICSR 2011, LNCS 6727, pp. 151–166, 2011.

Designers usually perceive architecture variability from the perspective of variant features or variant design decisions that are mapped into configurations of architecture variation elements. Figure 1 shows a typical design of the optional feature *Log* in a PLA. The architecture is depicted using boxes for components, small boxes with arrows for interfaces (inward arrows represent supplier interfaces; outward ones represent client interfaces), lines for links and ellipses for connectors. Dashed lines indicate optional elements. In order to model architectural representation of *Log*, an optional component *Log*, an optional interface in component *OnlinePayment*, two optional links and an optional connector have to be introduced. As discussed in Section 2, a simple composition between two components may induce 2^{11} combinations of basic variation elements. It is difficult and error-prone to model, customize and modify a PLA at the level of individual variation elements. For example, if we select the optional client interface in component *OnlinePayment*, we must also select relevant connector, links and component *Log*, or else the architecture after customization will not be valid.

Fig. 1. A typical design of optional feature *Log*

We observed that in general it is the case that certain groups of variation elements must be configured together in certain way to ensure correctness of the product architecture. We refer to valid group of variation elements that must be managed together as variation construct in the rest of the paper. In the design shown in Figure 1, optional feature *Log* is mapped into a single variation construct, but in general we have many-to-many mappings between features and variation constructs in PLA, which means a variant feature may involve several variation constructs. We hypothesized that it might be easier for designers to work with variation constructs instead of variation elements. We thought that variation constructs can simplify PLA design and customization, and make it less error-prone.

To test the hypothesis, we developed architecture variability modeling and customization method, and a tool that implements the method. In the method, we specify rules to help identify valid combinations of variation elements, mostly from the aspect of syntax. Then we further identify useful variation constructs according to some principles and clarify their different intention of variability design, as basic blocks for variability design and customization. We have successfully applied the proposed method in the development and maintenance of a medium-size financial product line. Our experience indicates that by raising the level of variability modeling and management not only do we reduce the design and customization effort, but also better ensure consistent configuration of architectural variation elements.

The remainder of this paper is organized as follows. Section 2 analyzes the problems in architectural-level variability design and customization after some background introduction. Section 3 defines PLA variation rules based on a PLA meta-model. Section 4 introduces our variation constructs with some examples. Section 5 presents our prototype tool implemented and evaluates our method with a case study on an enterprise product line. Finally, Section 6 discusses related work before Section 7 draws our conclusions.

2 Background and Problem Analysis

Software architecture reveals abstract views of the structure, behavior, and key properties of a software system [2]. In our work, we concentrate of structural architectural views that are typically expressed in terms of components, connectors, and constraints on the interactions among components. Different from single product architecture, product line architecture (PLA) defines a reference architecture shared by a family of products in a given business domain [3, 18, 19]. Architectures for custom products are derived from PLA. To enable such derivation, PLA must accommodate concepts of variability.

ADLs provide notational frameworks for architecture modeling. Examples of popular ADLs include Acme [4], C2 [5], Darwin [6], Rapide [7], UniCon [8], and Wright [9]. Among few ADLs that support PLA modeling we found xADL 2.0 [1], Koala [10] and ABC/ADL [25]. ADLs for PLA support *variation elements* to model product-specific differences. Typical variation elements are optional component/interface/connector/link and alternative component. During PLA customization, the application architect determines whether an optional element should be selected or not, and which variant of an alternative element is to be included in the product architecture.

At the level of variation elements, the number of possible customizations explodes in combinatorial way. Any two interacting components may involve as many as nine variation elements, namely the two components, one connector, four interfaces and two links; the two components can further be alternative (with variants). Among 2^{11} combinations of those variation elements, only a small number is valid. As an example, Figure 2 shows an invalid design for the optional feature *Log*. In comparison with the design in Figure 1, we can see that the mandatory connection between optional component *Log* and its client *OnlinePayment* component are used in Figure 2. Design of Figure 2 does not correctly reflect the interaction between the optional component *Log* and its client *OnlinePayment*. Furthermore, if the component *Log* is removed during customization, it is likely to overlook the necessary customization to its clients, for example, leaving a dangling link in the product architecture. For this problem, we expect to identify a set of rules to help eliminate those invalid combinations.

Fig. 2. A meaningless design of optional feature *Log*

The other problem is that different valid combinations of variation elements may have similar structures but different meanings. For example, design of Figure 3 is similar to Figure 1, but the meaning is quite different. In Figure 1, mandatory *OnlinePayment* service is provided with or without logging. On the contrary, in the design of Figure 3 *OnlinePayment* is an optional service, but it must be provided with logging if *OnlinePayment* is selected.

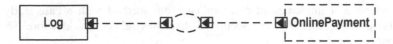

Fig. 3. A design of optional feature *OnlinePayment*

In the next section, we introduce the concept of variation construct to combat the above problems.

3 PLA Meta-model and Variation Combination Rules

This section first presents a PLA meta-model defining architecture modeling concepts found in many ADLs. Then based on the meta-model, we derive a set of rules that can be used to identify valid combinations of variation elements.

3.1 PLA Meta-model

To present our approach in ADL-independent way, we define essential PLA modeling elements as a meta-model shown in Figure 4. Architecture modeling elements include components, connectors, interfaces and links. Each component can have a possibly empty set of supplier interfaces and client interfaces. A connector must be connected to at least one supplier component and one client component via its interfaces. Each link establishes connection from a client interface to a supplier interface. The additional constraint to links in the meta-model prescribes that links can only be established between component interfaces and client interfaces. That means components can only be composed via connectors.

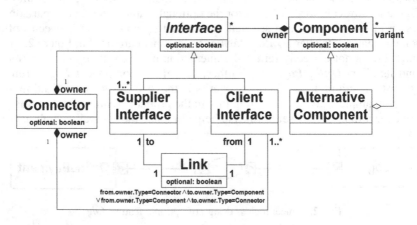

Fig. 4. A meta-model of product line architecture

Variability in PLA is represented by optional and alternative architecture elements. Components, connectors, interfaces and links can be optional. For simplicity, we assume that only a component can be alternative. Some ADLs (e.g., xADL 2.0 [1]) include alternative connectors, but they are not frequently used.

An optional component or connector may be selected or removed during PLA customization. When de-selected, all corresponding interfaces of an optional element must be removed. It should be noted that a component/connector being optional does not imply that its interfaces must also be optional. An optional interface can be selected or removed for its owner component or connector: a removed supplier interface means the service is not provided; a removed client interface means the service request is not activated. Optional links usually are used together with optional components, connectors or interfaces to represent optional interactions. An alternative component has 0 to multiple variant components for customization. If no predefined variant is provided, it can be regarded as an abstract component with product-specific implementation that can only be provided in application engineering.

3.2 Rules to Identify Valid Combinations of Variation Elements

Some valid combinations of variation elements are implied by PLA meta-model. For example, the rules annotated for link in Figure 4. Here we further explore constraints related to combination of variation elements as shown in Table 1. The predicate op(*ele*) denotes that architectural element *ele* is optional, and alt(*ele*) denotes that *ele* is alternative.

Table 1. Rules for variation constructs

R1	*link*∈Link ∧ (op(*link.from*)∨op(*link.to*)∨op(*link.from.owner*)∨op(*link.to.owner*)) → op(*link*)
R2	*link*∈Link ∧ op(*link*) → op(*link.from*)∨op(*link.from.owner*)
R3	*serIF*∈SupplierInterface ∧ op(*serIF*) ∧ *serIF.owner*.Type=Connector → ∃ *serIF'* ∈ SupplierInterface ∧ *serIF'*≠*serIF* ∧ *serIF'*.owner=*serIF.owner*
R4	*cliIF* ∈ ClientInterface ∧ op(*cliIF*) ∧ *cliIF.owner*.Type=Connector → ∃ *cliIF'* ∈ ClientInterface ∧ *cliIF'* ≠ *cliIF* ∧ *cliIF'*.owner= *cliIF.owner*
R5	*serIF*∈SupplierInterface ∧ op(*serIF*) ∧ *serIF.owner*.Type=Component → alt(*serIF.owner*)

PLA variation constraints are derived from general observations about what forms a correct configuration of variation elements during customization. First, links cannot be dangling, i.e., a link must not be selected unless either of the interfaces it connects to is selected during PLA customization. This constraint makes the first rule (R1) in Table 1, stating that for each link *link*, if either of the interfaces or either of the components it connects to is optional, it must be optional.

Second, if we select a client interface then we must also select a corresponding service provider for it. The second rule (R2) in Table 1 is derived from this point: if a link is optional, the interface or the component at its client side must be optional.

Third, to ensure a connector connects to at least one supplier component and one client component, a supplier (client) interface of a connector must be mandatory if it is the only supplier (client) interface. This constraint is reflected by the third and fourth rules (R3, R4) in Table 1.

Fourth, an optional supplier interface means the service can be provided or not. This usually tells that the owner component has several variants and they are not consistent in providing the service. The fifth rule (R5) describes this constraint.

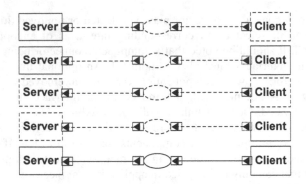

Fig. 5. The set of variation constructs with the constraint of one-to-one connector

With these rules, we can formally eliminate most invalid combinations of variation elements. For example, the combination in Figure 2 can be determined to be invalid according to rule R1. We developed a tool to identify valid combinations of variation elements, i.e. variation constructs. For a composition between two components without alternative components, the tool produces 44 variation constructs, and all of them are meaningful according to our validation.

It should be emphasized that these rules are only the minimum constraint set with the PLA meta-model given in Figure 4. Given additional specific architectural styles, more rules can also be extended. For example, if each connector is restricted to be shared by exact two components, a much stronger rule telling that connector interfaces cannot be optional can be derived from the third and fourth rule. Then we can identify a set of 5 variation constructs as shown in Figure 5 according to rule R1-R5.

4 Variation Constructs in PLA

In our method, a variation construct is defined as a group of architectural elements in a PLA that represent a meaningful functional variation point in the architecture and must be managed together as a whole in PLA evolution and customization. In PLA design, variation constructs can be instantiated and composed with other variation construct instances. And instances of variation constructs can overlap, that is, one architectural element can belong to two or more instances of variation constructs.

In this section, we first introduce the principles in identifying useful variation constructs, then present those identified variation constructs according to the categorization of optional construct and alternative construct with some examples. Those examples are extracted from the Wingsoft Financial Management System Product Line (WFMS-PL). The initial version of WFMS-PL was developed in 2003 and it has evolved into a product line with more than 100 customers today, including major universities in China such as Fudan University, Shanghai Jiaotong University, Zhejiang University [13].

4.1 Principles in Identifying Useful Variation Constructs

The rules given in 3.2 specify the minimum constraint set of valid combinations of variation elements. For example, as mentioned in 3.2, we can identify 44 variation constructs for a composition between two components without alternative components. They are still a little more than a compact variation construct set for reuse, and we also found some of those variation constructs are not as useful as others. Therefore for those combinations satisfying all the rules, we still need to identify useful variation constructs with clarified variability meaning for developers to use.

There are some principles that can be used as guidance to identify variation constructs. These principles involve both the syntax aspect and semantic aspect, i.e. the intention of the design, of architectural variability modeling.

The first principle (P1) is reusing modeling elements among connections as many as possible. In our construct library, both the link and the connector can be reused. The third variation construct of Figure 7 presents such an example. Its link between the connector and *ExceptionHandle* component is used by two connections. Not only can this principle reduce the variation elements but it can also enable the connector to coordinate the interactions between *ExceptionHandle* component and the other parts of the system.

The second principle (P2) is to clearly distinguish the two different intentions of optional interface in alternative components. The first intention is to represent the optional attribute of the component's function that is consistently involved in all the variant components. The second one is to indicate that the interface is only provided by a part of the variants of the alternative component. As the two different intentions have quite different instructions on component implementation, they should be distinguished in the PLA design and reflected in different constructs. For example, for the latter case, the dependence between the variant component and the other parts of the system should be eliminated.

The third principle (P3) is that optional interactions between two components should be modeled at the client side using optional client interface rather than the supplier side. This kind of optional interactions usually reflect internal variation points within components. Then a supplier interface can only be optional when the interface is introduced by different behaviors of the variants of an alternative component (see rule R5 in Table 1). In that case, the optional supplier interface is defined to eliminate the dependency between an alternative component and other parts of the system.

Guided by these principles, we propose to identify different kinds of meaningful combinations of variation elements as architecture-level variation constructs, and further support PLA variability design and customization by variation constructs rather than individual variation elements. In this paper, we report our initial study on the variation constructs between two interacting components. The constructs are divided into two categories according to the two typical kinds of architectural variation points, i.e. optional constructs and alternative constructs. In the following subsections, we will describe variation constructs of the two categories with some typical examples from our case study.

4.2 Optional Constructs

An optional construct means it can be selected or removed during PLA customization. In the PLA, an optional construct is usually modeled using optional component and optional composition between components. An optional composition denotes that the interaction between two components can be selectively included in specific products, and is usually modeled as optional interfaces, connectors and likes.

Figure 6 shows three examples that use optional component to model an optional construct. The first example represents the situation that optional component provide optional feature for the system, implying that only some products require to log the online payment history. According to rule R1 and R2 (see Table 1), an optional component *Log* is introduced, together with an optional connector and two optional links, to model the optional feature *Log*. These two rules are elementary, and almost all the constructs involve the application of them. Note that the interface in *Log* component is mandatory. However, the interface in its client component *OnlinePayment* is optional, since the availability of *Log* is not known until the customization phase. According to the third principle (P3), this kind of variation points is better to be modeled in the client side rather than in the supplier side. Optional components sometimes may invoke other parts of system, which is the case in the second example. The optional component *AdditionalCharge* reflects the fact that only some products need to charge additional fee. Since the charge strategy is very complex, *AdditionalCharge* delegates to another component *CommonOperation* to calculate the tax rate.

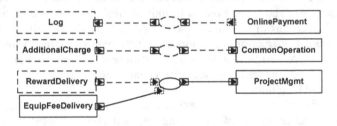

Fig. 6. Optional constructs by optional component

The connectors in the above two examples are both optional, and only serve the connection for the optional component. In some cases the connector for optional construct is at least used once, it should then be mandatory. As shown in the third example of Figure 6, *RewardDelivery* provides online delivery of additional reward for staffs and students in university. If selected, the component *RewardDelivery* depends on the service provided by the component *ProjectMgmt* to deduct the amount from corresponding project fund. As some universities tend to deliver salary offline, *RewardDelivery* is designed to be optional. The amount deduction service provided by *Project* is also required by other mandatory components such as *EquipFeeDelivery*, so the connector is at least necessary by one component. According to the first principle (P1), the connector is modeled to be mandatory. The only entrance of amount deduction service also brings benefit of easy management for payment control.

Optional composition represents finer-grained variability than optional component. Figure 7 shows three examples that use optional composition to model optional construct. In the first example, *Budget* and *ProjectMgmt* are two mandatory business components for budget management and project management respectively. *Budget*, when is executed for project budget making, involves an internal variation point of whether performing balance control (provided by *ProjectMgmt*) or not. According to P3, the optional client interface of *Budget* and related optional connector and links are employed to model this internal variation point. The component *Initiation* in the second example is responsible for initializing the system's basic information, such as the mode of payment and the student state. The initialization of the student state is optional, which is also a fine-grained variation point and modeled as an optional interface in component *Initiation*. The difference from the first example is that the service provided via the supplier interface of *Utility* is also required by other mandatory components. According to R3 that a supplier (client) interface of a connector must be mandatory if it is the only supplier (client) interface, the interface in the connector which links to *Utility* must be mandatory. So according to P1, the connector and the composition to *Utility* are modeled as mandatory elements. Optional composition can also exist between optional components. As an interface will be removed together with its owner, the interfaces of an optional component usually do not need to be modeled to be optional. But sometimes an interface of an optional component should still be modeled to be optional to represent another finer-grained variation point. As shown in the third example in Figure 7, WFMS-PL can support normal payment as well as web service payment. The exceptions thrown by the component *WebService-Payment* can be handled inside itself or by the *ExceptionHandle* component. That means the client interface of *WebServicePayment* may be removed even when *WebServicePayment* is selected, so the interface and related link and connector interface are modeled to be optional.

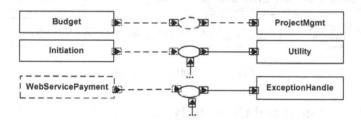

Fig. 7. Optional constructs by optional compositions

4.3 Alternative Constructs

An alternative construct means that it can be replaced by different variants during application customization. Figure 8 presents three examples that use alternative components to model an alternative construct. Alternative component is shown in a large box containing variants in smaller boxes. The first example describes the case that all the variants of a component exhibit the same interface. WFMS-PL support many banks that the application engineers can configure and adopt a subset of them in their product. The interfaces of different banks are the same as each other. There is no need to introduce additional variation elements to the *Bank* component for this alternative construct since the selection of different variants does not impact the rest of the system.

However, as shown in the second and third examples in Figure 8, there are also some cases in which only part of the variants of an alternative component provide certain services. For example, as shown in the second example of Figure 8, in WFMS-PL there are three different modes of fee payment, i.e. *ByItem*, *ByYear* and *ByYearOrder*. *ByItem* means user can pay their fee item by item. *ByYear* means user can only pay the fee year by year (each fee item belongs to one year) in any order. *ByYearOrder* means user can only pay year by year following the time order. Only the variant *ByYearOrder* may raise exception and requires the service provided by *ExceptionHandle*. According to P2, the alternative component must use optional interfaces to identify those interfaces that are not exposed by all of its variants [11]. Only if the variant *ByYearOrder* is selected, the optional interface in *FeeItemSelection* will be selected as well. Similarly, in the third example in Figure 8 only the variant *Operation* of the alternative component *LockFeeItem* provides the interface for *OnlinePayment*. In contrast to general principle P3 that the variability is better to be modeled in the client side rather than in the supplier side, it is interesting to note that the variability introduced by the *Operation* variant of the *LockFeeItem* component is modeled on the supplier side. This is because that this optional interface is introduced for eliminating the unnecessary dependencies between the other variants of the component *LockFeeItem* (e.g. *Delegation*) and the rest of the system (e.g. *OnlinePayment*). This kind of variability cannot be moved to the client side.

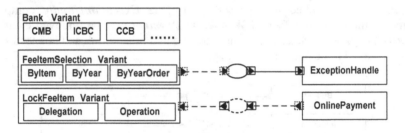

Fig. 8. Alternative Constructs

5 Implementation and Case Study

5.1 Implementation

In order to validate the proposed approach, we developed an Architecture Centric Software Product Line (ACSPL) tool that supports construct-based variability management, as shown in Figure 9. The tool is equipped with a graphical editor for PLA modeling (the upper right editor in Figure 9). In the lower left view, the tool lists all the instances of variation constructs in the PLA under development. In the construct view, the construct instances are divided into two categories, i.e. optional construct and alternative construct. Each construct instance contains all its related variation elements. The user can apply adaptive, corrective, and perfective [12] operations to the constructs and their contained variation elements, such as adding or removing a construct, changing the construct type.

(1) Add a variation construct

This situation happens when developer is designing a new variant feature. In ACSPL, developer has two options modeling this requirement. The first one is the traditional way in which developer edits the variation elements individually. The second one is to select an intention such as optional construct by optional connection and choose from candidate constructs provided by the tool. Then a skeleton variation construct will be added by the tool.

(2) Remove a variation construct

Removing a variation construct does not mean to remove the construct's elements but the elements' variability. With ACSPL, developer just needs to operate on one construct to eliminate the variability of all the relevant variation elements. After this operation, optional element becomes mandatory and alternative component to selected variants.

(3) Change the type of variation construct

This situation happens in PLA evolution [24]. For example, the need for more fine-grained control over a variation point could requires changing the type of variation construct from optional component construct category to optional composition construct category. In traditional way, in order to keep consistency, developer firstly needs to remove all the related elements' variability and then applies the change operations. ACSPL have documented the structures of the constructs, developer can be ensured the operation is consistency applied and also can clearly see the change impact before bringing it into effect.

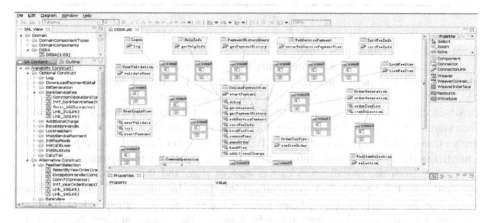

Fig. 9. Architecture Centric Software Product Line (ACSPL) Tool

5.2 Case Study

We have developed and maintained Wingsoft Financial Management System Product Line (WFMS-PL) using the proposed construct-based variability management approach. We have identified 21 key variation constructs during the development and evolution of WFMS-PL. The 22 variants of the key constructs have also been identified. Among the current 43 constructs in the catalog, the instances of 7 constructs, which is shown in Table 2, account for 70 percent of construct instances identified in the WFMS-PL.

The variation constructs raise the level of abstraction in PLA design and customization. We no longer model and manage variability at the detailed level of variation elements and their relationships. We only need to manage 53 variation constructs and

Table 2. Different Constructs used in WFMS

Variability Constructs	#Instance
	11
	7
Variant Component — variant1, variant2	6
	5
Variant Component — variant1, variant2	4
	3
	3
Others	14

42 relationships among them, in comparison with the 217 individual variation elements and 279 relationships among them.

In the past, in order to keep the consistency of the product architecture, variation elements usually inherit variability from its contained or linked elements. For example, a link connect to an optional interface is inherited optional. Thus they are selected or unselected together in the customization phase. This can certainly solve a part of inconsistency evolution problem. But not all the relations between variation elements are so transparent. As shown in Figure 10, the component *Initiation* is responsible for initializing the system's basic information, such as the mode of payment and the student state. Both the initialization of the student state and the mode of payment are optional, which is modeled as two optional interfaces in component *Initiation*. Since the connector is mandatory, it takes time to figure out the correspondent relations between two sides of the connector, which makes the evolution error prone. If the construct is introduced and becomes the management unit, in the lower left view of Figure 9, all the correlated variation elements are listed explicitly and this alleviates the inconsistency problem. Compared with traditional way, variation construct also gains benefits that variation elements in a construct can be different granularity. If the interface's variability is inherited from its contained components, they will be selected or unselected according to their components. But in some cases, the optional component is included and its optional interface is unselected. On the other hand, if the construct is the basic management unit, a variation element can be contained by many constructs and unless all the constructs are unselected the variation element is unselected. Thus the elements in one construct may have different bound conditions and granularities.

The core assets of the WFMS-PL were designed and implemented by few *domain engineers*. The maintainer of the system is changed continually. Thus it takes significant amount of time for a new member of the project team to familiarize himself with the system and all possible variants. Through our case study, we find out that there exists certain connection between the construct and the implementation. For example, construct like Figure 1 is implemented through reflection mechanism in WFMS-PL. Thus with our construct, developer can not only understand the architecture easily but also get some insights of the implementation, which can greatly speed up their learning process.

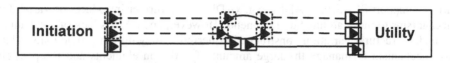

Fig. 10. An error prone situation of customization

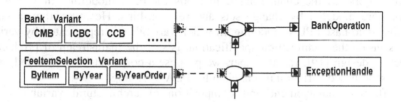

Fig. 11. Syntactically same but semantically different

Furthermore, the variation constructs help to reveal the distinctive meanings of the variability designs in PLA and eliminate the ambiguity. Take the two construct instances in Figure 11 as an example. The two instances are syntactically same in that they involve the same set of variation elements. However, the optional interface in alternative component *Bank* is exposed by all its variants, such as *CMB* and *ICBC*. This optional interface is introduced because some customers have to pay the fees for the bank online service while others do not. In contrast, the optional interface in alternative component *FeeItemSelection* is introduced because it is only exposed by the variant *SelectByYearOrder*. The variant *ByYear* and *ByItem* do not provide this interface. Clearly, the semantics of the two cases are completely different. In fact, they are the instances of the two different variation constructs from optional construct category and alternative construct category respectively.

Although we need more systematic quantitative study, our experience indicates that, by categorizing the variation constructs and providing the tool support, the proposed approach provides not only an efficient way to document and manage the variation points in PLA, but also help to flatten the learning curve of the new comers who joined the project later and reduce the errors due to the inconsistent modifications to variation points.

6 Related Work

As a fundamental aspect of software product line, variability management has attracted a lot of research. Among them, some focus on the development of variability model, e.g. OVM (Orthogonal Variability Model) [14] and PuLSE [15]. The others aim at variation implementation mechanism, e.g. XVCL [16]. However, architecture-level variation management is much less explored.

In the past two decades, many architecture description languages (ADLs), e.g. xADL2.0 [1] and ACME [4], have been proposed to support formal architecture modeling and analysis. In these ADLs, the architectural elements, such as component, connector, interface (port) and link are commonly used to model software architecture. To support PLA, some ADLs, e.g. xADL2.0 [1], further introduce the variability mechanisms to these architectural elements. However, such ADLs lack of mechanism to model structural variation constructs. Furthermore, they do not provide any effective mechanism to manage the large amount of variation elements and the possibly even larger number of dependencies between these variation elements [17].

In order to improve architecture-level variability management, Hendrickson et al. [18] have proposed the change-based methods for PLA modeling, in which PLA variations are modeled by change sets and relationships. However, they acknowledged that state-based PLA modeling, in which variability is represented by variation elements inside the architectural specification, is still the mainstream of product line architecture design [19]. In this paper, we propose a construct-based method, which provides state-based variation mechanism for PLA modeling.

For effective management and composition of architectural variability, Neil Loughran et al [20] have proposed a variability modeling language (VML). VML supports compositions involving both fine-grained and coarse-grained variabilities in an orthogonal fashion. With our method, VML will reference variation constructs instead of primitive variation elements. Thus our approach can complement this approach rather than replace it.

There has been some work on using patterns to model variability in product lines. The proposed patterns [21, 22] work close to the system implementation. For example, they use adapter pattern to model the alternative function [21]. In contrast, our variation constructs are at a higher level of abstraction. We focus on the variation constructs in component based product line architecture, consisting of components and their interactions represented by interfaces and connectors.

7   Conclusion and Future Work

In this paper, we presented an architectural variability modeling method by structural construct for the design and customization of software product line architecture (PLA). With our method, the architect can conceive and model the variability design for each variant feature by structural construct rather than individual variation element. The proposed approached has been implemented in a software product line tool and has been evaluated on an industrial financial system. Our preliminary results indicate that the raising of variability modeling level by structural constructs improves PLA design and customization by reducing the complexity and inconsistency of the variability modeling.

We plan to extend this work in two directions. First, the current construct catalog has been extracted and validated on the WFMS-PL. But we believe that they would be applicable in other software product lines, since the principles underlying these constructs are not specific to a given system. We plan to further refine and enrich the current construct catalog with more subject systems. Furthermore, the current variation constructs involve only two components and their interactions. We are also interested in extending the concept to the constructs involving multiple components.

Second, we plan to explore the backward and forward traceability between the architecture-level variation constructs and the variation points in the analysis models, such as feature models [23], and in the product line implementations, such as XVCL [16]. We believe that architecture-level variation constructs can serve as an intermediate layer that helps to trace and manage the variations across different levels of abstraction. We would like to investigate if they can facilitate the consistent feature-driven derivation of application products. Furthermore, we want to investigate if they can improve the evolution of software product line, e.g. helping to populate variation points with new variants, to prune old, no longer used, variants, as well as to distribute new and/or changed variants to the already installed products.

Acknowledgments. This work is supported by National Natural Science Foundation of China under Grant No. 90818009, Shanghai Committee of Science and Technology, China under Grant No. 08DZ2271800 and 09DZ2272800, Shanghai Leading Academic Discipline Project under Grant No. B114.

References

1. Dashofy, E.M., van der Hoek, A., Taylor, R.N.: A comprehensive approach for the development of modular software architecture description languages. ACM Transactions on Software Engineering and Methodology 14(2), 199–245 (2005)
2. Medvidovic, N., Taylor, R.N.: A Classification and Comparison Framework for Software Architecture De-scription Languages. IEEE Transactions on Software Engineering 26(1), 70–93 (2000)
3. Clements, P., Northrop, L.M.: Software Product Lines: Practices and Patterns. Addison-Wesley, New York (2002)
4. Garlan, D., Monroe, R., Wile, D.: ACME: An Architecture Description Interchange Language. In: Proceedings of the 1997 Conference of the Centre for Advanced Studies on Collaborative Research, CASCON (1997)
5. Medvidovic, N., Oreizy, P., Robbins, J.E., Taylor, R.N.: Using object-oriented typing to support architectural design in the C2 style. In: Proceedings of the 4th ACM Symposium on the Foundations of Software Engineering, FSE (1996)
6. Magee, J., Kramer, J.: Dynamic Structure in Software Architectures. In: Proceedings of the 4th Symposium on the Foundations of Software Engineering (1996)
7. Luckham, D.C., Vera, J.: An Event-Based Architecture Definition Language. IEEE Transactions on Software Engineering 21(9), 717–734 (1995)
8. Shaw, M., et al.: Abstractions for Software Architecture and Tools to Support Them. IEEE Transactions on Software Engineering 21(4), 314–335 (1995)
9. Allen, R., Garlan, D.: A Formal Basis for Architectural Connection. ACM Transactions on Software Engineering and Methodology 6(3), 213–249 (1997)
10. van Ommering, R., et al.: The Koala Component Model for Consumer Electronics Software. Computer 33(3), 78–85 (2000)

11. Roshandel, R., van der Hoek, A., Mikic-Rakic, M., Medvidovic, N.: Mae—a system model and environment for managing architectural evolution. ACM Transactions on Software Engineering and Methodology 13(2), 240–276 (2004)
12. Swanson, E.B.: The dimensions of maintenance. In: Proceedings of the 2nd International Conference on Software Engineering (ICSE), pp. 492–497 (1976)
13. Ye, P., Peng, X., Xue, Y., Jarzabek, S.: A Case Study of Variation Mechanism in an Industrial Product Line. In: Edwards, S.H., Kulczycki, G. (eds.) ICSR 2009. LNCS, vol. 5791, pp. 126–136. Springer, Heidelberg (2009)
14. Pohl, K., Metzger, A.: Variability management in software product line engineering. In: Proceedings of the 28th International Conference on Software Engineering, ICSE (2006)
15. Schmid, K., John, I.: A customizable approach to full lifecycle variability management. Science of Computer Programming 53(3), 259–284 (2004)
16. Jarzabek, S., Bassett, P., Zhang, H., Zhang, W.: XVCL: XML-based variant configuration language. In: Proceedings of the 25th International Conference on Software Engineering, ICSE (2003)
17. Deelstra, S., Sinnema, M., Bosch, J.: Experiences in Software Product Families: Problems and Issues During Product Derivation. In: Nord, R.L. (ed.) SPLC 2004. LNCS, vol. 3154, pp. 165–182. Springer, Heidelberg (2004)
18. Hendrickson, S.A., van der Hoek, A.: Modeling Product Line Architectures Through Change Sets and Relationships. In: Proceedings of the 29th International Conference on Software Engineering (ICSE), Minneapolis, USA, pp. 189–198 (2007)
19. López, N., Casallas, R., van der Hoek, A.: Issues in Mapping Change-Based Product Line Architectures to Configuration Management Systems. In: Proceedings of the 13th Software Product Lines Conference (SPLC), pp. 21–30 (2009)
20. Loughran, N., Sánchez, P., Garcia, A., Fuentes, L.: Language Support for Managing Variability in Architectural Models. In: Pautasso, C., Tanter, É. (eds.) SC 2008. LNCS, vol. 4954, pp. 36–51. Springer, Heidelberg (2008)
21. Keepance, B., Mannion, M.: Using patterns to model variability in product families. IEEE Software 16(4), 102–108 (1999)
22. Jiang, J., Ruokonen, A., Systä, T.: Pattern-based variability management in Web service development. In: Proceedings of the 3rd European Conference on Web Services, ECOWS 2005 (2005)
23. Kang, K.C., Cohen, S.G., Hess, J.A., Novak, W.E., Spencer Peterson, A.: Feature-Oriented Domain Analysis (FODA) Feasibility Study. Technical Report CMU/SEI-90-TR-21, Software Engineering Institute, Carnegie Mellon University, Pittsburgh, PA
24. Peng, X., Shen, L., Zhao, W.: An Architecture-based Evolution Management Method for Software Product Line. In: Proceedings of the 21st International Conference on Software Engineering and Knowledge Engineering, SEKE (2009)
25. Mei, H., Chen, F., Wang, Q., Feng, Y.-D.: ABC/ADL: An ADL Supporting Component Composition. In: George, C.W., Miao, H. (eds.) ICFEM 2002. LNCS, vol. 2495, p. 38. Springer, Heidelberg (2002)

Code Reuse with
Language Oriented Programming*

David H. Lorenz and Boaz Rosenan

Open University of Israel
1 University Rd., P.O. Box 808, Raanana 43107 Israel
lorenz@openu.ac.il, brosenan@cslab.openu.ac.il

Abstract. There is a gap between our ability to reuse high-level concepts in software design and our ability to reuse the code implementing them. Language Oriented Programming (LOP) is a software development paradigm that aims to close this gap, through extensive use of Domain Specific Languages (DSLs). With LOP, the high-level reusable concepts become reusable DSL constructs, and their translation into code level concepts is done in the DSL implementation. Particular products are implemented using DSL code, thus reusing only high-level concepts. In this paper we provide a comparison between two implementation approaches for LOP: (a) using external DSLs with a projectional language workbench (MPS); and (b) using internal DSLs with an LOP language (Cedalion). To demonstrate how reuse is achieved in each approach, we present a small case study, where LOP is used to build a Software Product Line (SPL) of calculator software.

1 Introduction

A key issue with software reuse is the gap between concept reuse and code reuse. Many abstract concepts, such as a state machine, are often reused across substantially different software products. However, on the code level, their implementations are tangled with details of particular products and often cannot be reused.

This loss of reuse can be attributed to the abstraction gap between the high-level (concept level) and the low-level (code level) representations of the solution. When programmers implement a high-level concept, such as a state machine, they "compile" the high-level concept into code in a manual process. The product of this process is code that integrates, often in an inseparable manner, the reusable knowledge of how to code such a concept in the programming language in use (e.g., a state machine design patterns), with the specifics of the particular instance of the concept (e.g., a particular instance of a state machine).

One solution to this problem is the use of *Domain-Specific Languages (DSLs)*. Programmers use DSLs to code high-level concepts directly. The DSL implementation is responsible for specifying the meaning of these concepts in terms

---

* This research was supported in part by the *Israel Science Foundation (ISF)* under grant No. 926/08.

K. Schmid (Ed.): ICSR 2011, LNCS 6727, pp. 167–182, 2011.

of lower-level concepts. This can be done either by compiling the DSL code into code in some pre-existing language, or by interpreting it. Either way, the application code now consists of two parts: the DSL code and the DSL implementation. The DSL code conveys the specifics of the application, which is generally not reusable but very concise. The DSL implementation conveys the knowledge of expressing high-level concepts in terms of low-level ones, which is often complicated, but highly reusable. This method thus allows us to take reusable concepts and turn them into reusable code, expressed as the DSL implementation.

Indeed, DSLs can be used to solve this abstraction gap and achieve higher code reusability. However, for this method to take effect in real-life software development, it has to be applied systematically throughout the code. Real-life software is complex and diverse. It usually uses many kinds of high-level concepts. Some are globally relevant (e.g., a state machine), but some are only relevant to an industry or a particular software product-line (SPL).

Using DSLs for these concepts can allow reusing the logic behind them. This means that DSLs must be developed for various aspects of the software, and that these DSLs need to be able to interact, in the places where one high-level concept touches another, e.g., when a network event (one high-level concept) triggers a state transition in a state machine (another high-level concept). Having such interactions requires that the DSLs be implemented over some common platform that allows DSLs to interact, both syntactically and semantically. This approach to software development, which advocates the use of interoperable DSLs to write software, is called *Language Oriented Programming* (*LOP*) [11,1,2].

The main challenge for realizing LOP in real-life software lies in the need to develop and use DSLs. Here, the choice of techniques and tools used for DSL implementation bears a great significance on the practicality of LOP. For example, the traditional approach of using standard compiler-generator tools such as Lex and Yacc or ANTLR to implement DSLs can work properly for a pre-determined, limited set of concepts, but will not allow DSLs to be defined as separate, reusable but interoperable components.

One important decision one needs to make is the choice between internal and external DSLs [2]. *External DSLs* are DSLs implemented in form of a compiler, translator or interpreter for the DSLs, while *internal DSLs* (or *embedded DSLs* [3]) DSLs are "sub-languages" defined from within a host language. Internal and external DSLs have inherent trade-offs. On the one hand, external DSLs provide more freedom in defining syntax and semantics, but place the burden of implementing the language on the DSL developer. On the other hand, internal DSLs are much easier to implement, as they reuse most of the facilities provided by the host language, but are constrained by its syntax and semantics. In addition, DSL interoperability is supported naturally by internal DSLs (where all the DSLs are actually code in the same host language), while interoperability is much harder to achieve using external DSLs.

To date, two approaches have been presented to overcome these trade-offs, namely *language workbenches* and *LOP languages*. Both of these approaches allow to develop one kind of DSLs, while mitigating its limitations relative to the other kind:

Language Workbenches. Language workbenches are integrated development environments (IDEs) for developing external DSLs. They ease the task of defining and implementing DSLs by providing (meta) DSLs dedicated for that task. They provide some tooling (auto-completion, definition search, etc.) for the DSLs for free, or at very little cost, by leveraging the DSL definition. Language workbenches, in contrast to other compiler-generation tools, are made to support DSL interoperability. The most notable language workbenches are MPS [1] and the Intentional Domain Workbench [8]. They both use *projectional editing*, an approach were the program is a model edited through a view, as a replacement for using text editing and parsing. This allows syntactic integration of DSLs without causing ambiguity. With projectional editing, disambiguation is done when entering the code, e.g., by selecting the intended construct from a list or a menu.

LOP Languages. This is a new concept presented by our group [7]. These are programming languages oriented towards LOP, similarly to how object-oriented programming languages are oriented towards OOP. By our definition, LOP languages are made to host internal DSLs, while providing two important features previously associated with language workbenches and external DSLs. These are: projectional editing, and the ability to define and enforce DSL schemata. The Cedalion language [5] is an example of such an LOP language, based on logic programming for hosting internal DSLs, with a static type system to provide a basic notion of DSL schema.

The main difference between these two approaches is in the relationships between languages in each framework. In language workbench we can identify three: the DSL code, the DSL implementation (the meta level), and the workbench provided DSLs for implementing DSLs (the meta-meta level). LOP languages, on the other hand, provide all these function from within a single programming language. In a way, this is their advantage, allowing reuse across these levels.

In this work we implemented twice, as a case study, a simple SPL of *calculator software*, using two LOP techniques. One of the implementations is based on external DSLs and the other on internal DSLs. The differences between the two implementations provides a comparison in terms of the cost of reuse between external and internal DSL. It also provides a deeper understanding of LOP and how LOP can generally address the issue of code reuse in SPLs.

Specifically, we implemented the complete SPL in MPS and another complete implementation in Cedalion. We present the two implementations and discuss the pros and cons of each method. The choice of MPS and Cedalion as the implementation tools for this paper was made due the fact that their main difference is in the choice of external (MPS) versus internal (Cedalion) DSLs, thus providing a comparison between these two approaches. In other LOP respects they are similar (projectional editing, DSL schema).We concentrate on the cost of achieving code reuse in these two approaches. We conclude that both approaches indeed support reusability by providing easy-to-use DSLs that hide the complexity of translating high-level concepts into low-level, executable ones. However, the difference between these LOP approaches lies in the DSL implementation. Implementing internal DSLs over a declarative language is easier and more straightforward than implementing external DSLs over an imperative language.

2   Case Study: Calculator Product Line

To get the feel of how practical and useful LOP can be, and to study the implications of using internal versus external DSLs, we present here a small comparative case study, where we use LOP to create a tiny SPL for calculator software. Our measurements will be both qualitative (how well did we manage to reuse code) and quantitative (the cost, in terms of implementation time). We conduct this study using two tools: the MPS language workbench, and the Cedalion LOP language.

Meta-Programming System (MPS). This is a projectional language workbench (i.e., a language workbench using projectional editing) developed by Dmitriev and his team at Jetbrain's [1]. It is mostly open source, and can be freely downloaded. This made it a good candidate for this case study. Its website contains examples and tutorials to help new users get up-to-speed. It features relatively mature and very powerful projectional editing capabilities, overcoming some of the usability problems traditionally associated with projectional editing. DSL implementation is typically done by generating code in a language called the "base language," which is, for all practical purposes, Java. Implementing a DSL in MPS requires creating templates and conversions for all DSL constructs into lower-level languages, and eventually, into the base language.

Cedalion. Cedalion is an LOP programming language, based on logic programming. Logic programming provides a declarative way to define DSL semantics, while its static type system provides a structural definition (a schema) for the DSL. Like MPS, it features projectional editing, which allows syntactic freedom for DSL developers, without the danger of creating ambiguities, since disambiguation is done when entering the code. Cedalion is open source (http://cedalion.sourceforge.net). Its projectional editor is implemented as an Eclipse plug-in, using a Prolog back-end. Cedalion, however, is a research tool developed as a proof-of-concept and as such lacks the maturity that MPS provides. Nevertheless, Cedalion is more than capable to implement the case study at hand.

2.1   The Problem Statement

To examine the value of LOP for code reuse, and to compare between internal and external DSLs for this purpose, we define a problem, which we shall solve using the above tools. The problem statement is as follows:

Develop an SPL of calculator software. All calculators have a key-pad and a line-display. On the key-pad there are numerous keys for digits, operators and functions. Pressing these keys simply append characters to the line-display. There is also an "execute" or "=" button, which, when pressed, replaces the expression in the display with either the number to which the expression evaluates to, or the string "Syntax Error", if the expression is invalid.

Since we are interested in a SPL, we refer to a whole product-line of such calculators. These calculators differ in their choice of operators, functions, and even digits (e.g., a hexadecimal calculator), and how they evaluate to numbers. Our goal in this case study would be to try and reuse as much code as possible between different calculators in this SPL.

2.2   General Guidelines

In this case study we focus on the part of the software that parses and evaluates the string into a value, assuming the rest of the software (e.g., the line editing) are inherently reusable between different calculators.

We will implement these calculators using LOP. This means that we will first identify the high-level concepts we need to describe *a calculator*, regardless of the specific instance (scientific, financial, etc.). We then define a DSL to express these concepts formally, and implement it. In this case study we ignore any pre-existing DSLs that may address these concepts, since we would like to aim for the real-life scenario where such DSLs are often unavailable or inapplicable for various reasons. We then implement each calculator using the DSL we developed. These implementations are expected to be concise and very high-level, expressing the syntax of each particular calculator. All the logic common across calculators is expressed in the DSL implementation. Reuse of calculator features expected to be common to different calculators (such as the parsing of numbers and basic arithmetic operations) is beyond the scope of the case study, and will be addressed briefly in Sections 3.3 and 4.2.

3   SPL Implementation in MPS

We now describe the calculator SPL implementation in MPS. Due to space limitation we keep the MPS-related implementation details as brief as possible.

3.1   Defining the DSL

We begin by analyzing our calculator SPL, in order to figure out what kind of DSL(s) we need to define for it. Our software needs to do two things: (1) parse a string, according to some grammar; and (2) calculate a numeric value based on that parsing. We therefore wish to implement our calculator using a DSL that combines a grammar (context-free) and the evaluation of expressions. This is somewhat similar to an attribute grammar, where each production rule is associated with a single value. Existing DSLs, such as Yacc [4] can be considered here. However, as stated in Section 2.2, for the purpose of the case study we ignore pre-existing DSLs and implement the ones we need. For the purpose of this discussion we consider the '+' operator. Its syntax can be defined as:

$$expr ::= expr, \text{ }'+', \text{ } multExpr \tag{1}$$

We would evaluate $expr$ for Eq. 1 by summing the values of the derived $expr$ and $multExpr$ non-terminals. This could be formulated as:

$$expr ::= a = expr, \text{ }'+', \text{ } b = multExpr \text{ } \{a + b\} \tag{2}$$

by binding the result of evaluating both arguments with variables a and b (using the $=$ operator), and then specifying that the entire phrase evaluates to $a + b$, inside the curly braces.

This notation is clear and concise, however, making it executable is far from trivial. The grammar in Eq. 1 has a head recursion, making it non-LL (this is actually an LR grammar). Parsing LR grammars is significantly harder than parsing LL grammars. LL grammars can be parsed using recursive descent, with reasonable effort. Generating a parser for even a subclass of LR (such as LALR(1)) is a much harder task [4]. We therefore would like to restrict ourselves to LL grammars, and for that we need to avoid head recursion. To make Eq. 1 an LL grammar, we need to replace the head recursion with a tail recursion:

$$\begin{aligned} expr ::= multExpr, \text{ } exprSuffix \\ exprSuffix ::= '+', \text{ } expr \end{aligned} \tag{3}$$

This changes the way we calculate the value. We need to adopt a top-down approach for the evaluation. Such calculation can be formalized as follows:

$$\begin{aligned} expr ::= a = multExpr, \text{ } s = exprSuffix(a) \text{ } \{s\} \\ exprSuffix(a) ::= '+', \text{ } b = expr \text{ } \{a + b\} \end{aligned} \tag{4}$$

An $expr$ consists of a prefix ($multExpr$) and a suffix ($exprSuffix$). We first parse the prefix and bind its value to variable a. Then we parse the suffix, providing it the value of a as argument. The suffix modifies the value by adding the right-hand value (variable b) to the parameter a. Finally, $expr$ returns the value returned from the suffix.

The notation used in the example in Eq. 4 is sufficient for expressing the logic of an entire calculator in our case study.

DSL Schema. Now that we understand what our DSL looks like, we need to break it down and understanding which constructs our DSL has, and more importantly, how they are classified. The notation in Eq. 4 holds four "families" of constructs: Rules, Patterns, Reducibles and Expressions. Most important is the distinction between patterns and reducibles. Both patterns and reducibles define languages of strings, however, a reducible reduces a string to a single value, whereas a pattern reduces a string into a set of variable bindings.

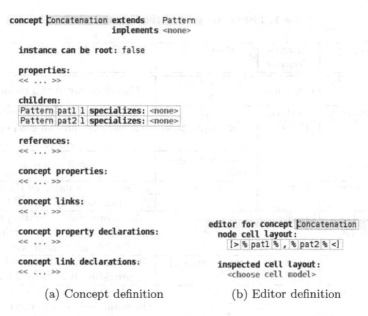

(a) Concept definition   (b) Editor definition

Fig. 1. Definition of the Concatenation concept in MPS

For example, $'+', e = expr$ is a pattern, as it produces the bindings for e, while the more complete term $'+', e = expr\{p + e\}$ is reducible, since it defines a single value $(p + e)$ for the string being parsed.

DSLs in MPS can rely on other languages. In this case, we use the *Expression* concept defined in the MPS *base-language* [1] as our expression type, so our language will inherit the wealth of expressions supported by the base language with no effort on our part. We do, however, need to define two expression concepts of our own: a reference to an argument (such as p in the term $\{p + e\}$ in Eq. 4), and to a bound variable (such as e in the term $\{p + e\}$ in Eq. 4). These new expression concepts will integrate seamlessly into base-language expression concepts such as the '+' expression.

In MPS, a DSL schema is defined by defining the language's *structure model*. This model consists of *concepts*, which are each defined using its own form. The concept definition resembles a class definition. It contains the concept's name, base-concept, implemented interfaces, child concepts, referenced concepts, properties, etc. For child and referenced concepts, cardinality should be provided. Table 1 lists the concept in our DSL. Figure 1a shows the definition of *Concatenation*, as an example for a concept definition. Note that this is a screenshot and not code listing, due to MPS's projectional nature.

Defining the Editors. To allow projectional editing, we need to define how each concept is visualized and edited. In MPS we do this by defining an *editor model*. Figure 1b shows the editor definition for the *Concatenation* concept.

Table 1. List of concepts in the Grammar DSL

Concept	Base Concept	Projection	Description
Alternative	Reducible	$\begin{array}{c} a \; | \\ b \end{array}$	Choice between two reducibles
Concatenation	Pattern	a, b	Concatenation of two patterns
Empty	Pattern	$< empty >$	A pattern matching an empty string
Grammar	-	grammar *name* *rules*...	A full grammar
NamedPattern	Pattern	$v = r$	Assigning a name to the value produced by reducible r
NamedPattern Reference	Expression	*name*	An expression evaluating to the value returned from parsing the reducible associated with name
NonTerminal	Reducible	$name(args...)$	References the rule named *name*, providing it arguments *args*
PatternValue	Reducible	$p\{e\}$	Evaluates to the value of e, with the variable bindings received from p
Rule	-	$name(args...)::=r$	A production rule in the grammar
RuleArgReference	Expression	*name*	An expression evaluating to the value of an argument given to the rule
RuleArgument	-	*name*	A formal argument for a rule
Terminal	Pattern	$'string'$	A pattern matching a constant string

Language Refinements. Now the language is defined, although we have not yet implemented it. However, two refinements are in order:

1. Limiting the scope of rule arguments to the rule they are defined in, and limiting the scope of variables to the pattern they are defined in. These are done by defining a *constraints model* for these concepts.
2. Making the type of both variables and arguments "double," when used in expressions. In addition, expressions associated with patterns must also evaluate to "double." These rules are specified in a *type system model*.

We omit screenshot of these definitions due to space limitations.

3.2 Implementing the DSL

A generator translates the DSL code into a lower-level, executable language, making the DSL executable. This translation defines the semantics of our DSL. Before implementing a generator we need to decide on a target language. In MPS, if Java is an acceptable output language, the MPS *base-language* [1] will be a natural choice. This is an adaptation of Java to MPS including most of its features (MPS1.1 does not yet support generics), but like all other MPS-based languages, it is edited using a projectional editor.

The more interesting question we need to ask is how do we wish to see our DSL program translated to that target language (i.e., Java). In our case, this means how do we wish to implement a parser or evaluator in Java (or a Java-like language). We already mentioned that we prefer top-down parsing (LL) over bottom-up (LR), since the latter requires some heavy algorithms which we wish to avoid in this case. Therefore, we need to understand how to implement a recursive descent parser in Java. There are several ways to do that with performance–simplicity trade-offs. Here we prefer simplicity over performance, and specifically we prefer the simplicity of the *generator*, and not necessarily that of the *generated code*.

The biggest challenge in this translation is the need for backtracking. In this case, backtracking is used to support look-ahead. With backtracking, the parser can go forward several characters following a certain alternative, not find what it is looking for, and then backtrack to the point when it made the choice and re-parse the text using a new alternative. This technique is expected to be simpler (in terms of generator code) then a possible alternative of turning the non-deterministic state machine into a deterministic one, with no backtracking. One of the main challenges of introducing backtracking is with regard to variable bindings. In our DSL we bind values to variables. These values may change due to backtracking. We need a way to save not only the state of parsing, but also the value of variables, and restore them when backtracking. Some declarative languages, such as Prolog, provide natural support for backtracking. Variable bindings in these languages obey backtracking. In fact, variables in these languages do not change their value with time *except* with backtracking.

The semantics of Java (and hence the MPS base-language) does not have natural support for backtracking. Therefore, one of our challenges would be to build backtracking "from scratch."

Implementing a Generator. Here we define the semantics of our DSL. This is done using *mapping rules* and *reduction rules*. Mapping rules define how concepts in the model map into top-level concepts in the generated code. A class in the base-language is a top-level concept, so we map each grammar to a class, using a mapping rule. The mapping rule specifies a template of the class, which lays out the general structure of a class generated to implement a grammar. This template uses macros to customize the output class based on the properties and children of the grammar. One kind of macro, *COPY_SRC*, is used to copy child nodes into place in the template. This "copying" includes reduction where needed, following the reduction rules specified for the generator. *Reduction rules* define how a DSL concept is translated to lower-level concepts, usually concepts of the base language. In our DSL, reducibles and patterns have reduction rules, transforming them into expressions in the base-language, resulting in an object implementing *IReducible* and *IPattern* respectively. Figure 2 shows the reduction rule associated with the *Concatenation* concept. It produces an instance that

```
┌concept     Concatenation┐ --> <T new IPattern() {                                    T>
│inheritors false         │      private Parser.IPattern pat1 = $COPY_SRC$[null];
└condition  <always>      ┘      private Parser.IPattern pat2 = $COPY_SRC$[null];

                                  public void parse(String string, Map bindings, final Parser.IBindingTarget
                                      target) {
                                    final Parser.IPattern pat2_ = this.pat2;
                                    this.pat1.parse(string, bindings, new IBindingTarget() {
                                      public void handleBinding(String residue, Map bindings) {
                                        pat2_.parse(residue, bindings, target);
                                      }
                                      <add members (ctrl+space)>
                                    });
                                  }
                                  <add members (ctrl+space)>
                                }
```

Fig. 2. Reduction rule for *Concatenation*

```
grammar CalculatorGrammar
digit ( ) ::= ' 0 ' { 0 } |
              ' 1 ' { 1 } |
              ' 2 ' { 2 } |
              ' 3 ' { 3 } |
              ' 4 ' { 4 } |
              ' 5 ' { 5 } |
              ' 6 ' { 6 } |
              ' 7 ' { 7 } |
              ' 8 ' { 8 } |
              ' 9 ' { 9 }
integer ( numToTheLeft ) ::= firstDigit = digit ( ) , restOfNumber = integer ( numToTheLeft * 10 + firstDigit ) {
                                0 + restOfNumber } |
                           <empty> { numToTheLeft }
number ( ) ::= wholePart = integer ( 0 ) , fractionPart = fractionOpt ( 0.1 ) { wholePart + fractionPart }
fractionOpt ( multiplier ) ::= ' . ' , fraction = fraction ( multiplier ) { 0 + fraction } |
                             <empty> { 0 }
fraction ( multiplier ) ::= firstDigit = digit ( ) , restOfFraction = fraction ( multiplier / 10 ) {
                                firstDigit * multiplier + restOfFraction } |
                          <empty> { 0 }
expr ( ) ::= primary = multExpr ( ) , suffix = exprSuffix ( primary ) { 0 + suffix }
exprSuffix ( primary ) ::= ' + ' , other = expr ( ) { primary + other } |
                           ' - ' , other = expr ( ) { primary - other } |
                         <empty> { primary }
multExpr ( ) ::= primary = atomicExpr ( ) , suffix = multSuffix ( primary ) { 0 + suffix }
multSuffix ( primary ) ::= ' * ' , other = multExpr ( ) { primary * other } |
                           ' / ' , other = multExpr ( ) { primary / other } |
                         <empty> { primary }
atomicExpr ( ) ::= number ( ) |
                   ' ( ' , value = expr ( ) , ' ) ' { 0 + value }
```

Fig. 3. A calculator implementation

when getting a string it will first pass it through the *IPattern* associated with its left-hand argument, passing each result (received using a callback) to the *IPattern* associated with its right-hand argument. The *COPY_SRC* macros replace the *null* values with the reduction of the left and right-hand arguments of the concatenation.

3.3   Implementing the Calculator

Now that our DSL is defined and implemented we can move forward to using it to implement a concrete calculator. Figure 3 shows an implementation of a simple calculator, accepting numbers, the four basic arithmetic operations and parentheses. This definition is indeed short, concise, and contains nothing of the *algorithm* required to actually parse the string and to evaluate it. It only contains the *rules* by which this will be done.

Each member of our product line should have such a definition, defining its precise syntax and semantics. Since all implementation details are encapsulated in the DSL definition (the generator model), they are fully reused between these SPL instances.

DSL Code Reuse. As concise as it may be, with complex enough calculators it may not be enough to reuse the logic hidden in the DSL implementation. DSL code duplication may become a problem as well. For example, the features defined in Figure 3 may be desired in all calculators. Scientific calculators may add, e.g., trigonometric functions, and financial calculators may add percentage calculations; but both will keep this core behavior. One simple solution for that would be to use inheritance, thus the scientific and financial calculator grammars will inherit from the basic calculator grammar, adding their own specific functionality. However, inheritance can go only a certain way. Supporting an assortment of calculator, each with an arbitrary selection of features will not work well with inheritance. Völter [9] presents an approach to SPL engineering of DSL code in projectional language workbenches, and has implemented it in MPS. With his approach, DSL code can be annotated with feature-specific markers. A configuration selecting the desired features controls code generation, so that only the code that contributes to desired features takes effect. This approach can be applied here, associating grammar rules with features. Consequently, by enabling and disabling features we can control the insertion and removal of grammar rules.

4   SPL Implementation in Cedalion

4.1   Defining and Implementing the DSL

We wish to define and implement a DSL similar to the one described in Section 3.1, but this time, we use the internal DSL approach, where we implement each language construct directly, and not by implementing a code generator for the language. This difference allowed us to separate the language definition into two separate DSLs: (1) A "generic" DSL for BNF grammars, and (2) an extension of that DSL to support evaluation ("Functional BNF", or FBNF). The concepts of *Pattern* and *Reducible* exist here too, but the "generic" BNF DSL only supports patterns, while the FBNF DSL introduces reducibles. FBNF uses Cedalion's *Functional* DSL (a functional programming language over Cedalion) for expressions. Table 2 shows all concepts in both DSLs. There are only five of them (four in BNF and one in FBNF). This is due to the fact that some concepts (e.g., variables, alternatives) are inherent in Cedalion, due to its logic programming nature. Other concepts, such as the *name(args...)* reducible, will be defined concretely for each reducible type, in the calculator definitions.

Figure 4 shows how a concept (in this case, A, B), is defined and implemented in Cedalion. The first line is the type signature (comparable with the *concept definition* in MPS). It defines A, B to be a pattern, given that both A and B are patterns. The second line is the projection definition, comparable with MPS's

Table 2. List of concepts in the Cedalion BNF DSL

DSL	Concept	Type	Description
BNF	A, B	pattern	Concatenation of two patterns
BNF	ε	pattern	A pattern matching an empty string
BNF	$head ::= body$	statement	A production rule. Both *head* and *body* are of type *pattern*.
BNF	$'string'$	pattern	A pattern matching a constant string
FBNF	$Reducible \rightarrow^{Type} Expression$	pattern	A pattern that associates a Reducible with an Expression of type Type.

- *A* , *B* :: pattern ↪ [*A* :: pattern , *B* :: pattern]
- *A* , *B* :: pattern ↠ "[⟨ *A* :: pattern ⟩ , " , " , ⟨ *B* :: pattern ⟩]
- , is an alias for *A* , *B* :: pattern
- *A* , *B* ⇒ *Text* / *Residue* :-
  - *A* ⇒ *Text* / *Mid* ,
  - *B* ⇒ *Mid* / *Residue*

Fig. 4. Implementation of the *conc* concept in Cedalion

editor definition. It states that this concept shall be displayed as a horizontal list (the tiny "h") of visuals, starting with a placeholder for the projection of A, followed by a comma, followed by a placeholder for the projection of B. The third line defines an alias for this concept, allowing the user to type a comma and get auto-completion suggesting this concept. The last line defines the semantics of A, B. It does so in a Prolog-like manner, by contributing a clause to the *Pattern* ⇒ *Text/Residue* predicate. This predicate states that *Pattern* derives a prefix *Pref* of *Text*, such that *Text* = *Pref · Residue*. The clause here parses *Text* as A, B by first parsing *Text* as A, taking the residue *Mid* and parsing it as B. The residue now is the overall residue. Similar definitions exist for all the other concepts. Backtracking and variable bindings are handled implicitly, as they are inherent in logic programming, simplifying the implementation significantly.

4.2 Implementing the Calculator

Figure 5a shows part of the implementation of a simple calculator in Cedalion, using the BNF and FBNF DSLs we defined. We omitted the part that defines the syntax of numbers, due to space limitations. This definition is more elaborate then the one in Figure 3 due to the need to specify type signatures for all reducibles. Unlike MPS, where concept definitions exist only in the DSL definition, in Cedalion the DSL code is allowed and encouraged to define new concepts. This allows safe usage of not only DSL constructs, but also of concepts defined by

- expr :: reducable (number) ↪ []
- expr → ᵐᵘᵐᵇᵉʳ **Suffix** ::= multExpr → ᵐᵘᵐᵇᵉʳ **Primary** , exprSuffix (Primary) → ᵐᵘᵐᵇᵉʳ Suffix
- exprSuffix (**Primary**) :: reducable (number) ↪ [Primary :: expr (number)]
- exprSuffix (**Primary**) → ᵐᵘᵐᵇᵉʳ Primary + **Other** ::= ' + ' , multExpr → ᵐᵘᵐᵇᵉʳ Other
- exprSuffix (**Primary**) → ᵐᵘᵐᵇᵉʳ Primary - **Other** ::= ' - ' , multExpr → ᵐᵘᵐᵇᵉʳ Other
- exprSuffix (**Primary**) → ᵐᵘᵐᵇᵉʳ Primary ::= ε
- multExpr :: reducable (number) ↪ []
- multExpr → ᵐᵘᵐᵇᵉʳ **Suffix** ::= atomicExpr → ᵐᵘᵐᵇᵉʳ **Primary** , multSuffix (Primary) → ᵐᵘᵐᵇᵉʳ Suffix
- multSuffix (**Primary**) :: reducable (number) ↪ [Primary :: expr (number)]
- multSuffix (**Primary**) → ᵐᵘᵐᵇᵉʳ Primary * **Other** ::= ' * ' , atomicExpr → ᵐᵘᵐᵇᵉʳ Other
- multSuffix (**Primary**) → ᵐᵘᵐᵇᵉʳ Primary / **Other** ::= ' / ' , atomicExpr → ᵐᵘᵐᵇᵉʳ Other
- multSuffix (**Primary**) → ᵐᵘᵐᵇᵉʳ Primary ::= ε
- atomicExpr :: reducable (number) ↪ []
- atomicExpr → ᵐᵘᵐᵇᵉʳ **Value** ::= number → ᵐᵘᵐᵇᵉʳ Value
- atomicExpr → ᵐᵘᵐᵇᵉʳ **Value** ::= ' (' , expr → ᵐᵘᵐᵇᵉʳ Value , ') '

(a) General expression syntax in Cedalion

* atomicExpr → ᵐᵘᵐᵇᵉʳ sin (X) ::= ' sin ' , atomicExpr → ᵐᵘᵐᵇᵉʳ X
  if scientific is enabled

* atomicExpr → ᵐᵘᵐᵇᵉʳ cos (X) ::= ' cos ' , atomicExpr → ᵐᵘᵐᵇᵉʳ X
  if scientific is enabled

- // scientific is enabled
- financial is enabled

(b) Trigonometric functions for scientific calculators   (c)   Configuration example

Fig. 5. Calculator implementation in Cedalion

the user, relieving the DSL developer from specifying custom type system rules. While insisting on having type signatures present in the code, Cedalion offers to add them automatically. The syntax here is slightly different then the one we defined with MPS, because while the DSL in MPS was designed as one monolithic DSL, here we see a composition of two DSLs, trying to reuse their language constructs as best we can. This is why we have the $Reducible \rightarrow^{Type} Expression$ concept on both sides of the production rules (on the right, replacing the MPS *NamedPattern* concept, and on the left, replacing the *PatternValue* concept (see Table 1). The *Alternative* in the MPS implementation is not needed here, as different statements (or in this case, production rules), are taken as having an *or* relation, due to the nature of logic programming.

DSL Code Reuse. As in Section 3.3, two approaches can be considered here: grammar inheritance or associating rules with features. Since our BNF DSL does not have a concept of a grammar, the first option is inapplicable (recall that this option has significant drawbacks). However, associating rules with features is easy, and can be done from outside the DSL [9]. Even though only full statement can be associated with features, with feature variability [9] this is not a limitation here, because we only intend to do so with full production rules, which are statements. Figure 5b shows how do we support trigonometric functions only if the *scientific* feature is enabled. Figure 5c shows a configuration, where the *financial* feature is enabled, but the *scientific* feature is not.

5   Results, Discussion and Related Work

In previous sections we described a case study, where we used two different tools: MPS and Cedalion, representing two different approaches to DSLs, external using imperative base languages and internal using a declarative host language, to construct a SPL of calculator software, to achieve the goal of maximum code reuse between products. Indeed, the use of DSLs (regardless of their implementation approach) improved reusability by placing the complexity in a shared asset, the DSL implementation. The particular assets in both implementations are stated in a high-level language, capturing the high-level concepts of the problem domain. With methods for associating DSL code with specific features, we can maximize code reuse even at the DSL level, bringing code duplication to zero. We therefore can conclude that we have achieved our goal of code reuse through LOP.

But at what cost? Here the choice of tools takes effect. We measured the time it took to implement and test the first, simplest calculator (four arithmetic operations and parentheses), including the time it took to define and implement the DSL behind it. With MPS it took us about eight hours of work, most of which were dedicated to creating the generator, which was not trivial (implementing backtracking and variable bindings that adhere to backtracking in a Java-like language). In Cedalion it took about two hours. The main challenge there was dealing with the tool's sensitivity to user errors (i.e., its tendency to crash due to them). As evidence for this difference in effort, one can look at the complexity of the DSLs we defined in both tools. It takes significantly less time to implement five constructs than to implement twelve. Moreover, backtracking and variable binding were given for free by the host language. No type system extensions were needed, apart from defining a type signature for each construct. Once the DSLs were defined and implemented, using them was relatively similar in effort. MPS is more mature and therefore is more usable. Cedalion requires type signatures for each new concept (including ones defined in DSL code), which takes a little effort and makes the code a bit more elaborate. However, these differences are minor relative to the difference in effort in implementing DSLs. We therefore conclude that from the view point of this case study, internal DSLs seam to be a more cost effective for achieving code reuse through LOP.

5.1   Threats to Validity

In this work we used implementation time to measure cost efficiency. It may be argued that our familiarity with Cedalion introduced a bias in its favor. However, we took that into account, and familiarized ourselves with MPS well enough before starting this case study, so that the eight hours the implementation took did not include any of the "learning curve."

Another concern that may rise is the fact that we defined the case study ourselves, and it may therefore be biased in favor of internal DSLs, and Cedalion in particular. Specifically, the need for backtracking and variable bindings turns the tables in favor of Cedalion. However, these concepts are needed for many declarative notations. This is why they are so fundamental in logic programming. We chose this case study because it is relatively small and self contained, and at the same time not trivial.

5.2   Related Work

The first notable work on code reuse through systematic use of DSLs was done by Neighbor [6]. This work introduces Draco, a generative DSL framework. Draco's limitation in comparison with MPS and Cedalion is in its dependence on parsing, which is sensitive to conflicts that can arise when fusing the syntax of several DSLs together.

The term LOP has been coined by Ward [11], who mentioned reuse as one of its primary goals. It was then used by Dmitriev [1] and Fowler [2]. Their notion of LOP is a bit different than Ward's, as they emphasis the need for DSL interoperability. DSL interoperability widens the opportunities for code reuse as the DSLs become small, reusable components. However, Dmitriev [1] and Fowler [2] do not explicitly mention code reuse as a goal for LOP.

At the heart of this paper is a comparison of two approaches to LOP: internal and external DSLs. To our knowledge, not many such comparisons have been proposed. The Language Workbench Competition (LWC) [10] provides a suggestion for comparison between language workbenches. It provides a common task that should be implemented on different workbenches to allow learning about their trade-offs. However, this task does not tell a full story. It specifies a particular DSL, but does not specify the semantics for that DSL. As a result, we found the LWC not helpful for assessing reuse, and therefore turned to define our own.

6   Conclusion

In this paper, we demonstrated how LOP can be used for code reuse, allowing a separation-of-concerns between the generic, reusable high-level concepts used to describe the problem and its solution, and the concrete definition of a particular instance in a SPL. We showed that by defining DSLs to capture high-level concepts we hide the complexity of transforming them into low-level concepts inside the DSL implementation. The DSL implementation becomes an asset shared across the SPL.

This LOP goal was achieved regardless of the choice of approach, internal DSLs over a declarative language or external DSLs over an imperative language. However, the cost of doing that differs significantly. In our case study, using internal DSLs proved to be nearly four times more cost-effective than using external DSLs. While the numbers may vary based on the nature of the SPL and the ratio between the size of the DSL implementations and the amount of DSL code, the advantage of using internal DSLs is evident.

From a reuse perspective, internal DSLs provide an additional advantage. Our ability to construct our DSL from two different DSLs (BNF and FBNF) in the Cedalion implementation opens opportunities for reuse, since the BNF DSL can be used by itself, possibly for totally different kinds of products, and in conjunction with other DSLs. With MPS and external DSLs, combining DSLs is also possible, however, because of the code generation nature of the tool, we could not support such a separation in our case study. We actually started with a generic BNF DSL, but found it inapplicable for our needs, since it did not support variable bindings.

The case study in this paper provides the reader unfamiliar with LOP with a sense of how LOP can be leveraged for code reuse, and how language workbenches and LOP languages can help performing that task. Our case study shows an advantage for using declarative over the use of imperative programming as a base language. Surprisingly, despite this demonstrated (dis)advantage, the current state of the art is implementing LOP mainly using imperative languages (through language workbenches), instead of using declarative languages such as Cedalion.

Acknowledgement. We thank Michał Śmiałek for his helpful comments.

References

1. Dmitriev, S.: Language oriented programming: The next programming paradigm. JetBrains on Board 1(2) (2004)
2. Fowler, M.: Language workbenches: The killer-app for domain specific languages (2005), http://www.martinfowler.com/articles/languageWorkbench.html
3. Hudak, P.: Building domain-specific embedded languages. ACM Computing Surveys (CSUR) 28(4es) (1996)
4. Johnson, S.C.: Yacc: Yet another compiler-compiler. Technical Report CSTR32, Bell Laboratories, Murray Hill, NJ (1975)
5. Lorenz, D.H., Rosenan, B.: Cedalion: A language-oriented programming language. In: IBM Programming Languages and Development Environments Seminar, Haifa, Israel (April 2010)
6. Neighbors, J.M.: The Draco approach to constructing software from reusable components. IEEE Trans. Software Eng. 10(5), 564–574 (1984)
7. Rosenan, B.: Designing language-oriented programming languages. In: Companion to the ACM International Conference on Systems, Programming Languages, and Applications: Software for Humanity (SPLASH 2010), pp. 207–208. ACM, Reno (2010)
8. Simonyi, C., Christerson, M., Clifford, S.: Intentional software. ACM SIGPLAN Notices 41(10), 451–464 (2006)
9. Völter, M.: Implementing feature variability for models and code with projectional language workbenches. In: Proceedings of the 2nd International Workshop on Feature-Oriented Software Development (FOSD 2010), pp. 41–48. ACM, Eindhoven (2010)
10. Völter, M., Visser, E., Kelly, S., Hulshout, A., Warmer, J., Molina, P.J., Merkle, B., Thoms, K.: Language workbench competition (2011), http://www.languageworkbenches.net
11. Ward, M.P.: Language-oriented programming. Software-Concepts and Tools 15(4), 147–161 (1994)

Achieving Reuse with Pluggable Software Units*

Fernando J. Barros

Departamento de Engenharia Informática
Universidade de Coimbra
Coimbra, Portugal
barros@dei.uc.pt

Abstract. In this paper we present a solution to software reuse based
on Pluggable Units (PUs) that can be used to compose new applications
from existing parts. Although this goal has been achieved in hardware
design through the creation of integrated circuits (ICs), the attempts to
build a software equivalent were not fully successful. Pluggable units are
a full fledged software implementation of the IC concept while providing
new features not existing in hardware, namely the ability to compose
software hierarchically. An application example is provided in JU3E, a
new Java-based language supporting pluggable units and in JWIDGET,
a pluggable version of Java/Swing.

1 Introduction

Increasing software productivity was identified as one of the grand challenges
facing Information Technologies [1]. Although many tools and development processes have been created, the efficient exploitation of reusable code looks the
most encouraging way to greatly increase programmer productivity [1].

Reuse has been achieved in many areas, and it has the potential of reducing costs and dramatically improve productivity. Nowadays, standardization is
common in the computer hardware industry leading to large cost reductions.
The main responsible for hardware standardization and reuse was the creation
of Integrated Circuits (ICs) that has allowed the mass production of electronic
devices at low cost and the development of new hardware based on existing ICs.

Although the IC paradigm looks promising for achieving cost reduction in
software development, software ICs were never fully achieved [31] and adopted
by the software industry [30]. Moreover, pessimistic authors argued that software
is intrinsically different from hardware and, thus, software reuse may be never
fully accomplished [12].

Hierarchical and modular principles have been used as a powerful heuristic
for handling complex problems [8]. We have adapted these concepts to programming language design and we have developed Connectons [9], a formalism that
defines independent and reusable software units. Connectons merge a modular

* This work is supported by the Portuguese Foundation for Science and Technology,
under grant PTDC/EIA-EIA/100752/2008.

K. Schmid (Ed.): ICSR 2011, LNCS 6727, pp. 183–191, 2011.

and hierarchal description, with request-reply communication protocol [9]. The result is a new language based on independent and pluggable (software) units (PUs) that allows the development of applications by assembling existing software. Pluggable units provide a realization of software ICs, taking the concept to a level that was not achieved by hardware ICs. These features include the ability to define PUs by composition of other PUs being the result indistinguishable from a *basic* PU. Another characteristic is the ability to change the composition and coupling of software ICs during runtime operation. This feature also allows PUs to be moved across networks of PUs [10].

In this paper we introduce JUSE, an implementation of pluggable software units in the Java/Groovy language. We demonstrate the use of JUSE with a simple application and we show that JUSE yields to simpler and reusable software when compared with the corresponding solution based on object-oriented using design patterns [15]. Other approaches have been developed to tackle software reuse with software components. This related work is described in Section 3.

This paper focus on some of the key aspects enabling software reuse. The benefits of reuse on quality, productivity and lead-time reduction have been demonstrated [18, 20, 23, 28].

2   Pluggable Software Units

Pluggable (software) units (PUs) provide a realization of independent and reusable software. PUs permit the development of software by composition of existing assets enabling the benefits associated with software reuse [28].

We define two types of pluggable software units: basic and network. Basic PUs provide method invocation, whereas networks are a composition of PUs providing message passing operations. Network composition and coupling is dynamic permitting the definition of self-adaptive topologies [10].

To manage complex systems, PUs can be hierarchically composed being the resultant pluggable unit indistinguishable from a basic PU. This ability permits to handle, in a homogeneous form, both basic and network software units. The network is managed by a special PU termed here by *network executive*.

Pluggable software units are supported by JUSE, a Java/Groovy implementation of PUs. We show that PUs provide full reuse support for two reasons. First, reuse is achieved by removing any external dependency from PUs definition. This enables the definition of PUs independently from the context they will be used. Second, the combination of arbitrary PUs is greatly simplified by the introduction of adapting filters that can transform parameters between incompatible interfaces [9]. These two features offer the basic framework for a solution to the reuse problem. JUSE implements most of the concept defined in Connectons [9], and it provides a similar implementation to the original Smalltalk realization. Both versions are based on the Meta-Object Protocol (MOP) and current work is being made to improve MOP performance. The PU concept is orthogonal to thread-based programming and actually no threads are required to JUSE applications. Threads can obviously be used, but JUSE does not offer any particular support for thread synchronization that need to be enforced through conventional constructs. Also, under development is the type system, already described in Connectons [9], in order to make JUSE more amenable to syntax checking. A detailed description of the Smalltalk version of PUs can be found in [9]. JUSE uses a similar implementation based on MOP.

2.1 Basic Pluggable Unit

We start the description of the basic pluggable units by defining the Pull PU. This unit performs the following sequence of actions: a) send a request; b) receive the answer; c) send a new request with this answer; c) receive a new answer; d) return the last answer. To fulfill the specification we define the input gate get, and two output gates get and send as depicted in Figure 1.

Fig. 1. The Pull software unit

JUSE definition of the Pull software unit is shown in Listing 1.1. Class Connecton is the base class of all PUs. This class defines variable out used to access all external PUs.

```
public class Pull extends Connecton {                                              1
    public GateCollection inGates() {return super.inGates().add("get")}             2
    public GateCollection outGates() {return super.outGates().add("get").add("send")} 3
    public Object get() {                                                           4
        Object value = out.get();                                                   5
        Object answer = out.send(value);                                            6
        return answer;                                                              7
    }                                                                               8
}                                                                                   9
```

Listing 1.1. Pull definition in JUSE

Method inGates defines Pull input gates while method outGates defines PU output gates. For each input gate we need to define the corresponding *action* (method). Output gates provide the construct to achieve the independence of software units and they are used to discriminate massages sent through the pseudo-variable out. The actual invocation of external actions depends on the context the PU is inserted.

Action get defines the Pull behavior. Line 5 gets a value from the output gate get. This value is sent through gate send (Line 6). The answer is returned in Line 7. In spite of its simplicity, the Pull PU combines *Event-Based Programming* (EBP), point-to-point communication and request-reply communication.

EBP would require the creation of an event to request a value, the creation of an additional event to signal the answer, and finally, the creation of a new event to send the answer. PUs effectively combine request-reply communication with fully independence, characteristic of EBP, to achieve a framework that extends object-oriented programming without incurring in the cumbersome specifications of EBP.

At this point, we emphasize that the definition of the Pull unit is *completely* independent from any other software units, making it *fully* reusable, since it does not depend on any external entity.

The definition of PUs imposes strongly typed gates with input and output signatures [9]. However, this typing system poses no constraint on gate linkage since PUs enable the definition of both forward and reverse filters to make the match between incompatible signatures as we show in the next Section.

2.2   Network Pluggable Unit

Pluggable units can be composed to define networks of software units. To demonstrate the concept of *network* pluggable software unit we describe here the audio system presented in [15] and originally designed with the Model-View-Controller pattern. We model this application as a composition of reusable software units, as shown in JUSE/CAD depicted in Figure 2. The corresponding JUSE definition of the Audio application is made in Listing 1.2.

Application rendering is depicted in Figure 3, where the left frame defines the beat value and the right frame shows the last value sampled from the audio volume. CButtons have the output gate buttonUp that signal a mouse click. The Sampler PU stores the current sampling rate (or beat). The beat can be entered directly through the CTextField and set when the users presses button Set. The beat can also be changed by the Up/Down buttons that increment/decrement its value by one unit. The Sampler uses the beat value to sample the audio volume. This value is read by the Sampler and then displayed on a progress bar. The Audio Executive (top-left unit) is responsible for defining the topology of the network pluggable unit. This unit also supports the run time adaptation of the topology.

This application was developed using the JWIDGET library. JWIDGET wraps Swing objects, like JFrame and JButton, and Swing events in order to achieve a pluggable version of GUI widgets. JWIDGET enables the seamless integration of GUI elements in any application since no event model is required for the GUI, making the overall application homogenous and based on the same communication paradigm.

Same PUs have incompatible interfaces and require adaptation. This is the case of CTextField that requires a String to be displayed. Since the Sampler produces int values, a filter [9], is required to make the matching between String and int types. This adaptation involves the method toString(), as defined in Listing 1.2, Line 21. In general, filters (forward and reverse) can make the match of any two signatures, freeing the user from creating additional PUs to act as adapters.

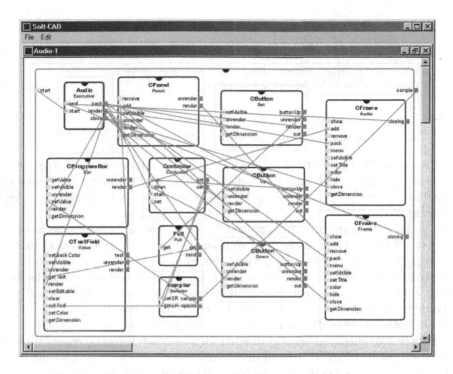

Fig. 2. Audio software topology represented in JUse/CAD

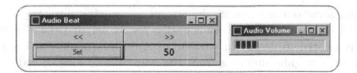

Fig. 3. Audio volume GUI

```
public void topology() {                                                         1
    super.topology();                                                            2
    add(CFrame, "Frame", {CFrame frame -> frame.setTitle("Audio Volume")});      3
    add(CFrame, "Audio", {CFrame frame -> frame.setTitle("Audio Beat")});        4
    add(CButton, "Up");                                                          5
    add(CButton, "Down");                                                        6
    add(CButton, "Set");                                                         7
    add(Controller, "Controller");                                              8
    add(CProgressBar, "Bar");                                                    9
    add(CTextField, "Value");                                                   10
    add(Sampler, "Sampler");                                                    11
    add(Pull, "Pull");                                                          12
    ...                                                                         13
    link("Up", "buttonUp", "Controller", "up");                                14
    link("Down", "buttonUp", "Controller", "down");                            15
    link("Set", "buttonUp", "Pull", "get");                                    16
    link("Pull", "get", "Value", "getText");                                   17
    link("Pull", "send", "Controller", "set");                                 18
```

```
link("Controller", "set", "Sampler", "setSR");                              19
link("Controller", "get", "Sampler", "getSR");                              20
link("Controller", "set", "Value", "setText", "{[int x]->[x.toString()]}", "{Object    21
    x->x}");
link("Sampler", "update", "Bar", "setValue");                               22
link("Sampler", "sample", "Network", "sample");                             23
    ...                                                                     24
}                                                                           25
```

Listing 1.2. JUSE definition of the `Audio` application

The `Audio` PU can be be developed using a text editor or, in alternative, in the CAD of Figure 2, an interactive manipulation tool that simplifies topology definition. A new CAD is currently being developed in a widespread rich client platform.

In spite of its simplicity, this application shows several keys aspects involved in software reuse. Some of the PUs composing the application already existed in JWIDGET. Only two new PUs were created to develop the application. The `Sampler` PU stores the sampling rate and it is specific of this software. The logic of the application is unique, requiring also the development of a specific software topology, materialized in the creation of a new `Executive` PU.

The `Audio` network PU is reusable by design and it can be used in other projects that require read/display a signal. In particular, it can be reused through inheritance of topology as defined in [9]. In general a software project involving PUs reuses existing code, requires the creation of new code that can be latter reused, and the development of code very specific to a domain with little possibility of reuse.

Although, some domain specific languages approaches, like AppInventor [4], address GUI development they are actually very different from JWIDGET and not directly related to JUSE. In particular, AppInventor does not support the concept of output gate suffering from the same limitations of object-oriented programming in enabling large scale reuse. In fact, AppInventor uses the event paradigm to support GUI development being, is this aspect, similar to more conventional systems like Java/Swing.

3   Related Work

Hierarchical and modular principles have been used as a powerful heuristic for handling complex problems in many fields. One of the first formal descriptions of modular decomposition have been made in the area of General Systems Theory [22, 34]. An earlier use of modularly in software was made in [17], where a synchronous programming language was defined.

The main limitation of general systems formalism is due to its asynchronous nature that is not compliant with the request-reply communication protocol used by most programming languages. This feature added to the imposition of a determinist execution of timed systems, prevents systems theory to be used in practice in software engineering [8].

Software engineering first mention modularity is made in [26]. However, this work did not go beyond general principles, since no implementation or a formal definition was provided. The decomposition of software into modules has later been advocated in software engineering [11]. On this latter work, however, the hierarchical decomposition of software has not been really introduced but rather hierarchy is used as synonymous of layered (software). Again no working definition of modularity was provided.

Pluggable units relate to the overlapping areas of software architectures [21] and software components [19]. Formal definitions of software architectures have been created [3, 5, 25, 13]. Likewise systems theory representations, these formalisms based on CSP, synchronous programming or π-calculus are not compliant with the request-reply communication protocol, imposing awkward software specifications. Given these limitations, most formal models are of little use for developing software applications.

To overcome the limitations of formal descriptions, so called Architecture Definition Languages (ADLs) have been developed [16, 21, 29]. However, ADLs are mainly façades decoupling specification from implementation as pointed in [2]. ADLs need thus to be translated into a programming language. This process is, in some aspects, similar to the one used by the Unified Modeling Language [6] with the limitations and drawbacks of separating specification from implementation [32].

Many current approaches are generative [13, 14, 33], with the inherent limitations. We also consider that generative approaches make it difficult to develop libraries of independent and reusable software units as we have achieved with the JWIDGET library described in the last section. In fact we found that GUIs are commonly treated as monolithic systems that need to be generated to every application [32]. Little evidence has been provided that GUIs are currently being developed in software architectures from reusable and independent widgets. An excellent overview of the plethora of existing ADLs and their limitations is given in [7].

To bridge the gap between specification and implementation, hierarchical and modular constructs have been introduced into existing programming languages [2]. However, this approach does not provide the general support to modular hierarchal software as provided by PUs. Limitations include the lack of filters and input/output functions defined by PUs [9]. Additionally, ArchJava does not provide full support for topology adaptation. In particular this system does not support operators to remove component and links, being incapable to represent mobile PUs as defined in [10].

We found it difficult to compare JUSE with related approaches since research papers do not, in general, provide detailed solutions to well defined problems like, for example, those addressed by design patterns. Exceptions include, for example, Aspect Programming [27], and the Scala language [24] that describe how to represent several design patterns. Taking, for example, the Observer pattern, we found that that PUs provide a simpler and more reusable solution [9], than the alternative representations provided in [24, 27].

Components are often pointed as providing supporting independent and composable software units [31]. However, no agreement on the definition of component has been established. In particular, the definition of component given in [31] points to an entity without permanent state. This is incompatible with our definition of PUs as given in [9]. For this reason we choose to not use this overloaded and ambiguous term.

4   Conclusions

Pluggable units (PUs) provide independent and fully reusable software. PUs implement the concept of IC in software, taking it to limits not yet attainable by hardware ICs. PUs enable software creation by composition of existing parts avoiding the costly development of software from scratch. We conjecture that reusable software units will enable a new software development cycle enabling improved programmer productivity, as large repositories of reusable software units become available in the different application domains. JUSE provides a Java/Groovy implementation of pluggable software units leveraging systematic reusable to software engineers. We are currently developing several libraries in order to show the ability of pluggable units to represent arbitrary systems.

References

1. Gartner identifies seven grand challenges facing IT (2008),
   http://www.gartner.com/it/page.jsp?id=643117
2. Aldrich, J., Chambers, C., Notkin, D.: ArchJava: Connecting software architecture to implementation. In: International Conference on Software Engineering, pp. 187–197 (2002)
3. Allen, R., Garlan, D.: A formal basis for architectural connection. ACM Transactions on Software Engineering and Methodology 6(3), 213–249 (1997)
4. AppInventor, http://appinventor.googlelabs.com/
5. Arbab, F.: Reo: A channel-based coordination model for component composition. Mathematical Structures in Computer Science 14, 329–366 (2004)
6. Arlow, J., Neustadt, I.: UML 2 and the Unified Process: Practical Object-Oriented Analysis and Design. Addison, London (2005)
7. Barais, O., Meur, A., Duchien, L., Lawall, J.: Software architecture evolution. In: Software Evolution, pp. 233–262. Springer, Heidelberg (2008)
8. Barros, F.: Modeling formalisms for dynamic structure systems. ACM Transactions on Modeling and Computer Simulation 7(12), 505–515 (1997)
9. Barros, F.: System and method for programming using independent and reusable software units. US Patent 6851104 B1 (Filed August 2000) (February 2005)
10. Barros, F.: Representing hierarchical mobility in software architectures. In: International Workshop on Software Engineering for Adaptive and Self-Managing Systems (2007)
11. Batory, D., O'Malley, S.: The design and implementation of hierarchical software systems with reusable components. ACM Transactions on Software Engineering and Methodology 1(4), 355–398 (1992)

12. Brooks, F.: No silver bullet: Essence and accidents of software engineering. In: Information Processing 1986, pp. 1069–1076 (1986)
13. Bruneton, E., Coupaye, T., Leclercq, M., Quéma, V., Stefani, J.: The FRACTAL component model and its support in Java. Software Practice and Experience 36(11-12), 1257–1284 (2006)
14. Bureš, T., Hnětynka, P., Plášil, F.: Dynamic reconfiguration and access to services in hierarchical component models. In: International Conference on Software Engineering Research, Management and Apllications, pp. 40–48 (2006)
15. Freeman, E., Freeman, E., Sierra, K., Bates, B.: Head First Design Patterns. O' Reilly, Sebastopol (2004)
16. Garlan, D., Monroe, R., Wile, D.: ACME: An architecture description interchange language. In: Conference of the Centre for Advanced Studies on Collaborative Research (1997)
17. Kahn, G.: The semantics of a simple language for parallel programming. In: Information Processing, pp. 471–475 (1974)
18. Khoshgoftaar, T., Allen, E., Kalaichelvan, K., Goel, N.: The impact of software evolution and reuse on software quality. Empirical Software Enginnering, 31–44 (1996)
19. Lau, K.-K., Wang, Z.: Software component models. IEEE Transactions on Software Engineering 33(10), 709–724 (2007)
20. Lim, W.: The effects of reuse on quality, productivity, and economics. IEEE Software, 23–30 (1994)
21. Medvidovic, N., Taylor, R.: A classification and comparison framework for software architecture description languages. IEEE Transactions on Software Engineering 26(1), 70–93 (2000)
22. Mesarovic, M., Takahara, Y.: General Systems Theory: A Mathematical Foundation. Academic Press, London (1975)
23. Mohagheghi, P., Conradi, R.: Quality, productivity, and economics benefits of software reuse: A review of industrial studies. Empirical Software Engineering 12, 471–516 (2007)
24. Odersky, M., Zenger, M.: Scalable component abstractions. In: Object-Oriented Programming Systems Languages and Applications, pp. 41–57 (2005)
25. Oquendo, F.: Formally modelling software architectures with the UML 2.0 profile for π-ADL. ACM SIGSOFT Software Engineering Notes 31(1), 1–13 (2006)
26. Parnas, D.: On the criteria to be used in decomposing systems into modules. Communications of the ACM 15(12), 1053–1058 (1972)
27. Pawlak, R., Seinturier, L., Retaillé, J.-P.: Foundations of AOP for J2EE Development. A-Press (2006)
28. Sametinger, J.: Software Engineering with Reusable Components. Springer, Heidelberg (1997)
29. Shaw, M., Clements, P.: The golden age of software architectures: A comprehensive survey. Technical Report CMU-ISRI-06-101, Carnegie-Mellon University, USA (2006)
30. Sommerville, I.: Software Engineering 8. Addison-Wesley, Reading (2007)
31. Szyperski, C.: Component Software: Beyond Object-Oriented Software. Addison-Wesley, Reading (1998)
32. Taylor, R., Medvidović, N., Dashofy, E.: Software Architecture. Wiley, Chichester (2010)
33. van Ommering, R., van der Linden, F., Kramer, J., Magee, J.: The Koala component model for consumer electronics software. Computer 33(3), 75–85 (2000)
34. Wymore, A.: A Mathematical Theory of Systems Engineering: The Elements. Krieger (1967)

Eight Practical Considerations in Applying Feature Modeling for Product Lines

Juha Savolainen[1], Mikko Raatikainen[2], and Tomi Männistö[2]

[1] Nokia Research Center, Itämerenkatu 11-13, 00180 Helsinki, Finland
juha.e.savolainen@nokia.com
[2] Software Business and Engineering Institute, Aalto University, PL 19210 Aalto, Finland
{Mikko.Raatikainen,Tomi.Mannisto}@aalto.fi

Abstract. Feature modeling has enjoyed success as a widely used variability modeling method in companies utilizing product lines. A number of different feature modeling methods have been proposed with expanded notational concepts and ability to model various dependencies among features. Despite popular usage and relatively simple concepts, different feature modeling methods tend not to explicate their purposes and assumptions and, in particular, how exactly the model is intended to be used. Consequently, many practitioners have a hard time evaluating whether a particular method is good for their purposes. In this paper, we intend to discuss the practical considerations when applying feature models. On the one hand, discussion of these considerations in research papers would clarify the intent of a proposed method. On the other hand, the considerations could help practitioners in clarifying the guiding principles for their feature modeling. In total, we expose eight points of practical considerations that are rarely discussed in research papers. These observations are based our experience of practice and research carried out in close cooperation with several companies.

Keywords: feature modeling, industrial experience, software architecture.

1 Introduction

Feature modeling is a popular variability modeling approach in software product lines, which is an approach to reuse software among product variants. In general, a feature in a feature model refers to an end-user visible characteristic of a system, or a distinguishable characteristic of a concept (e.g., system, component, and so on) that is relevant to some stakeholder of the concept [2]. Therefore, feature models are also a meaningful means to represent variability both internally and externally, e.g., to engineers as well as to customer.

Recently, research has focused on feature modeling languages that include formal semantics, parsimony, and much expressive power. In addition, tools supporting these languages in analysis, use, and construction have been developed. In fact, since the emergence of the original feature modeling approach, FODA [1], several extensions have been developed [2,3,4], various formalizations of feature models have been developed [5,6,7], and comparisons have been made [8] that all contribute to these

K. Schmid (Ed.): ICSR 2011, LNCS 6727, pp. 192–206, 2011.
© Springer-Verlag Berlin Heidelberg 2011

targets. Currently, the resulting feature models are able to express modeled software unambiguously and parsimoniously.

However, from practitioners' point of view, a central criterion of any method is utility. Here, utility means adhering to dictionary-definition, i.e., fitness for some desirable purpose or valuable end [11], including costs and benefits. To increase utility, less expressive modeling notations can be used that are also easier to use or easier in maintenance (cf. [9]). For example, sometimes a feature model on a whiteboard is the best model for the purpose of maximizing utility. Although, at least in the long term, engineering research tries to fulfill the needs of the practice, the state of the art in feature modeling seems to be that there are several considerations that are rarely addressed from the point of view of practitioners in the research. Therefore, practitioners have challenges in assessing the methods and models for their specific needs. Often, these considerations are implicit and represent a choice between equally valid alternatives having practical implications. The choice depends on the application domain, context, usage, and other factors. A universally applicable feature modeling approach is unlikely to exist. Rather, different methods address different considerations in different ways.

In this paper, we identify eight practical considerations that should be considered when developing a new feature model or using an existing one or applying feature modeling in practice. Despite not being extensive, the considerations are relevant for the utility of a feature model according to our experience in practice and research carried out in close cooperation with several companies. We argue that the considerations are also worth taking into account by researchers developing new or extending existing feature modeling methods. The considerations are discussed in light of an example of a mobile phone product line.

2 The Eight Considerations

2.1 Cost–Benefit

The most fundamental consideration in feature modeling is what is cost-efficiently meaningful to model. From the practical point of view, a feature model is an investment in terms of work effort. Too many details without a clear usage of these details lead to wasted work that could have been used better otherwise. Having a good model provides clear benefits, such as better manageability and understanding. However, if only a sketch of a product line is needed for communication, why make a complete feature model with fancy constraints? The point of choice is how much and what to model.

Our experience is that existing feature modeling concepts and tools make it possible to construct a feature model of practically any software. However, despite being possible, the cost-efficiency of such modeling efforts remains questionable. On the one hand, constructing a model itself can be laborious. On the other hand, the understanding and use of the model can be impractical.

Besides making a decision on how much should be modeled, even a larger investment consideration is often the actual maintenance of the model when, e.g., software, domain, or business decisions change. Each change can spread to the feature model and force large changes that are expensive to make. That is, although modeling itself can be laborious, it is still relatively easy and cheap to develop a comprehensive feature model compared to the costs required to maintain the same model. Our experience is that, even in complex situations, the creation of a feature model may well succeed but then fail in the maintenance. In fact, even in simple situations, failures are usually based on maintenance and keeping the model up to date.

The cost-benefit analysis should be the responsibility not only of the companies but also of research on feature modeling methods, including notations. That is, any extension or other further development of methods or tools should be assessed in terms of cost-benefits.

Overall, making good choices regarding the cost and benefit is one of the most difficult decisions during product line development. Making good decisions requires an excellent understanding of the company's needs and available methods to suit those needs. Three central issues in feature modeling are the costs and benefits of constructing, using, and maintaining the model. The decision about how, what, and how much to model has an influence on many other following considerations.

2.2 Completeness

A consideration closely related to how much to model in terms of cost-benefit is the completeness of a feature model. A feature model specifies the constraints of the ways in which the features can be combined. Ultimately, the feature model may be so restrictive that it represents only correct feature configurations; i.e., every feature configuration derived from the feature model represents a correct product variant. However, if not all constraints are defined, derivation can typically produce at least all correct configurations but also some incorrect ones.

Typically, increasing completeness adds something, such as constraints, to the feature model and makes a model contain more information, making it more complex to understand. Increasing complexity also increases the likelihood of introducing errors in the model as well as making the long-term management of the model harder. The more constraints the model has, the more opportunities for changes are also present. This is especially true if one chooses to model constraints that do not have a solid technical or domain background.

An advantage of modeling all details is that various automations can be conveniently applied, such as automatically deriving the different variants, the analysis of correctness of feature configurations against the feature model, or finding out whether some constraints in the feature model are obsolete. In practice, automation requires a large number of different products to justify the investment in modeling all details. An example of such automatic derivation is when sales representatives or customers do the derivation. However, even with an incomplete feature model, analysis and derivation can be carried out, although the outcome needs to be carefully assessed.

Typically, in industrial product lines, the feature model is not complete. In particular, some of the most obvious decisions are left to the product manager to take care of when making decisions about the product features. A feature model includes non-trivial dependencies and constraints.

The challenge with respect to constructing a complete feature model is not in the capabilities of methods or notations. Rather, the challenge for research and practice is the usability of methods, notations, and supporting tools.

2.3 Stakeholders

An important question in a feature modeling is: what stakeholders is the feature model meant for, and what are their concerns for the model? The feature model is intended for a specific purpose and stakeholders. In practice, employees construct and use the feature model, although tools such as analysis tools can be used as well.

Feature modeling was, originally, an approach to model a problem or solution domain and, typically, a tool of software engineers or other technical designers. However, a feature model can also be used by a wider audience. An example is using a feature model in internal product segmentation within product management or even for marketing or sales. That is, the stakeholders of the feature model can include product developers, product managers, sales, and even customers or users.

In the case of non-technical use, a feature model may be a sketch intended to help in, e.g., product planning or work organization. Such a model does not strive for completeness and unambiguousness but, rather, to communicate the main ideas of the product line. A feature model can function as a tool in the communication and elaboration of product line planning, even with non-technical stakeholders. Especially in such a case, the simplicity and clarity of the feature model overweight rigor. A model is useless if it is too complex or detailed to be understood by the relevant stakeholder.

If a feature model is used as a basis for product architecture, more rigor needs to be put into the modeling, e.g., in terms of constraints and correct structure. When the model is used in technical planning, even automated tool assistance can be applied and analyses carried out that require a certain level of correctness of the model.

A key point is the differences of these stakeholders who have a different background as well as different knowledge of the domain and the product line. A detailed technical model is not necessarily understandable or meaningful to non-technical stakeholders since they are not necessarily familiar with the details of software implementation. The details of technical constraints or relationships can create confusion, at best, among non-technical stakeholders. Even the feature modeling notations can be unintuitive for non-technical stakeholders. Respectively, technical stakeholders are not familiar with business constraints or what should be revealed to customers and how best to communicate with customers.

The stakeholders who are responsible for constructing and managing the model can be different from the stakeholders who benefit from the model. Consequently, researchers who propose a modeling method should consider and discuss who would construct and use the model. Similarly, the practitioners should think before starting to build models and clearly identify the stakeholders in their organization.

To sum up, there are stakeholders who, on the one hand, construct and maintain the model and, on the other hand, use the model. Each of these stakeholders has different knowledge about feature modeling in general and the product line in question.

2.4 Domain

An important question in feature modeling is whether a resulting feature model is intended to represent the problem or solution domain. The domain is not necessarily obvious from the model. If the feature model represents the problem domain, then the representation tries to capture the domain characteristics as the main features and their interactions. In a technical sense, features can be considered as corresponding with possible requirements. However, these requirements are general in the sense that they are not necessarily implemented yet or might not even be planned to be implemented in the product line. The feature model, including its constraints, thus, represents what is meaningful or feasible in the domain. The domain, per se, does not restrict the existence of the feature even if the feature combinations are not feasible commercially. For example, a domain model would not require a mobile phone to have a camera, although most, if not all, mobile phones today have a camera. However, a feature of making a phone call being optional does not make sense in a domain model of a mobile phone.

Alternatively, a feature model can represent the solution domain of a product line. The feature model, thus, corresponds with elements in the actual product line. The feature model excludes the characteristics of the domain that are not considered as being within the scope of the product line. The constraints and relationships are based on the decisions made about the product line. The decisions can be based on various reasons, including but not limited to technical constraints and product strategies.

Another consideration related to the usage of a feature model is the horizon to the future that the model is intended to capture. A feature model may aim to represent only the current situation of the product line, e.g., the variability as it exists now. As a result, when the software product line changes, respectively, the feature model needs to change. However, a feature model can also represent planned or roadmapped software, thus capturing future variability. When a feature model is used in derivation, the nature derivation differs so that, if the feature model represents current product line features, selection means selecting and adapting features, whereas, in the case of future plans, feature selection means that selected features need to be implemented.

Whether a feature model represents the problem or solution domain is relevant to research in developing the feature modeling methods. Methods that result in a feature model should include, in addition to notations, a means to study a domain. For practitioners, the question is relevant especially when selecting the feature modeling method and, during the use of the resulting model, understanding whether the model represents a domain or product line.

2.5 Commonality

A feature model can be intended to focus only on those features that vary. In this case, the details of common functionality provided by all products in a product line are not represented in the feature model. Representing only variability may be problematic, e.g., if a customer makes decisions about her purchases on the basis of a feature model. For example, a music player can be present in all mobile phones of a product line and, therefore, as a common feature, it would not be included in a feature model representing only varying features. However, if a customer makes a decision about her phone on a basis of a feature model and she wants to listen to music with her mobile phone, then the common music playing feature should be included in the feature model. A compromise approach is that commonalities are expressed at the higher level of abstraction without describing the details to make the model more understandable.

Alternatively, a feature model can represent the model of an entire product line, including mandatory and variable features. Such a feature model, thus, provides documentation of all features of the entire product line. Each product's individual model, derived from the feature model, includes all features of the product. For example, if a customer does derivation, it is meaningful to show all features, including common features, rather than only the varying features. A feature model can then be used to represent the entire software rather than UML or some other common modeling method that could have been used. In fact, few existing modeling methods for software provide, per se, a means of modeling variability. Rather, extensions or misuse of constructs are needed to represent variability. An advantage of modeling the entire software is to have all features in place, whereas a disadvantage is that the model size increases, especially if variability focuses only on a specific part of software, which is typically the case.

The question of how much a feature model represents is a particular challenge for notations and tools. When representing an entire model, it might be reasonable for only part of a model to be shown or for a model to consist of several fragments since models can become large. In the case of representing only variability, the variability needs to be associated with a specific part of the software since only a fraction of the software is represented in the feature model.

2.6 Correspondence

Another consideration is the elements that the features in a feature model correspond to. Typically, a feature corresponds to requirements or high-level implementation elements such as hardware components or static or dynamic software components. Rarely, features correspond to low-level implementation artifacts. Rather, means other than features can be used to specify details such as attributes of the features or constructs beyond feature modeling. For example, software can have a large number of parameters or other adaptation means that are not feasible to represent in a feature model.

A feature model can even consist of several different feature models at different levels of detail or granularity, as described above. For example, one feature model can represent a specific part of the software where all details in the component level are modeled, whereas another model represents another part of the software where general architectural components are modeled. The former model, then, typically describes variability, whereas the latter describes common parts, as described above. Alternatively, one feature model represents the general architectural components, whereas other models, such as UML diagrams, represent the details of each architectural component. Consequently, besides general rules for what the feature models represent, if there are several feature models, it needs to be taken into account that the feature models might not be equal and do not need to be equal.

Another point of view is that a feature model has a specific structure that is aligned toward something. One option is to align the feature model with the software structure. In the case of structuring the feature model with the software, most, if not all, real features are in the leaf nodes. Here, real features are the features that have been provided with an actual implementation in software. All other features exist only to structure the real features, as in software packages that organize real features.

These structuring features represent the structure of the software, and the leaf nodes represent real choices in software. When a feature model is aligned with the software structure, there is a mapping from the features to the software components. The mapping does not need to be one-to-one, as more complex mappings can be used as well. Aligning the feature model to the software structure tends to create models that are very close to the actual software implementation. Each of these software components may be organized such that they can be independently switched on or off using, for example, compile time flags.

Although alignment with software is relatively common, a feature model can be aligned with other concerns such as market segmentation or marketing decisions.

The key considerations for research and practice are that the feature modeling method provides necessary constructs that can be used to represent modeled elements, such as software components. There can be even a need to provide mapping between the modeled elements and the feature model.

2.7 Constraints

Feature modeling includes a structure that organizes the features into a hierarchy and constraints for resolving variability. That is, selecting a child feature typically means that the parent feature should also be selected. This relationship represents a mandatory feature. Typically, the features are structured as a tree, where some constraints are represented in the structure of the tree, whereas the remaining constraints must be specified by some other means, such as cross-branch relations between the nodes of the tree. The decomposition criterion used when constructing a feature tree has a significant impact on what constraints can be represented in the structure of the tree. In the worst case, the structure of the software and the best structure to represent the constraints may be contradictory. In these cases, the main dependencies exist in cross-branch relationships that tend to be less obvious from the model.

If cross-branch relations are allowed in the feature tree, there are a number of alternatives to represent them. First, one can use a set of rules to represent constraints that cannot be represented as the structure of the tree. Second, a separate model can be created to represent all feature dependencies. Separating the feature dependencies into their own model simplifies the management of dependencies and allows the dependencies to be considered separately. This is particularly useful if the main feature structure is composed primarily of optional features. This would mean that nearly all constraints on the selection of features originate from the feature dependency model. If the feature dependencies are represented separately from the feature model, overlapping specifications can easily happen. However, it is important to remember that, in more complex feature trees, there is no direct link between something being mandatory and being always selected. If any feature between a mandatory feature and its root feature is non-mandatory, then, in practice, this feature can be excluded from the product configuration. That is, this feature may not be selected regardless of being mandatory. The requirement relationship between two features does often a better job of highlighting the fact that this relationship applies only between these features and that this is dependent on the actual selection of features.

An alternative to the tree structure is to use more general data models to represent variability constraints. Some researchers [15] use a graph to represent variability among features. While this is clearly a more general approach, it has not enjoyed adaptation from the industry, most likely because feature trees are easier to understand and analyze than a general graph form.

The challenge of constraints is highlighted by the fact that the constraints can emerge from various sources such as business decisions, including marketing and product segmentation, restrictions enforced by technology, or the architectural constraints of existing software. Some of the constraints can be soft, meaning that the constraint can but should not be violated. Consequently, the source and nature of constraints vary largely, but all of them need to be taken into account to achieve a complete model.

As a result of the heterogeneity of the sources of the constraints, one can include even duplicate information in the feature model when both variability and feature dependencies are modeled. Clearly, including the same constraint twice is a wasted effort. However, sometimes, duplicate work can actually be beneficial from the evolution perspective. If two different constraints actually communicate different rationales, combining them may be a mistake. If an organization has a clear understanding of the role of variability and dependencies, it may be able to model marketing decisions using variability in the structure and functional dependencies and technical limitations using feature dependencies. Thus, these two aspects communicate different rationales and may help evolution through a better understanding of the interplay between marketing requirements and technical solutions.

The challenges are, thus, managing and representing constraints efficiently. The heterogeneity of the sources of the constraints also should be taken into account, e.g., by separating the different source as concerns.

2.8 Notation

The feature models used in practice need to be understandable to the product experts. This requires that the modeling method allows for the expression of domain variability in a natural manner so that the concepts and structures used match the practical way of describing products. However, as described earlier, there are also other usages, such as analyses and automated derivation. The issue is what concepts and notations best serve the different usages.

As a comparison, in a comparative field of research, that of product configuration, approaches with multiple levels of abstraction in the development of configuration modeling concepts have been used. For example, to keep the definition of the semantics clear, a specific product configuration modeling language (PCML) has been defined based on the conceptualization introduced in [18]. As the PCML is still somewhat clumsy to use in actual modeling and tool development, more appropriate modeling concepts are used in configuration models, and they are then mapped to PCML. The semantics for PCML and the consequent ability to make inferences are provided by a mapping to a general knowledge representation language that is particularly suitable for configuration tasks (namely WCRL) [19]. In fact, the general knowledge representation language used is, further, given semantics by mapping them to a propositional logic. This multitude of levels helps in separating the modeling concerns of the product experts of a particular company, configuration modeling experts and tool developers, researchers or developers providing or extending the semantics for the variability modeling and configuration tools, and the inference engine developers.

The point we want to make here is not to suggest a specific approach but to raise questions about the various concerns and needs for modeling. For example, different variability expressions, such as optional, alternative, or exclusive alternative features, can be defined with a smaller set of general concepts and still used to model the product variants in a natural manner. Similarly, it may make sense to define a set of typical feature dependencies for the use of product experts, such as Requires and Is-incompatible-with, although they can be expressed by means of a more generic constraints, e.g., "not A OR B" and "not (A AND B)."

Another, potentially even more important, point is to be clear about the need for and usefulness of particular modeling concepts. A generic logic is more powerful in the sense that it allows the expression of a large variety of constraints between features. However, being general does not imply usefulness. From the perspective of a practitioner, the selection of two constraints, such as Requires and Is-incompatible-with, is probably better than the opportunity to write arbitrary Boolean expressions. This means that extending a feature modeling approach to allow larger expressivity is not self-evidently an improvement.

By providing the aforementioned multiple levels of abstraction and mappings between them, different concepts and notations can be tailored to modelers, non-technical persons doing product derivation, and tools assisting with feature modeling. When the underlying semantics of the model have appropriate semantics, the power of existing theories and tools can be used to manipulate the models and automate the derivation tasks. The latter can be provided by various logical formalisms and related approaches, such as constraint satisfaction methods or propositional logic, which clearly are not suitable modeling approaches for most product experts.

The key consideration in selecting the notation for variability modeling is to provide as much syntactical and notational support as possible for expressing the variability in an effective manner from the perspective of a practitioner without making the assumption that more flexibility and generality would be better.

3 Discussion

This paper intends to improve understanding of the considerations that need to be taken into account when using feature modeling methods in practice in a company. In addition, the considerations provide researchers working with feature modeling with a set of considerations to keep in mind when assessing the utility of their work. A summary of the considerations with the most important question about each consideration is provided in Table 1.

To concretize the considerations, we use a simple example from the mobile phone domain, shown in Figure 1, which has three features: Camera, Flash, and Redeye reduction. The notation that is typically used in feature modeling specifies that all these features are optional, meaning that features can be selected or left out. Both Camera and Flash have two further alternative sub-features, meaning that, if the parent is selected, exactly one of the sub-features needs to be selected.

Table 1. Summary of the eight considerations

Consideration	Key questions
Cost-benefit	What is the optimal model in terms of cost-benefit when taking into account construction, usage, and maintenance?
Completeness	How complete is the feature model?
Stakeholders	Who puts effort into and who gains the benefits of the model? What knowledge about feature modeling methods in general and the product line in question do the stakeholders have?
Domain	Does the model represent the problem or solution domain? Does the model represent a current or planned product line?
Commonality	How much commonality is represented?
Correspondence	What elements of the product line does the feature model correspond to?
Constraints	What do the constraints represent?
Notation	What constructs and representation should different stakeholders use?

From this simple model, one can derive 18 different configurations of a mobile phone. However, a number of these configurations do not represent choices that would be derived in practice. It is hard to imagine a mobile phone with a range-adaptable flash without a camera. In addition, this model allows the derivation of a mobile phone without any other features than the root. Nevertheless, the model is relatively simple and communicates the basic features of the mobile phone product line.

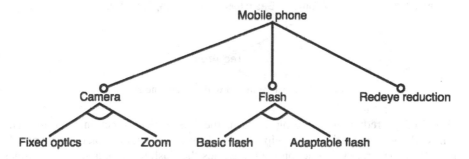

Fig. 1. A simple feature model

When considering only the domain, one could deduct that a mobile phone may or may not have a camera. A camera is not a necessary feature of a mobile phone. In that respect, the feature model in Figure 1 can be considered a domain. In addition, in the case of a mobile phone domain, a feature model represents all the possible cameras that are meaningful for a mobile phone, such as fixed optics and optical zoom still cameras. A feature model of a current mobile phone product line would be restricted, at least in the low-end models, to fixed optics cameras.

Figure 1 represents the domain also in a manner that allows the derivation of products that are not meaningful. To increase the completeness of the model, one can add more constraints to the selection of features, e.g., by removing optionality or adding cross-branch dependencies. Figure 2 shows a modified feature model in which Camera has become a mandatory feature and two dependencies have been added: Redeye reduction requires Flash and Zoom requires Adaptable flash.

Making Camera mandatory is a marketing decision. One can easily envision a mobile phone without a camera, but it has been decided that, from this product line, no mobile phones without a camera will be derived. Zoom requiring Adaptable flash seems to be partially a marketing decision, but with a solid technical basis. Having a basic flash with a zoom lens will affect the user's ability to take good pictures inside buildings or in darkness outside when using the zoom feature. However, one could still use zoom when taking pictures outside in daylight. It seems, though, that the marketing department has decided not to sell mobile phones with Zoom but without Adaptable flash. Such a decision can also affect implementation so that basic flash does not even support redeye reduction.

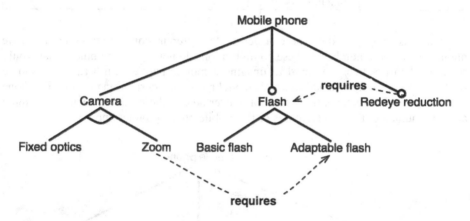

Fig. 2. A feature model with dependencies

For Redeye reduction requiring a Flash, there is a clear functional reason. The intent of Redeye reduction is to help avoid red eyes when taking pictures of people with a flash. The redeye reduction feature guides the flash to blink a number of times to reduce the chance of the eyes appearing red in the final pictures. Including Redeye reduction in mobile phones without a Flash is unnecessary. However, if the Redeye reduction were a pure software feature, then it could be independently selected, if so chosen for marketing reasons. Consequently, the added constraints are a mix of technical and marketing decisions. The resulting model restricts the range of possible feature configurations to be derived. In addition to the variability in the feature structure, one can further add constraints to the model in terms of feature dependencies. One such possibility is shown in Figure 3. Here, Flash has become a mandatory feature. In addition, two new dependencies have been added. Camera now requires Flash and Fixed optics requires Basic flash.

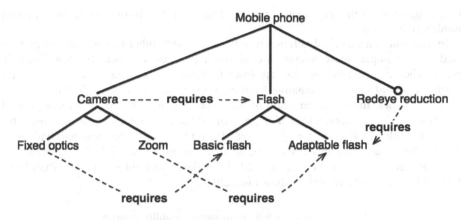

Fig. 3. "Complete" feature model

The fact that Camera requires Flash appears to be mainly a marketing decision. It says that we want the customers to know that, if they buy a mobile phone from this product line, they will always have a camera with a flash. However, because Flash has also been defined as mandatory, these specification overlap. This happens because Camera is mandatory and, in this small example, it is always selected. When Camera requires Flash, in theory, making Flash mandatory is redundant, or the requirement relationship between Camera and Flash could be removed.

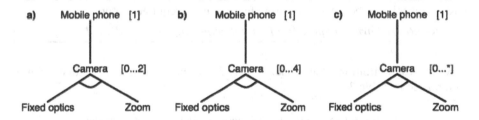

Fig. 4. Three different ways to represent a camera feature

There are many viewpoints on how to model the camera feature in the mobile phone product line. For simplicity, we reduce the feature model here only to the camera part. If we choose to model the cardinalities based on the *current product line*, we could decide to model them as shown in Figure 4a. This model defines that a mobile phone can have zero, one, or two cameras. Two cameras are typical in mobile devices that allow video conferencing features. The second option is to choose to model *software and hardware capabilities*. Based on the understanding of the software architecture and the multimedia middleware, one could model the features as shown in Figure 4b. The model says that, based on the combination of current software and hardware, one could have up to four cameras. Naturally, after introducing a new hardware platform, one could be forced to change the upper limit of the cardinality. Finally, we could choose to model the *software implementation* such that the exact number of cameras is not restricted, which is shown in Figure 4c.

This is because, in the implementation, one can theoretically instantiate an unlimited number of cameras.

In addition to a graphical notation of a feature model, other representations may be used. For example, the concepts offered for a practitioner could be those used in Fig. 3. They can be listed as: concept (root feature), feature, feature-tree, mandatory feature, optional feature, alternative features, and requires constraint. In a tool, e.g., a feature modeler, the implementation of the concept can be based on a more general mechanism. For example, a general expression of the form *FeatRel(f, S, min, max)* for defining a relation from feature *f* to a set of features *S* with *min* and *max* values to express how many features need to be selected from the set *S* if *f* is selected. To continue our example, the concepts needed for the model shown in Fig. 3 could be defined by means of *FeatRel*, as shown in Table 2.

Table 2. Textual definitions of some variability concepts

Mandatory feature relation between a parent feature and a child feature: *MandRel(parent, child) = FeatRel(parent, {child}, 1, 1)*
Optional feature relation between a parent and a child feature: *OptRel(parent, child) = FeatRel(parent, {child}, 0, 1)*

Alternative features:
   AltRel(parent, {alternative1, …, alternativeN}) =
   FeatRel(parent, {alternative1, …, alternativeN}, 1, 1)

Requires relation between a requiring feature and a required feature: *ReqRel(requiring, required) = FeatRel(requiring, {required}, 1, 1)*

With these definitions, the model of Fig. 3 can be expressed in textual form, as exemplified in Table 3.

Table 3. Example of a textual representation of a feature model

MandRel(Mobile phone, Camera),   *MandRel(Mobile phone, Flash),*   *OptRel(Mobile phone, Redeye reduction),*   *AltRel(Camera, {Fixed optics, Zoom}),*   *ReqRel(Camera, Flash), …*

Such textual representation makes the processing, storing, and transfer easy and understandable, e.g., between modeling tools and derivation support tools.

Finally, the complete feature model can be represented to a customer who is making a purchasing decision to communicate the choices she can make. However, the incomplete feature models can result in the customer's selecting and desiring a configuration that is not meaningful or desired. Showing the feature trees can also be confusing. As an alternative, the features can be represented to a customer so that she can select either fixed or zoom optics and an optional redeye reduction feature. Marketing has determined that the user is not interested in selecting the flash, but the flash will be automatically selected on the basis of optics. In addition, the choices are restricted so that, if redeye reduction is selected, then zoom will be selected automatically. If the user first selects fixed optics and then tries to select redeye, her selection is not accepted and an explanation is provided about the conflict. Respectively, if the user selects redeye reduction first, she cannot select fixed optics.

4 Conclusion

We have described eight considerations in applying feature modeling. However, there are also other approaches to represent variability. For example, there can even be a separate model that is not feature-specific for modeling variability, as in the case of an orthogonal variability model [12] or Covamof [13]. A similar approach to representing variability in a separate model is also in the decision models [14]. Feature modeling can be also compared with creating a configuration in the manufacturing industry. One such approach is exemplified by a configurator called WeCoTin [16].

Another approach is to define the domain-related concepts from the perspective of the practical variability modeling and give them the semantics by means of mapping to a particular logical formalism. Comparative approaches can be found from programming languages and domain-specific languages that provide a mapping for lower-level constructs. However, the mapping may be non-trivial, thus making the semantics hard to understand from the mapping and, therefore, make the further development of the model difficult.

Compared with these related approaches, some of the considerations seem to be relevant. For example, a decision model needs to be complete to be meaningful, so completeness consideration is not relevant. However, the consideration of stakeholders is also relevant in decision models. Nevertheless, the applicability of the presented eight considerations can be applicable in other approaches but needs to be assessed.

To sum up, since feature modeling has been used extensively, it may appear as a well-understood and fully known set of methods. However, in practice, engineers must face a number of issues when applying feature modeling for real product lines. Based on our experience, we have exposed eight practical considerations for applying feature modeling.

This work has been based on doing feature and variability modeling projects in several different companies accompanied with more basic research about variability modeling concepts. In different projects, a widely different approach for features modeling has been used with good results. However, we were initially surprised by the inability of practitioners to evaluate feature models. After consideration, it has become obvious that determining whether a feature model is good and appropriate in the current context is a complex and difficult question.

We hope that this paper will help researchers to better explain how they expect their results to be used and to give better insight into the challenges faced by the practitioners in their daily work. Practitioners, it is hoped, will gain a better understanding of the various concerns that affect how to apply feature modeling in their organizations.

References

[1] Kang, K.C., Kim, S., Lee, J., Kim, K., Shin, E., Huh, M.: FORM: A Feature-Oriented Reuse Method with Domain-Specific Reference Architectures. Annals of Software Engineering 5, 143–168 (1998)

[2] Griss, M., Favaro, J., d'Alessandro, M.: Integrating Feature Modelling with the RSEB. In: Proceedings of the Fifth International Conference on Software Reuse 1998, pp. 76–85 (1998)

[3] Czarnecki, K., Eisenecker, U.W.: Generative Programming. Addison-Wesley, Boston (2000)

[4] Czarnecki, K., Bednasch, T., Unger, P., Eisenecker, U.: Generative Programming for Embedded Software: An Industrial Experience Report. In: Generative Programming and Component Engineering 2002, pp. 156–172 (2002)

[5] Janota, M., Kiniry, J.: Reasoning about Feature Models in Higher-Order Logic. In: Software Product Line Conference, vol. 1, pp. 13–22 (2007)

[6] Asikainen, T., Männistö, T., Soininen, T.: A Unified Conceptual Foundation for Feature Modelling. In: Software Product Line Conference, pp. 31–40 (2006)

[7] Heymans, P., Schobbens, P.-Y., Trigaux, J.-C., Matulevicius, R., Classen, A., Bontemps, Y.: Towards the Comparative Evaluation of Feature Diagram Languages. In: SVM-WS (2007)

[8] Schobbens, P.-Y., Heymans, P., Trigaux, J.-C., Bontemps, Y.: Generic Semantics of Feature Diagrams Computer Networks, pp. 456–479. Elsevier, Amsterdam (2007)

[9] Niiniluoto, I.: The aim and structure of applied research. Erkenntnis 38, 121 (1993)

[10] Asikainen, T., Männistö, T.: Nivel—A metamodelling language with a formal semantics. Software and Systems Modeling 8(4), 521–549 (2009)

[11] Oxford English Dictionary (2010), http://www.oed.com

[12] Pohl, K., Böckle, G., van der Linden, F.: Software Product Line Engineering: Foundations, Principles, and Techniques. Springer, Heidelberg (2005)

[13] Sinnema, M., Deelstra, S., Hoekstra, P.: The COVAMOF Derivation Process. In: International Conference on Software Reuse, ICSR (2005)

[14] Rabiser, R., Grunbacher, P., Dhungana, D.: Supporting Product Derivation by Adapting and Augmenting Variability Models. In: SPLC, pp. 141–150 (2007)

[15] Mannion, M.: Using first-order logic for product line model validation. In: Chastek, G.J. (ed.) SPLC 2002. LNCS, vol. 2379, pp. 176–187. Springer, Heidelberg (2002)

[16] Tiihonen, J., Soininen, T., Niemelä, I., Sulonen, R.: A Practical Tool for Masscustomising Configurable Products. In: ICED 2003 (2003)

[17] Ferber, S., Haag, J., Savolainen, J.: Feature interaction and dependencies: Modeling features for reengineering a legacy product line. In: Chastek, G.J. (ed.) SPLC 2002. LNCS, vol. 2379, pp. 235–256. Springer, Heidelberg (2002)

[18] Soininen, T., Tiihonen, J., Männistö, T., Sulonen, R.: Towards a General Ontology of Configuration. AI EDAM 12(04), 357–372 (1998)

[19] Soininen, T., Niemelä, I., Tiihonen, J., Sulonen, R.: Representing Configuration Knowledge with Weight Constraint Rules. In: AAAI Spring Symposium on Answer Set Programming: Towards Efficient and Scalable Knowledge (2001)

On the Extent and Nature of Software Reuse in Open Source Java Projects

Lars Heinemann, Florian Deissenboeck, Mario Gleirscher,
Benjamin Hummel, and Maximilian Irlbeck

Institut für Informatik, Technische Universität München, Germany
{heineman,deissenb,gleirsch,hummelb,irlbeck}@in.tum.de

Abstract. Code repositories on the Internet provide a tremendous amount of freely available open source code that can be reused for building new software. It has been argued that only software reuse can bring the gain of productivity in software construction demanded by the market. However, knowledge about the extent of reuse in software projects is only sparse. To remedy this, we report on an empirical study about software reuse in 20 open source Java projects with a total of 3.3 MLOC. The study investigates (1) whether open source projects reuse third party code and (2) how much white-box and black-box reuse occurs. To answer these questions, we utilize static dependency analysis for quantifying black-box reuse and code clone detection for detecting white-box reuse from a corpus with 6.1 MLOC of reusable Java libraries. Our results indicate that software reuse is common among open source Java projects and that black-box reuse is the predominant form of reuse.

1 Introduction

Software reuse involves the use of existing software artifacts for the construction of new software [9]. Reuse has multiple positive effects on the competitiveness of a development organization. By reusing mature software components, the overall quality of the resulting software product is increased. Moreover, the development costs as well as the time to market are reduced [7, 11]. Finally, maintenance costs are reduced, since maintenance tasks concerning the reused parts are "outsourced" to other organizations. It has even been stated that there are few alternatives to software reuse that are capable of providing the gain of productivity and quality in software projects demanded by the industry [15].

Today, practitioners and researchers alike fret about the failure of reuse in form of a software components subindustry as imagined by McIlroy over 40 years ago [13]. Newer approaches, such as software product lines [2] or the development of product specific modeling languages and code generation [8], typically focus on reuse within a single product family and a single development organization. However, reuse of existing third party code is—from our observation—a common practice in almost all software projects of significant size. Software repositories on the Internet provide a tremendous amount of freely reusable source code, frameworks and libraries for many recurring problems. Popular examples are

K. Schmid (Ed.): ICSR 2011, LNCS 6727, pp. 207–222, 2011.
© Springer-Verlag Berlin Heidelberg 2011

the frameworks for web applications provided by the Apache Foundation and the Eclipse platform for the development of rich client applications. Due to its ubiquitous availability in software development, the Internet itself has become an interesting reuse repository for software projects [3, 6]. Search engines like Google Code Search[1] provide powerful search capabilities and direct access to millions of source code files written in a multitude of programming languages. Open source software repositories like Sourceforge[2], which currently hosts almost a quarter million projects, offer the possibility for open source software projects to conveniently share their code with a world-wide audience.

Research problem. Despite the widely recognized importance of software reuse and its proven positive effects on quality, productivity and time to market, it remains largely unknown to what extent current software projects make use of the extensive reuse opportunities provided by code repositories on the Internet. Literature is scarce on how much software reuse occurs in software projects. It is also unclear how much code is reused in black-box or white-box fashion. We consider this lack of empirical knowledge about the extent and nature of software reuse in practice problematic and argue that a solid basis of data is required in order to assess the success of software reuse.

Contribution. This paper extends the empirical knowledge about the extent and nature of code reuse in open source projects. Concretely, we present quantitative data on reuse in 20 open source projects that was acquired with different types of static analysis techniques. The data describes the reuse rate of each project and the relation between white-box and black-box reuse. The provided data helps to substantiate the academical discussion about the success or failure of software reuse and supports practitioners by providing them with a benchmark for software reuse in 20 successful open source projects.

2   Terms

This section briefly introduces the fundamental terms this study is based on.

Software reuse. In this paper, we use a rather simple notion of software reuse: software reuse is considered as the utilization of code developed by third parties besides the functionality provided by the operating system and the programming platform.

We distinguish between two reuse strategies, namely *black-box* and *white-box* reuse. Our definitions of these strategies follow the notions from [17].

White-box reuse. We consider the reuse of code to be of the white-box type, if it is incorporated in the project files in source form, *i. e.*, the internals of the reused code are exposed to the developers of the software. This implies that the

---

[1] http://www.google.com/codesearch
[2] http://sourceforge.net

code may potentially be modified. The reuse rate for white-box reuse is defined as the ratio between the amount of reused lines of code and the total amount of lines of code (incl. reused source code).

Black-box reuse. We consider the reuse of code to be of the black-box type, if it is incorporated in the project in binary form, *i. e.*, the internals of the reused code are hidden from the developers and maintainers of the software. This implies that the code is reused *as is*, *i. e.*, without modifications. For black-box reuse the reuse rate is given by the ratio between the size of the reused binary code and the size of the binary code of the whole software system (incl. reused binary code).

3 Methodology

This section describes the empirical study that was performed to analyze the extent and nature of software reuse in open source projects.

3.1 Study Design

We use the Goal-Question-Metric template from [20] for defining this study:

> We analyze *open source projects* for the purpose of *understanding the state of the practice in software reuse* with respect to *its extent and nature* from the viewpoint of *the developers and maintainers* in the context of *Java open source software*.

To achieve this, we investigate the following three research questions.

RQ 1 Do open source projects reuse software? The first question of the study asks whether open source projects reuse software at all, according to our definition.

RQ 2 How much white-box reuse occurs? For those projects that do reuse existing software, we ask how much of the code is reused in a white-box fashion as defined in Section 2. We use as metrics the number of copied lines of code from external sources as well as the reuse rate for white-box reuse.

RQ 3 How much black-box reuse occurs? We further ask how much of the code is reused in a black-box fashion according to our definition. For this question we use as metrics the aggregated byte code size of the reused classes from external libraries and the reuse rate for black-box reuse. Although not covered by our definition of software reuse, we separately measure the numbers for black-box reuse of the Java API, since one could argue that this is also a form of software reuse.

3.2 Study Objects

This section describes how we selected the projects that were analyzed in the study and how they were preprocessed in advance to the reuse analyses.

Table 1. The 20 studied Java applications

System	Version	Description	LOC	Size (KB)
Azureus/Vuze	4504	P2P File Sharing Client	786,865	22,761
Buddi	3.4.0.3	Budgeting Program	27,690	1,149
DavMail	3.8.5-1480	Mail Gateway	29,545	932
DrJava	stable-20100913-r5387	Java Programming Env.	160,256	6,199
FreeMind	0.9.0 RC 9	Mind Mapper	71,133	2,352
HSQLDB	1.8.1.3	Relational Database Engine	144,394	2,032
iReport-Designer	3.7.5	Visual Reporting Tool	338,819	10,783
JabRef	2.6	BibTeX Reference Manager	109,373	3,598
JEdit	4.3.2	Text Editor	176,672	4,010
MediathekView	2.2.0	Media Center Management	23,789	933
Mobile Atlas Creator	1.8 beta 2	Atlas Creation Tool	36,701	1,259
OpenProj	1.4	Project Management	151,910	3,885
PDF Split and Merge	0.0.6	PDF Manipulation Tool	411	17
RODIN	2.0 RC 1	Service Development	273,080	8,834
soapUI	3.6	Web Service Testing Tool	238,375	9,712
SQuirreL SQL Client	Snapshot-20100918_1811	Graphical SQL Client	328,156	10,918
subsonic	4.1	Web-based Music Streamer	30,641	1,050
Sweet Home 3D	2.6	Interior Design Application	77,336	3,498
TV-Browser	3.0 RC 1	TV Guide	187,216	6,064
YouTube Downloader	1.9	Video Download Utility	2,969	99
Overall			3,195,331	100,085

Selection Process. We chose 20 projects from the open source software repository Sourceforge as study objects. Sourceforge is the largest repository of open source applications on the Internet. It currently hosts 240,000 software projects and has 2.6 million users[3].

We used the following procedure for selecting the study objects[4]. We searched for Java projects with the development status *Production/Stable*. We then sorted the resulting list descending by number of weekly downloads. We stepped through the list beginning from the top and selected each project that was a standalone application, purely implemented in Java, based on the Java SE Platform and had a source download. All of the 20 study objects selected by this procedure were among the 50 most downloaded projects. Thereby, we obtained a set of successful projects in terms of user acceptance. The application domains of the projects were diverse and included accounting, file sharing, e-mail, software development and visualization. The size of the downloaded packages (zipped files) had a broad variety, ranging from 40 KB to 53 MB.

Table 1 shows overview information about the study objects. The *LOC* column denotes the total number of lines in Java source files in the downloaded and preprocessed source package as described below. The *Size* column shows the bytecode sizes of the study objects.

Preprocessing. We deleted test code from the projects following a set of simple heuristics (e.g. folders named test/tests). In few cases, we had to remove code that was not compilable. For one project we omitted code that referenced a commercial library.

---

[3] http://sourceforge.net/about
[4] The project selection was performed on October 5th, 2010.

Table 2. The 22 libraries used as potential sources for white-box reuse

Library	Description	Version	LOC
ANTLR	Parser Generator	3.2	66,864
Apache Ant	Build Support	1.8.1	251,315
Apache Commons	Utility Methods	5/Oct/2010	1,221,669
log4j	Logging	1.2.16	68,612
ASM	Byte-Code Analysis	3.3	3,710
Batik	SVG Rendering and Manipulation	1.7	366,507
BCEL	Byte-Code Analysis	5.2	48,166
Eclipse	Rich Platform Framework	3.5	1,404,122
HSQLDB	Database	1.8.1.3	157,935
Jaxen	XML Parsing	1.1.3	48,451
JCommon	Utility Methods	1.0.16	67,807
JDOM	XML Parsing	1.1.1	32,575
Berkeley DB Java Edition	Database	4.0.103	367,715
JFreeChart	Chart Rendering	1.0.13	313,268
JGraphT	Graph Algorithms and Layout	0.8.1	41,887
JUNG	Graph Algorithms and Layout	2.0.1	67,024
Jython	Scripting Language	2.5.1	252,062
Lucene	Text Indexing	3.0.2	274,270
Spring Framework	J2EE Framework	3.0.3	619,334
SVNKit	Subversion Access	1.3.4	178,953
Velocity Engine	Template Engine	1.6.4	70,804
Xerces-J	XML Parsing	2.9.0	226,389
Overall			6,149,439

We also added missing libraries that we downloaded separately in order to make the source code compilable. We either obtained the libraries from the binary package of the project or from the library's website. In the latter case we chose the latest version of the library.

3.3   Study Implementation and Execution

This section details how the study was implemented and executed on the study objects. All automated analyses were implemented in Java on top of our open source quality analysis framework ConQAT[5], which provides—among others— clone detection algorithms and basis functionality for static code analysis.

Detecting White-Box Reuse. As white-box reuse involves copying external source code into the project's code, the sources of reuse are not limited to libraries available at compile time, but can virtually span all existing Java source code. The best approximation of *all existing Java source code* is probably provided by the indices of the large code search engines, such as Google Code Search or Koders. Unfortunately, access to these engines is typically limited and does not allow to search for large amounts of code, such as the 3 MLOC of our study objects. Consequently, we only considered a selection of commonly used Java libraries and frameworks as potential sources for white-box reuse. We selected 22 libraries which are commonly reused based on our experience with both own development projects and systems we analyzed during earlier studies. The libraries

---

[5] http://www.conqat.org

are listed in Table 2 and comprise more than 6 MLOC. For the sake of presentation, we treated the Apache Commons as a single library, although it consists of 39 individual libraries that are developed and versioned independently. The same holds for Eclipse, where we chose a selection of its plug-ins.

To find potentially copied code, we used our clone detection algorithm presented in [5] to find duplications between the selected libraries and the study objects. We computed all clones consisting of at least 15 statements with normalization of formatting and identifiers (type-2 clones), which allowed us to also find partially copied files (or files which are not fully identical due to further independent evolution), while keeping the rate of false positives low. All clones reported by our tool were also inspected manually, to remove any remaining false positives.

We complemented the clone detection approach by manual inspection of the source code of all study objects. The size of the study objects only allows a very shallow inspection, based on the names of files and directories (which correspond to Java packages). For this we scanned the directory trees of the projects for files residing in separate source folders or in packages that were significantly different from the package names used for the project itself. The files found this way were then inspected and their source identified based on header comments or a web search. Of course this step only can find large scale reuse, where multiple files are copied into a project and the original package names are preserved (which are typically different from the project's package names). However, during this inspection we are not limited to the 22 selected libraries, but potentially can find other reused code as well.

Detecting Black-Box Reuse. The primary way of black-box reuse in Java programs is the inclusion of libraries. Technically, these are Java Archive Files (JAR), which are zipped files containing the byte code of the Java types. Ideally, one would measure the reuse rate based on the source code of the libraries. However, obtaining the source code for such libraries is error-prone as many projects do not document the exact version of the used libraries. In certain cases, the source code of libraries is not available at all. To avoid these problems and prevent measurement inaccuracies, we performed the analysis of black-box reuse directly on the Java byte code stored in the JAR files.

While JAR files are the standard way of packaging reusable functionality in Java, the JAR files themselves are not directly reused. They merely represent a container for Java types (classes, interfaces, enumerations and annotations) that are referenced by other types. Hence, the type is the main entity of reuse in Java[6]. Our black-box reuse analysis determines which types from libraries are referenced from the types of the project code. The dependencies are defined by the Java Constant Pool [12], a part of the Java class file that holds information about all referenced types. References are method calls and all type usages, induced *e. g.*, by local variables or inheritance. Our analysis transitively traverses the

---

[6] In addition to JAR files, Java provides a *package* concept that resembles a logical modularization concept. Packages, however, cannot directly be reused.

dependency graph, *i. e.*, also those types that are indirectly referenced by reused types are included in the resulting set of reused types. The analysis approach ensures that in contrast to counting the whole library as reused code, only the subset that is actually referenced by the project is considered. The rationale for this is that a project can incorporate a large library but use only a small fraction of it. To quantify black-box reuse, the analysis measures the size of the reused types by computing their aggregated byte code size. The black-box analysis is based on the BCEL library[7] that provides byte code processing functionality.

Our analysis can lead to an overestimation of reuse as we always include whole types although only specific methods of a type may actually be reused. Moreover, a method may reference certain types but the method itself could be unreachable. On the other hand, our approach can lead to an underestimation of reuse as the implementations of interfaces are not considered as reused unless they are discovered on another path of the dependency search. Details regarding this potential error can be found in the section that discusses the threats to validity (Section 6).

Although reuse of the Java API is not covered by our definition of software reuse, we also measured reuse of the Java API, since potential variations in the reuse rates of the Java API are worthwhile to investigate. Since every Java class inherits from `java.lang.Object` and thereby (transitively) references a significant part of the Java API classes, even a trivial Java program exhibits— according to our analysis—a certain amount of black-box reuse. To determine this *baseline*, we performed the analysis for an artificial minimal Java program that only consists of an empty `main` method. This baseline of black-box reuse of the Java API consisted of 2,082 types and accounted for about 5 MB of byte code. We investigated the reason for this rather large baseline and found that `Object` has a reference to `Class` which in turn references `ClassLoader` and `SecurityManager`. These classes belong to the core functionality for running Java applications. Other referenced parts include the Reflection API and the Collection API. Due to the special role of the Java API, we captured the numbers for black-box reuse of the Java API separately. All black-box reuse analyses were performed with a Sun Java Runtime Environment for Linux 64 Bit in version 1.6.0.20.

4   Results

This section contains the results of the study in the order of the research questions.

4.1   RQ 1: Do Open Source Projects Reuse Software?

The reuse analyses revealed that 18 of the 20 projects do reuse software from third parties, *i. e.*, of the analyzed projects 90% reuse code. *HSQLDB* and *YouTube Downloader* were the only projects for which no reuse—neither black-box nor white-box—was found.

---

[7] http://jakarta.apache.org/bcel

4.2   RQ 2: How Much White-Box Reuse Occurs?

We attempt to answer this question by a combination of automatic techniques (clone detection) and manual inspections. The clone detection between the code of the study objects and the libraries from Table 2 reported 337 clone classes (*i. e.*, groups of clones) with 791 clone instances all together. These numbers only include clones between a study object and one or more libraries; clones within the study objects or the libraries were not considered. As we had *HSQLDB* both in our set of study objects and the libraries used, we discarded all clones between these two.

Manual inspection of these clones led to the observation that, typically, all clones are in just a few of the file pairs which are nearly completely covered by clones. So, the unit of reuse (as far as we found it) is the file/class level; single methods (or sets of methods) were not copied. Most of the copied files where not completely identical. These changes are caused either by minor modifications to the files after copying them to the study objects, or (more likely) due to different versions of the libraries used. As the differences between the files were minor, we counted the entire file as copied if the major part of it was covered by clones.

By manual inspection of the study objects we found entire libraries copied in four of the study objects. These libraries were either less well-known (GNU ritopt), no longer available as individual project (microstar XML parser), or not released as an individual project but rather extracted from another project (OSM JMapViewer). All of these could not be found by the clone detection algorithm, as the corresponding libraries were not part of our original set.

The results for the duplicated code found by clone detection and the code found during manual inspection are summarized in Table 3. The last column gives the overall amount of white-box reused code relative to the project's size

Table 3. Amount of white-box reuse found by clone detection and manual inspection

System	Clone Detection (LOC)	Manual Inspection (LOC)	Overall Percent
Azureus/Vuze	1040	57,086	7.39%
Buddi			—
DavMail			—
DrJava			—
FreeMind			—
HSQLDB			—
iReport-Designer	298		0.09%
JabRef		7,725	7.06%
JEdit	7,261	9,333	9.39%
MediathekView			—
Mobile Atlas Creator		2,577	7.02%
OpenProj	87		0.06%
PDF Split and Merge			—
RODIN	382		0.14%
soapUI	2,120		0.89%
SQuirreL SQL Client			—
subsonic			—
Sweet Home 3D			—
TV-Browser	513		0.27%
YouTube Downloader			—
Overall	11,701	76,721	*n.a.*

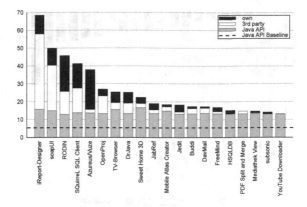

Fig. 1. Absolute bytecode size distribution (MB)

in LOC. For 11 of the 20 study objects no white-box reuse whatsoever could be proven. For another 5 of them, reuse is below 1%. However, there are also 4 projects with white-box reuse in the range of 7% to 10%. The overall LOC numbers shown in the last row indicate that the amount of code that results from copying entire libraries outnumbers by far the code reused by more selective copy&paste.

4.3   RQ 3: How Much Black-Box Reuse Occurs?

Figure 1 illustrates the absolute bytecode size distributions between the project code (own), the reused parts of the libraries (3rd party) and the Java API ordered descending by the total amount of bytecode. The horizontal line indicates the baseline usage of the Java API. The reuse of third party libraries ranged between 0 MB and 42.2 MB. The amount of reuse of the Java API was similar among the analyzed projects and ranged between 12.9 MB and 16.6 MB. The median was 2.4 MB for third party libraries and 13.3 MB for the Java API. The project *iReport-Designer* reused the most functionality in a black-box fashion both from libraries and from the Java API. The project with the smallest extent of black-box reuse was *YouTube Downloader*.

Figure 2 is based on the same data but shows the relative distributions of the bytecode size. The projects are ordered descending by the total amount of relative reuse. The relative reuse from third party libraries was 0% to 61.7% with a median of 11.8%. The relative amount of reused code from the Java API ranged between 23.0% and 99.3% with a median of 73.0%. Overall (third party and Java API combined), the relative amount of reused code ranged between 41.3% and 99.9% with a median of 85.4%. The project *iReport-Designer* had the highest black-box reuse rate. *YouTube Downloader* used the most code from the Java API relative to its own code size. For 19 of the 20 projects, the amount of reused code was larger than the amount of own code. Of the overall amount of reused code in the sample projects, 34% stemmed from third party libraries and 66% from the Java API.

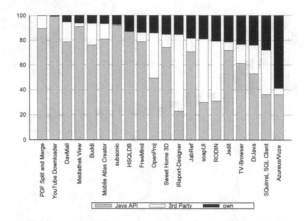

Fig. 2. Relative bytecode size distribution (%)

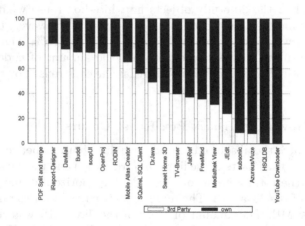

Fig. 3. Relative bytecode size distribution (%) without Java API

Figure 3 illustrates the relative byte code size distributions between the own code and third party libraries, *i. e.*, without considering the Java API as a reused library. The projects are ordered descending by reuse rate. The relative amount of reused library code ranged from 0% to 98.9% with a median of 45.1%. For 9 of the 20 projects the amount of reused code from third party libraries was larger than the amount of own code.

5   Discussion

The data presented in the previous sections lead to interesting insights into the current state of open source Java development, but also open new questions which were not part of our study setup. We discuss both in the following sections.

5.1 Extent of Reuse

Our study reveals that software reuse is common among open source Java projects, with black-box reuse as the predominant form. None of the 20 projects analyzed has less than 40% black-box reuse when including the Java API. Even when not considering the Java API the median reuse rate is still above 40% and only 4 projects are below the 10% threshold. Contrary, white-box reuse is only found in about half of the projects at all and never exceeds 10% of the code.

This difference can probably be explained by the increased maintenance efforts that are commonly associated with white-box reuse as described by Jacobson et al. [7] and Mili et al. [14]. The detailed results of RQ 2 also revealed that larger parts consisting of multiple files were mostly copied if either the originating library was no longer maintained or the files were never released as an individual library. In both cases the project's developers would have to maintain the reused code in any case, which removes the major criticism of white-box reuse.

It also seems that the amount of reused third party libraries seldom exceeds the amount of code reused from the Java API. The only projects for which this is not the case are *iReport-Designer*, *RODIN* and *soapUI*, from which the first two are built upon NetBeans respectively Eclipse, which provide rich platforms on top of the Java API.

Based on our data, it is obvious that the early visions of reusable components that only have to be connected by small amounts of glue code and would lead to reuse rates beyond 90% are not realistic today. On the other hand, the reuse rates we found are high enough to have a significant impact on the development effort. We would expect that reuse of software, as it is also fostered by the open source movement, has a huge contribution to the rich set of applications available today.

5.2 Influence of Project Size on Reuse Rate

The amount of reuse ranges significantly between the different projects. While *PDF Split and Merge* is just a very thin wrapper around existing libraries, there are also large projects which have (relatively) small reuse rates (*e. g.*, less than 10% for *Azureus* without counting the Java API).

Motivated by a study by Lee and Litecky [10], we investigated a possible correlation between code size and reuse rate in our data set. Their study was based on a survey in the domain of commercial Ada development on 73 samples and found a *negative influence* of software size on the rate of reuse. For the reuse rate without the Java API (only third party code) we found a Spearman correlation coefficient of 0.05 with the size of the project's own code (two-tailed p-value: 0.83). Thus, we can infer no dependence between these values. If we use the overall reuse rate (including the Java API), the Spearman coefficient is -0.93 (p-value < 0.0001), which indicates a significant and strong negative correlation. This confirms the results of [10] that project size typically reduces the reuse rate.

5.3 Types of Reused Functionality

It is interesting to investigate what kind of functionality is actually reused by software. Therefore, we tried to categorize all reused libraries into different groups of common functionality. Consequently, we analyzed the purpose of each reused library and divided them into seven categories (e. g., Networking, Text/XML, Rich Cient Platforms or Graphics/UI). To determine to which extent a certain type of functionality is reused we employed our black-box reuse detection algorithm presented in Section 3.3 to calculate the amount of bytecode for each library that is reused inside a project.

We observed that there is no predominant type of reused functionality and that nearly all projects are reusing functionality belonging to more than one category. We believe that there is no significant insight we can report except that reuse seems to be diverse among the categories and is not concentrated on a single purpose.

6 Threats to Validity

This section discusses potential threats to the internal and external validity of the results presented in this paper.

6.1 Internal Validity

The amount of reuse measured fundamentally depends on the definition of *software reuse* and the techniques used to measure it. We discuss possible flaws that can lead to an overestimation of the actual reuse, an underestimation, or otherwise threaten our results.

Overestimation of reuse. The measurement of white-box reuse used the results of a clone detection, which could contain false positives. Thus, not all reported clones indicate actual reuse. To mitigate this, we manually inspected the clones found. Additionally, for both the automatically and manually found duplicates, it is not known whether the code was copied *into* the study objects or rather *from* them. However, all findings were manually verified, for example by checking the header comments, we ensured that the code was actually copied from the library into the study object.

Our estimation of black-box reuse is based on static references in the bytecode. We consider a class as completely reused if it is referenced, which may not be the case. For example, the method holding the reference to another class might never be called. Another possibility would be to use dynamic analysis and execution traces to determine the amount of reused functionality. However, this approach has the disadvantage that only a finite subset of all execution traces could be considered, leading to a potentially large underestimation of reuse.

Underestimation of reuse. The application of clone detection was limited to a fixed set of libraries. Thus, copied code could be missed as the source it was taken from was not included in our comparison set. Additionally, the detector might miss actual clones (low recall) due to weak normalization settings. To adress this, we chose settings that yield higher recall (at the cost of precision). The manual inspection of the study objects' code for further white-box reuse is inherently incomplete; due to the large amounts of code only the most obvious copied parts could be found.

The static analysis used to determine black-box reuse misses certain dependencies, such as method calls performed via Java's reflection mechanism or classes that are loaded based on configuration information. Additionally, our analysis can not penetrate the boundaries created by Java interfaces. The actual implementations used at run-time (and their dependencies) might not be included in our reuse estimate. To mitigate this, one could search for an implementing class and include the first match into the further dependency search and the result set. However, preliminary experiments showed that this approach leads to a large overestimation. For example a command line program that references an interface that is also implemented by a UI class could lead us to the false conclusion that the program reuses UI code.

There are many other forms of software reuse that are not covered by our approach. One example are reusable generators. If a project uses a code generator to generate source code from models, this would not be detected as a form of reuse by our approach. Moreover, there are many other ways in which software components can interact with each other besides use dependencies in the source code. Examples are inter-process communication, web services that utilize other services via SOAP calls, or the integration of a database via an SQL interface.

6.2   External Validity

While we tried to use a comprehensible way of sampling the study objects, it is not clear to what extent they are representative for the class of open source Java programs. First, the choice of Sourceforge as source for the study objects could bias our selection, as a certain kind of open source developers could prefer other project repositories (such as Google Code). Second, we selected the projects from the 50 most downloaded ones, which could bias our results.

As the scope of the study are open source Java programs, transferability of the results to other programming languages or commercially developed software is unclear. Especially the programming language is expected to have a huge impact on reuse, as the availability of both open source and commercial reusable code heavily depends on the language used.

7   Related Work

Software reuse is a research field with an extensive body of literature. An overview of different reuse approaches can be found in the survey from Krueger [9]. In the following, we focus on empirical work that aims at quantifying the extent of software reuse in real software projects.

In [18], Sojer et al. investigate the usage of existing open source code for the development of new open source software by conducting a survey among 686 open source developers. They analyze the degree of code reuse with respect to developer and project characteristics. They report that software reuse plays an important role in open source development. Their study reveals that a mean of 30% of the implemented functionality in the projects of the survey participants is based on reused code. Since Sojer et al. use a survey to analyze the extent of code reuse, the results may be subject to inaccurate estimates of the respondents. Our approach analyzes the source code of the projects and therefore avoids this potential inaccuracy. Our results are confirmed by their study, since they also report that software reuse is common in open source projects.

Haefliger et al. [4] analyzed code reuse within six open source projects by performing interviews with developers as well as inspecting source code, code modification comments, mailing lists and project web pages. Their study revealed that all sample projects reuse software. Moreover, the authors found that by far the dominant form of reuse within their sample was black-box reuse. In the sample of 6 MLOC, 55 components which in total account for 16.9 MLOC were reused. Of the 6 MLOC, only about 38 kLOC were reused in a white-box fashion. The developers also confirmed that this form of reuse occurs only infrequently and in small quantities. Their study is related to ours, however the granularity for the black-box analysis was different. While they treated whole components as reusable entities, we measured the fraction of the library that is actually used. Since they use code repository commit comments for identifying white-box reuse, their results are sensitive with regards to the accuracy of these comments. In contrast, our method utilizes clone detection and is therefore not dependent on correct commit comments. Their study confirms our finding that black-box is the by far predominant form of reuse.

In [16], Mockus investigates large-scale code reuse in open source projects by identifying components that are reused among several projects. The approach looks for directories in the projects that share a certain fraction of files with equal names. He investigates how much of the files are reused among the sample projects and identify what type of components are reused the most. In the studied projects, about 50% of the files were used in more than one project. Libraries reused in a black-box fashion are not considered by his approach. While Mockus' work quantifies how often code entities are reused, our work quantifies the fraction of reused code compared to the own code within projects. Moreover, reused entities that are smaller than a group of files are not considered. However, their results are in line with our findings regarding the observation that code reuse is commonly practiced in open source projects.

In [10], Lee et al. report on an empirical study that investigates how organizations employ reuse technologies and how different criteria influence the reuse rate in organizations using Ada technologies. They surveyed 500 Ada professionals from the ACM Special Interest Group on Ada with a one-page questionnaire.

The authors determine the amount of reuse with a survey. Therefore their results may be inaccurate due to subjective judgement of the respondents. Again, our approach mitigates this risk by analyzing the source code of the project.

In [19], von Krogh et al. report on an exploratory study that analyzes knowledge reuse in open source software. The authors surveyed the developers of 15 open source projects to find out whether knowledge is reused among the projects and to identify conceptual categories of reuse. They analyze commit comments from the code repository to identify accredited lines of code as a direct form of knowledge reuse. Their study reveals that all the considered projects do reuse software components. Our observation that software reuse is common in open source development is therefore confirmed by their study. Like Haefliger et al., Krogh et al. rely on commit comments of the code repository with the already mentioned potential drawbacks.

Basili et al. [1] investigated the influence of reuse on productivity and quality in object-oriented systems. Within their study, they determine the reuse rate for 8 projects developed by students with a size ranging from about 5 kSLOCs to 14 kSLOCs. While they report reuse rates in a similar range as those from our results, they analyzed rather small programs written by students in the context of the study. In contrast to that, we analyzed open source projects.

8 Conclusions and Future Work

Software reuse, often called the holy grail of software engineering, has certainly not been found in the form of reusable components that simply need to be plugged together. However, our study not only shows that reuse is common in almost all open source Java projects but also that significant amounts of software are reused: Of the analyzed 20 projects 9 projects have reuse rates of more than 50%—even if reuse of the Java API is not considered. Reassuringly, these reuse rates are to a great extent realized through black-box reuse and not by copy&pasting source code.

We conclude that in the world of open-source Java development, high reuse rates are not a theoretical option but are achieved in practice. Especially, the availability of reusable functionality, which is a necessary prerequisite for reuse to occur, is well-established for the Java platform.

As a next step, we plan to extend our studies to other programming ecosystems and other development models. In particular, we are interested in the extent and nature of reuse for projects implemented in legacy languages like COBOL and PL/1 on the one hand and currently hyped languages like Python and Scala on the other hand. Moreover, our future studies will include commercial software systems to investigate to what extent the open-source development model promotes reuse.

Acknowledgment

The authors want to thank Elmar Juergens for inspiring discussions and helpful comments on the paper.

References

1. Basili, V., Briand, L., Melo, W.: How reuse influences productivity in object-oriented systems. Communications of the ACM 39(10), 116 (1996)
2. Clements, P., Northrop, L.M.: Software Product Lines: Practices and Patterns, 6th edn. Addison-Wesley, Reading (2007)
3. Frakes, W., Kang, K.: Software reuse research: Status and future. IEEE Transactions on Software Engineering 31(7), 529–536 (2005)
4. Haefliger, S., Von Krogh, G., Spaeth, S.: Code Reuse in Open Source Software. Management Science 54(1), 180–193 (2008)
5. Hummel, B., Juergens, E., Heinemann, L., Conradt, M.: Index-Based Code Clone Detection: Incremental, Distributed, Scalable. In: ICSM 2010 (2010)
6. Hummel, O., Atkinson, C.: Using the web as a reuse repository. In: Morisio, M. (ed.) ICSR 2006. LNCS, vol. 4039, pp. 298–311. Springer, Heidelberg (2006)
7. Jacobson, I., Griss, M., Jonsson, P.: Software reuse: architecture, process and organization for business success. Addison-Wesley, Reading (1997)
8. Kelly, S., Tolvanen, J.-P.: Domain-Specific Modeling. Wiley, Chichester (2008)
9. Krueger, C.: Software reuse. ACM Comput. Surv. 24(2), 131–183 (1992)
10. Lee, N., Litecky, C.: An empirical study of software reuse with special attention to Ada. IEEE Transactions on Software Engineering 23(9), 537–549 (1997)
11. Lim, W.: Effects of reuse on quality, productivity, and economics. IEEE Software 11(5), 23–30 (2002)
12. Lindholm, T., Yellin, F.: Java virtual machine specification. Addison-Wesley Longman Publishing Co., Inc., Boston (1999)
13. McIlroy, M., Buxton, J., Naur, P., Randell, B.: Mass produced software components. In: Software Engineering Concepts and Techniques, pp. 88–98 (1969)
14. Mili, H., Mili, A., Yacoub, S., Addy, E.: Reuse-Based Software Engineering: Techniques, Organizations, and Controls. Wiley Interscience, Hoboken (2001)
15. Mili, H., Mili, F., Mili, A.: Reusing software: Issues and research directions. IEEE Transactions on Software Engineering 21(6), 528–562 (1995)
16. Mockus, A.: Large-scale code reuse in open source software. In: FLOSS 2007 (2007)
17. Ravichandran, T., Rothenberger, M.: Software reuse strategies and component markets. Communications of the ACM 46(8), 109–114 (2003)
18. Sojer, M., Henkel, J.: Code Reuse in Open Source Software Development: Quantitative Evidence, Drivers, and Impediments. JAIS (to appear, 2011)
19. von Krogh, G., Spaeth, S., Haefliger, S.: Knowledge Reuse in Open Source Software: An Exploratory Study of 15 Open Source Projects. In: HICSS 2005 (2005)
20. Wohlin, C., Runeson, P., Höst, M.: Experimentation in software engineering: An introduction. Kluwer Academic, Dordrecht (2000)

University-Industry Collaboration Journey towards Product Lines

Stan Jarzabek[1], Ulf Pettersson[2], and Hongyu Zhang[3]

[1] School of Computing, National Univerisity of Singapore, Singapore
stan@comp.nus.edu.sg
[2] Technology Office, ST Electronics (Info-Software Systems) Pte. Ltd.
ulfp@stee.stengg.com
[3] School of Software, Tsinghua University, Beijing 100084, China
hongyu@tsinghua.edu.cn

Abstract. Product Lines for mission critical Command and Control systems was a starting point for a long lasting research collaboration between National University of Singapore (NUS) and ST Electronics (Info-Software Systems) Pte Ltd (STEE-InfoSoft). Collaboration was intensified by a joint research project, also involving University of Waterloo and Netron Inc. that led to development of reuse technology called XVCL. The contribution of this paper is twofold: First, we describe collaboration modes, factors that were critical to sustain collaboration, and benefits for university and industry gained over years. Among the main benefits, STEE-InfoSoft advanced its reuse practice by applying XVCL in several software Product Line projects, while NUS team received early feedback from STEE-InfoSoft which helped refine XVCL reuse methods and keep academic research in sync with industrial realities. Academic findings and industrial pilots have opened new unexpected research directions. Second, we draw lessons learned from many projects, to explain the general nature and significance of problems addressed with the XVCL approach.

Keywords: Software Product Lines, Industry collaboration, Variability management, Generative technique.

1 Introduction

Even though component-based reuse has yielded significant benefits in the past, the depth of success in the industry has been rather limited. While there are reuse success stories, even advanced Product Line reuse approach [6][7] has not penetrated the industrial software development deep enough to become a standard practice. Some problems with realizing reuse strategies have been reported [10].

ST Electronics (Info-Software Systems) Pte Ltd (STEE-InfoSoft) is a Singapore-based company developing turn-key software solutions in a wide range of domains, for local and international markets including defense and home-land security applications. In 1998, STEE-InfoSoft started a programme to develop a Common Application Platform (CAP) with the objective of providing fast and cost effective customized solutions in the Command and Control domain. Around the same time, a

K. Schmid (Ed.): ICSR 2011, LNCS 6727, pp. 223–237, 2011.
© Springer-Verlag Berlin Heidelberg 2011

collaboration agreement was signed between STEE-InfoSoft and National University of Singapore (NUS), as a vehicle for joint research. As a result, students from NUS were attached to the company to help in development of CAP.

CAP was built to form a foundation of reusable components designed to serve as low-level reuse libraries as well as higher-level services designed to facilitate implementation of design patterns. Even though the reuse solutions developed for CAP have been used in many projects across STEE-InfoSoft, and the programme has been considered as a big success, certain weaknesses of component-based reuse have been also exposed.

In particular, as STEE-InfoSoft deployed its reusable components to different customers, specific adaptations were often required in areas of business logic and almost always in the area of user interface. To address such customer specific variations, the underlying component platforms and conventional design techniques proved ineffective in defining generic solutions to avoid explosion of many similar components. Because of these difficulties, the reuse of CAP solutions was limited to functional areas where variations were few and could be easily managed with conventional design techniques, while for other areas cut-paste-modify was applied resulting in explosion of similar components. For those reasons, without complementary techniques, the component-based approach would not have been able to keep up with the customer evolving expectations of shorter time to market and more cost effective solutions.

We believe challenges that STEE-InfoSoft experienced to some extent affect other attempts to implement reuse strategies. Component-based reuse facilitated by modern component platforms is mostly limited to common services and middleware layers. Reuse potentials on a system-wide scale, especially in the application domain-specific areas of business logic and user interfaces, are more difficult to realize with component-based techniques. Furthermore, in our experience, the benefits of reuse and component platforms are mainly observed during new development, but are less evident in long-term evolution of successful products.

In an effort to overcome identified problems and better address customer expectations, STEE-InfoSoft and NUS teamed up with Netron Inc. (Toronto) and University of Waterloo to start a joint Singapore-Ontario research project in the area of "Software Reuse Framework for Reliable Mission-Critical Systems". Our intention was to evolve the frame-based Product Line techniques [3] used by Netron into a new language-independent and modern platform contexts, to facilitate development of Command and Control (C2) Product Lines. The result of this project was the XVCL language [21][12], the XVCL Processor and also the first pilot application of XVCL by STEE-InfoSoft in a C2 Environment.

By June 2002, the Singapore-Ontario project was over, but NUS and STEE-InfoSoft continued their collaboration at an increasing intensity level, even though the collaboration no longer was driven by any specific research project agreement. This collaboration resulted in several interesting XVCL projects that will be described in Section 4.

The contribution of this paper is twofold: *First*, we distil lessons-learned from 10-years of our project collaboration, focusing on collaboration modes, factors that were critical to sustain collaboration, and benefits for university and industry gained over years. Among the main benefits, STEE-InfoSoft advanced its reuse practice by applying XVCL in several software Product Line projects, while NUS team received early feedback from STEE-InfoSoft which helped refine XVCL reuse methods and keep academic research in sync with industrial realities. Academic findings and industrial pilots have opened new unexpected research directions.

Second, we generalize experiences from many projects, most of which we described in earlier papers. Based on that, we explain the general nature, significance and unique contribution of XVCL to the today's toolbox of software methods, and argue about the merits of the XVCL approach on a more general ground than we could do in earlier papers.

In Sections 2, we describe the history and models of our collaboration. In Section 3, we explain the process that led to formulation and application of variability technique of XVCL that was subject of our collaboration. In Section 4, we recap experiences from several projects with XVCL, highlighting the impact of the results and trade-offs involved in application of XVCL. We summarize lessons learned in Section 5. Conclusions end the paper.

2 The History of Collaboration

2.1 First Phase: MOU

Our collaboration started in 1998 when a Memorandum Of Understanding (MOU) was established between the School of Computing at the National University of Singapore (later referred to as NUS) and ST Electronics (Info-Software Systems) Pte Ltd (later referred to as STEE-InfoSoft).

Initial collaboration was facilitated through an Industrial Attachment, where Honours and Master students were attached to STEE-InfoSoft for research projects related to reuse frameworks. First few projects were focused on reliable use of DCOM (http://msdn.microsoft.com/library/) in Mission Critical Command and Control Systems. These first projects delivered concrete and useful benefits to both sides, helping STEE-InfoSoft in technology selection and helping NUS to bring industry-related projects to their students. Positive experiences acted as a booster for the collaborative spirit and brought the two sides closer together looking for more and bigger exploration in the area of Product Lines.

2.2 Second Phase: Singapore-Ontario Project

The governments of Singapore and Ontario, Canada, have established a joint research programme to boost collaboration among universities, and involving industrial partners from both countries. Under this research scheme, in 2000, we started a project to investigate methods for cost-effective, reuse-based development of reliable mission-critical software systems. The project involved four partners, namely NUS, STEE-InfoSoft, Netron Inc. (Toronto), and University of Waterloo. NUS provided software engineering and reuse expertise. University of Waterloo contributed in areas of software reliability – failure detection, fault tolerance and availability. STEE-InfoSoft has been developing command and control mission-critical systems for customers in Singapore (such as Ministry of Defense, police and civil defense) as well as abroad, and had extensive experience in mission-critical system domain.

STEE-InfoSoft was also a potential client for the technology we intended to develop in this project. Our Canadian industrial partner, Netron, Inc. contributed to our project with reuse tools and their rich experience in implementing reuse solutions in companies.

Before formulating the joint project proposal, we had already established a working relationship among project partners, though not all four of them together and not in the exact scope of the proposed project. NUS and University of Waterloo had been planning to pursue joint research on the interplay between reuse and reliability, during sabbatical leave of one of the authors at the University of Waterloo. As mentioned earlier, the link between STEE-InfoSoft and NUS was already established through the MOU and close collaboration was already in place. Finally, the NUS team worked with Frame Technology developed by Netron, Inc. before the joint Singapore-Ontario project, and had accumulated experiences in that area and described them in publications. These existing links helped a lot the four partners in two countries agree on common research goal, and on the approach to working towards the goal.

As our project progressed, the following three focus areas emerged:

> Definition of the XVCL language.
> Implementation of the XVCL Processor [21].
> XVCL-based pilot project [17].

Definition of the XVCL language was facilitated primarily through collaboration between NUS and Netron, where Netron shared their use of frame technologies both through visits to Singapore and through short attachments of NUS students at their Toronto office. The frame-related experiences and feedback provided by Netron (and in particular by Paul Bassett) was essential to the successful definition of a simple yet practical XVCL language.

Implementation of the XVCL Processor was done by students at NUS. As we chose XML as a vehicle for defining and then implementing XVCL, we could benefit from use of open-source components. In 2002, the resulting processor was also made public at SourceForge [21].

Experimentation with XVCL-based Product Lines was done through a pilot project for Computer Aided Dispatch (CAD) in the domain of Police and Fire emergency dispatch. This pilot project started with definition of use cases and study of feature variants both within a police system but also across other areas of the civil defense domain. We worked with software requirements (use cases). Use cases abstracted from real-world projects, contributed by the STEE-InfoSoft, established an understanding of requirements, while NUS students explored how XVCL could be applied to handle feature variants across the Product Line. Implementation was done jointly by NUS students and STEE-InfoSoft staff. The pilot project demonstrated that the XVCL approach was very capable of handling variants in CAD Product Lines, and the result formed an incubator for new experimentation and application of the XVCL technique.

These empirical studies were instrumental in gaining insights into the design of "flexible software", i.e., software that is easy to change and adapt to fit various reuse contexts. We tested the limits of what could be achieved to this end by conventional architecture-centric, OO and component-based programming techniques, and with this understanding it became possible to observe the value of meta-level enhancements implemented into the XVCL method.

In Singapore, overall control and evolution was facilitated through weekly (or bi weekly) research working sessions with participation from both NUS and STEE-InfoSoft. These sessions served as communication channel where:

➢ Result, ideas and findings were shared.
➢ Feedback was provided.
➢ Future work was brainstormed and outlined.

Working sessions served as a vehicle for sharing of experiences and findings well before publications were written, resulting in faster and more agile direction changes. We believe it helped us a lot to accelerate and effectively shape our research.

Initial sessions focused on clarifying requirements and documenting them in a standard way. Subsequent sessions concentrated on discussing novel approaches to modeling "requirements with variants" [15], as it was needed for reuse via Product Line approach, and on novel techniques for designing generic software architectures, capable of handling variant requirements in an effective and simple way.

Working sessions played an increasingly important coordination role as over time, more and more parallel and incremental projects branched out from the second phase.

Finally, working sessions have helped us to strengthen the partnership between NUS and STEE-InfoSoft, and served as a vehicle for continued collaboration beyond the second phase. Through these meetings, the collaboration entered into a third phase, where new projects were initiated, executed and shared without any formal agreement between the parties (apart from the general MOU).

2.3 Third Phase: Continuous Collaboration

In the third phase (still ongoing), we leverage on the XVCL technique to explore Product Lines and reuse in various domains, and we also venture into other research areas inspired by results we were getting on the way. The projects of the third phase are described in later sections, once we have briefly explained motivation and concepts of a XVCL approach to software development.

3 The Development of the XVCL Approach

In this section, we describe the role of our collaboration in development of the XVCL approach to variability management in software Product Lines. The three phases in XVCL development correspond to the three phases of our collaboration described in the previous section.

3.1 Initial Phase

In this phase, the idea of XVCL was initially formulated. XVCL is based on principles of Frame Technology™ by Netron, Inc. [3]. A number of frame-based systems have been implemented in industry and at universities, and we believe any of those systems can handle engineering problems we addressed in our projects. Frames have been extensively applied to maintain multi-million-line COBOL-based information systems. An independent assessment by QSM Associates, Inc. showed that frames could achieve up to 90% reuse, reduce project costs by over 84% and their time-to-market by 70%, when compared to industry norms [3].

The successes of Frame Technology motivated us to explore it further. Designed in 1970s and 1980s, frame commands and tools are very much influenced by the COBOL language and do not address many contemporary design methods and language features. Frame technology should be enhanced to blend into contemporary software development practices (such as architecture-centric, component-based product line development). We thus proposed XVCL to refines frame concepts into a general-purpose language and tool. XVCL can be applied on top of the contemporary programming paradigms to achieve enhanced flexibility and genericity. We also planned to apply XVCL to the practices of STEE-InfoSoft.

3.2 Second Phase

In this phase, the idea of XVCL was developed. In our studies, we found that similarities are omnipresent in software. We repeatedly apply similar design solutions to solve similar problems. In new, well-designed programs, we often find 50%-90% of code contained in similar program structures of various types and granularity, repeated many times (often called clones in the literature). For example, the extent of the redundant code in Java Buffer library was 68% [13], in parts of STL (C++) - over 50% [2], in J2EE Web Portals – 61% [22], and in certain ASP Web portal modules – up to 90% [17]. Similar results have been observed in studies of Open Source web projects [19]. Most of the repetitions that we found represented some important concepts from requirement or design spaces. In our judgment, repetitions were counter-productive for maintenance and signified untapped reuse opportunities.

Software similarities, especially large granularity, design-level similarity patterns, create opportunities for reuse within a given system, or even across similar systems. Unfortunately, at times, conventional methods – component based, architecture-centric approaches as well as language-level features such as generics – fail to provide effective means to reap benefits offered by software similarities. Common sense suggests that we should be able to express our design and code without unwanted repetitions, whenever we wish to do so.

The goal of XVCL is to provide a systematic treatment for the above problems. Developers still use one of the programming languages to define the behavioral core of their program solutions (e.g., user interfaces, business logic or databases). However, when repetitions become evidently counter-productive, and conventional techniques are not sufficient to achieve generic design, rather than using ad hoc solutions, developers can escape to the well thought-out mechanisms to deal with the problem. XVCL defines such mechanisms. XVCL complements conventional OO, component-based and modularization techniques to fully exploit the engineering potential of software similarities.

With XVCL, we represent each group of recurring similar program structures of significant importance with a *generic, adaptable structure*. XVCL representation maintains a complete picture of similarities and differences among specific program structures, instances of the generic structure, as well as their location in a program.

Variations among instances are specified as deltas from the generic structure and automatically propagated to the respective instances. These specifications are both human-readable and executable by the XVCL Processor. Based on the specifications, the Processor adapts generic structures to generate specific program structures in their required variant forms.

3.3 Third Phase

In this phase, we applied XVCL to several projects, including:

➤ Application of XVCL to strengthen conventional OO techniques in the area of generic design, demonstrated in studies on unifying similarity patterns in Java Buffer library [13] and STL [2].
➤ Application of XVCL to support a Web Portal Product Line [17] in Active Server Pages (http://msdn.microsoft.com/library/) environment.
➤ Application of XVCL for reconstruction and reuse within Web Portals in J2EE™ environment [22].
➤ Application of XVCL to manage variability in a role-playing game Product Line for mobile devices [24], which demonstrated that reuse may go hand-in-hand with improving, rather than compromising, the performance.
➤ Techniques for detecting design-level similar program structures, so-called structural clones [1], which extended current techniques focusing mainly on detecting similar code fragments.

The above projects already applied good practices of conventional software design, before considering XVCL. Still, the XVCL helped us to raise reuse rates, typically by 60%, which also led to significant simplification of the subject software and productivity improvements. These encouraging results triggered exploration into other research areas such as: tools/techniques to identify, classify and understand design-level similarity patterns in legacy code [1], tools for XVCL development (such as smart editor, static/dynamic analyzer, and debugger), and XVCL language integration into Integrated Development Environments such as Visual Studio .NET™ and JBuilder™.

4 Summary of Typical Projects

To highlight the significance of our results, we briefly discuss representative projects and variability problems we tackled with XVCL. The first project initiated our collaboration; in the second one, we show how variability technique can enhance design of class libraries; in the third project, STEE-InfoSoft's applied XVCL to manage variability in Web Portal Product Line.

4.1 Pilot CAD project

Internet-enabled Computer Aided Dispatch Systems (CAD for short) was our first pilot project. Fig. 1 depicts a basic operational scenario in a CAD system for Police. An Operator receives information about an incident and informs a Dispatcher about the incident. The Dispatcher examines the "Situation Display" that shows a map of the area where the incident happened. Then, the Dispatcher assigns a task of handling the incident to a Police Unit taking into account the distance of a Unit to the place of incident and possibly other criteria. The Police Unit approaches the place of incident and handles the problem. The Police Unit informs the Task Manager about the progress of action. The Task Manager monitors the situation and at the end – closes the case. The information about current and past incidents is stored in the database.

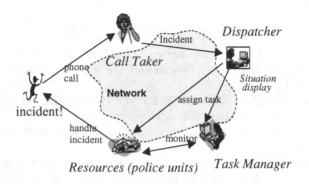

Fig. 1. CAD system for Police

CAD systems are used by police, fire & rescue, and health organizations. At the basic operational level, all CAD systems are similar – basically, they support the dispatch of units to incidents. However, there are also differences across CAD systems. The specific context of the operation (such as police or fire & rescue) results in many variations on the basic operational scheme. For example, CAD systems differ in rules of how resources are assigned to tasks, monitoring, reporting and timing requirements, specific information to be stored in a database, system component deployment strategies, reliability and availability requirements, and so on. If we ignore commonalities, then each CAD system in a specific context becomes a unique application that must be developed from scratch and maintained as a separate product – an expensive and inefficient solution. In our project, we applied a Product Line approach [6][7] to exploit commonalities and engineer CAD systems from a common base of reusable software assets, so-called Product Line architecture. We expected such a reuse-based approach to radically cut development and maintenance cost.

CAD systems offer high potential for reuse and, at the same time, pose important challenges for reliability. A typical CAD system must be pretty reliable – for example, 999 call reports should never be lost. So cost reduction must not come at the expense of reliability. CAD project allowed us to understand the interplay between reuse and reliability.

Basing CAD systems on internet, while meeting their real-time and reliability requirements in a manner that would allow high degree of software reuse posed significant research challenges for the project. Given that, and also the fact that we were applying XVCL for the first time, we kept the scope of CAD project simple: Java/XVCL CAD Product Line architecture contained 82 x-frames unifying groups of similar components in user interface and business logic layers. We addressed 24 variants that differentiated CAD systems. In each of the two new CAD systems developed based on the Java/XVCL Product Line architecture we achieved reuse ratios of 84%. Reuse ratio is defined as (Reused LOC) / (Total CAD LOC)*100%), where LOC are physical lines of code without blanks or comments. Further details of this project are described in [23].

The CAD project played two roles: First, it established trust and effective modes of collaboration among parties. We got a sense of benefits that collaboration could bring on both ends. Second, we could observe the strengths of conventional component-based techniques to support reuse, and also their limits in exploiting similarity patterns by means of generic design. We understood how mixed XVCL could help us overcome some of those limits.

4.2 Java Buffer Library and STL

These two projects allowed us to better see the roots of the similarity phenomenon and understand the essence of the problem we were addressing with XVCL in the context of OO techniques such as generics (or templates in C++), inheritance, abstract classes and dynamic binding. As we have described these results in detail in other publications [13][2], here we only recap the main findings.

Classes in the Buffer library JDK 1.5 differ in features such as a memory scheme: Heap or Direct; element type: byte, char, int, double, float, long, or short; access mode: writable or read-only; byte ordering: S – non-native or U – native; B – BigEndian or L – LittleEndian. Each legal combination of features yields a unique buffer class, with much similarity among classes. Analysis of similarity patterns in the Buffer library revealed seven groups of classes, each containing 7-13 classes similar to each other. Most of the variations among similar classes could be traced to feature combinations affecting classes or methods. Many similar classes or methods occurred due to the inability to unify variations in otherwise the same classes or methods.

Furthermore, any attempt to unify similarities would have to be synergistic with other design goals such as usability, conceptual clarity and good performance of buffer classes. In some situations, designers could introduce a new abstract class or a suitable design pattern to avoid repetitions. However, such a solution would compromise these goals, and therefore was not implemented. Java generics proved not effective in unifying similar classes either [13].

In a Java/XVCL solution, we could unify classes in each of the seven groups with generic x-frames. XVCL Processor generated Buffer classes from the Buffer class x-framework. This unification reduced program complexity as perceived by developers, also reducing the original code size by 68% percent. A controlled maintenance experiment revealed higher effort to maintain the original Buffer library as compared to its Java/XVCL representation: For example, the number of modifications to implement a new Complex buffer in Java/XVCL representation was 11, as compared to 91 modifications required for the same purpose in the original Java classes. Non-redundancy achieved by unifying similar classes made modifications easier, enhancing the visibility of ripple effects, and reducing the risk of update anomalies.

The Standard Template Library (STL) strengthened observations made in the Buffer Library [2]. Parameterization mechanism of C++ templates is more powerful than that of Java generics, due to light integration of templates with the C++ language core. STL uses the most advanced template features and design solutions (e.g., iterators), and is widely accepted in the research and industrial communities as a premier example of a generic programming methodology.

Still, we found much repetitions in some STL areas that could not be unified with conventional techniques. For example, four 'sorted' associative containers and four 'hashed' associative containers could be unified with two generic C++/XVCL containers, achieving 57% reduction in the related code. Stack and queue contained 37% of cloned code. Algorithms set union, intersection, difference, and symmetric difference (along with their overloaded versions) formed a set of eight clones that could be unified by a generic XVCL set operation, eliminating 52% of code.

4.3 Industrial Applications of XVCL

Web Portal (WP) Product Line was the first STEE-InfoSoft's application of XVCL in a business product and on a wider scale. A Team Collaboration Portal (TCP) was a starting point for this project. TCP was implemented in ASP. STEE-InfoSoft applied state-of-the-art design methods to maximize reusability of TCP in other contexts. Still, a number of problem areas were observed that could be improved by applying XVCL to increase the genericity of a conventional solution. The benefits of an ASP/XVCL solution for TCP were the following:

➤ Short time (less than 2 weeks) and small effort (2 persons) to transform the TCP into the first version of the ASP/XVCL solution.
➤ High productivity in building new portals from the ASP/XVCL solution. Based on the ASP/XVCL solution, STEE-InfoSoft could build new portal modules by writing as little as 10% of unique custom code, while the rest of code could be reused. This code reduction translated into an estimated eight-fold reduction of effort required to build new portals.
➤ Significant reduction of maintenance effort when enhancing individual portals. The overall managed code lines for nine portals were 22% less than the original single portal.
➤ Wide range of portals differing in a large number of inter-dependent features supported by the ASP/XVCL solution.

The reader may find full details of this project in [17]. In another industrial project, XVCL was applied to manage variability in a role-playing game Product Line for mobile devices [24]. This project demonstrated that reuse may go hand-in-hand with improving, rather than compromising, the performance.

4.4 Discussion of Project Experiences: Benefits and Trade-Offs

We believe the benefits observed in the above projects are not accidental, but are the result of effective treatment of some problems that are not easily solved with programming language and component platform mechanisms. At the same time, these problems have significant impact on software productivity.

With XVCL, we represent each of the important groups of similar program structures in a unique generic, but adaptable form, along with the information necessary to obtain its instances (i.e., specific program structures). Such a non-redundant program view reduces program complexity as perceived by developers, and reduces the risk of update anomalies which helps in maintenance. At the same time, non-redundancy is difficult to achieve with architecture-centric and component approaches alone.

XVCL program representation contains much information about program design that is useful for maintenance and reuse, in the form that is fully integrated with complete information about the subject program(s) itself. This, for example, includes explicit representation of a program design in terms of its subsystems, architecture, component layers, components and classes, down to every detail of code implementing the above program structures.

As a variation technique in the design of Software Product Line core assets, XVCL allows domain engineers to clearly mark the impact of variant features on product architecture and code components. Product developers can trace and understand this impact, and then use XVCL Processor to automatically generate custom products with required features.

An important add-in value that XVCL brings to component-based reuse is its ability to handle product-specific variants separately from generic, reusable components. This unique feature of XVCL allows developers to evolve the many products we have derived from the generic components according to the specific needs of their customers, without ever disconnecting them from the generic components. Product-specific variants do not pollute generic components, and do not affect other products derived from those components, if this is not required. This feature, along with the ability to represent any group of similar programs structures in a generic, adaptable form allows XVCL to exploit reuse opportunities that are often missed by conventional component-based design techniques.

Conventional component-based reuse is most effective when combined with architecture-centric, pattern-driven development which is now supported by the major platforms (such as .NET™ and J2EE™). Patterns lead to beneficial standardization of program solutions and are basic means to achieve reuse of common service components. Our projects demonstrated that further improvements are possible by applying XVCL on top of these modern development practices. By packaging patterns into XVCL structures we enhance the visibility of pattern application. In particular, XVCL representation shows the exact location of pattern application, as well as the exact differences among pattern instances in a program.

Industrial applications have demonstrated that XVCL technique is easy and fast to learn, and its benefit may outweigh the cost of the added complexity [17]. At the same time, the return on investment may be quick and substantial. Industrial applications have also revealed a number of further problems. Flexibility that we gain with XVCL does not come for free. As we relax the coupling between the parameterization mechanism and the rules (syntax and semantics) of the underlying programming language, the power of the parameterization mechanism increases. We can address genericity concerns without compromising program runtime properties. But as we move towards less restrictive parameterization mechanisms, we also decrease type-safety of parameterized program solutions.

Designing generic, reusable and maintainable solutions is always a challenge which requires more talent and skill than building a concrete program. XVCL is not a substitute for thinking, on contrary, it requires more thinking and up-front investment for future benefits. XVCL targets at long-lived programs that undergo extensive evolutionary changes, or need be tailored to needs of multiple customers.

XVCL software representation is expressed at two inter-mixed levels, in base programming language(s) and XVCL. This creates extra difficulties, especially for debugging. However, we must keep in mind that XVCL representation contains much useful information for maintenance and reuse, in addition to complete information about the subject program(s) itself. There is a great opportunity here for XVCL-support tools to help developers work with XVCL software representation.

The current form of XVCL can be seen as an assembly language for generic design. XVCL's explicit and direct articulation is the source of its expressive power, e.g., we can unify arbitrary types of variations across similar program structures, but it also adds a certain amount of complexity to the problem. Specification, analysis and validation methods for XVCL representations are yet to be discovered.

Engineering processes play an important role in industrial software development. Currently, we know how XVCL-enabled solutions can raise productivity of small teams of highly-skilled expert software developers. We have yet to learn what it takes to inject XVCL into more complex team structures and industrial development processes. Working on those issues is an important direction for our future work, but we realize difficulties involved.

Adopting a new technique always brings some overheads and XVCL is no different. It is essential to understand and evaluate trade-offs involved. In future we will also focus on empirical studies in various application domains and interpretation of the results and comparative studies of XVCL.

Other generative techniques such as AOP [16], MDSC [20] or AHEAD [5], exploit separation of concerns as means to simplify software development and maintenance. Separation of concerns makes software components more generic, reusable in multiple contexts, and easier to maintain. XVCL shares similar engineering goals with other generative techniques, but uses different means to achieve these goals. The emphasis on identifying any kinds of similarity patterns, and capability to unify arbitrary differences among similar program structures is a unique characteristic and contribution of XVCL, and frame principles in general.

5   Lessons Learned

We learned the following lessons from our collaboration:

- **The importance of early feedback on research progress from industry:** From the beginning of the project, we worked with requirements provided by our industry partner. We worked together on technical solutions, and on method formulation. Industry partner shared with research team the knowledge and constraints of industry practices which helped us modify our approach early to stay relevant to practice. We were meeting regularly, getting invaluable feedback. We think these were critical factors that allowed us to progress fast. Everybody involved in the project was benefiting. One PhD thesis, six Master thesis and many undergraduate research projects were completed during the initial three years of our collaboration, and many more sparked from the initial results. Three students involved in project were subsequently employed by ST Electronics (Info-Software Systems). Undergraduate students worked as interns in the company. The project responsibilities did not delay their degrees. On the contrary, helped them faster complete their theses. The fact that we could evaluate the effectiveness of our approach in real industrial environment could appear difficult initially, but was most beneficial in long run. In the course of our collaboration, STEE-InfoSoft advanced its reuse practice by applying XVCL in several software product line projects. NUS team received early feedback from STEE-InfoSoft which helped refine XVCL reuse methods and keep academic research in sync with industrial realities. Academic findings and industrial pilots have guided our research in new unexpected directions.

- **Broad, fundamental research base for collaboration:** Our collaboration evolved around reuse techniques for software Product Lines, a very broad and fundamental research theme, encompassing domain modelling, conventional design methods and variability management, in our case, realized by XVCL. XVCL is to software engineering what a Generic Application Platform is to software development. It is foundation method that can be applied on many technologies and application domains such as Command and Control, Web, or Hand held Applications. This characteristic helped us find a continuous flow of new projects and sustain collaborative research. This characteristic allowed us to progress from one project to another in cycles involving working on a project, assessing the results, extraction of ideas and formulating spin-off-new-project. Each time we learned something, we got ideas about new areas where benefits of XVCL might be significant. We think that in case of narrower, less fundamental (and more vertical) themes for collaborative research it may be difficult to sustain and find new projects time-after-time.

- **Free, problem-oriented, result-driven collaboration style:** It is most important to work on problems of mutual interest and benefit. Our collaboration was fueled by mutual interest of academic and industry partners in project findings. We believe this was a single most important factor to sustain high level of enthusiasm for collaboration in long-term. Often collaboration between university and industry is restricted to a certain topic/theme, with a well-planned schedule. Our collaboration was in a fairly informal, problem-oriented way, focusing on specific projects around XVCL. We made very little long-term plans for our collaborative work. We let the results so far and the current needs drive the selection of projects we embarked on. Such a relaxed and open attitude towards collaboration requires much trust. In return, we can always focus on our strengths, and not miss the best opportunities that current situation has to offer. For example, STEE-InfoSoft applied XVCL to support a Web Portal Product Line under unexpected business pressure, without much prior planning. The results were so good that NUS initiated a number of research studies in the Web domain that revealed unique opportunities for our techniques in this new domain. In a short time, we advanced our understanding of the interplay and synergy between advanced Web technologies and our technique, and learned what it took to turn these findings into further improvements of our approach.

- **The importance of effective communication:** Industrial people tend to describe problems in pragmatic terms, while academic people tend to use "jargons" from recent research conferences or journals. Therefore, it is important to achieve effective communications so that each party can understand the other's concerns and appreciate the other's efforts. Furthermore, our project involved people from multiple countries (Singaporean, Polish-Canadian, Swedish, Chinese, Myanmar, etc.), with different languages, social and cultural backgrounds. The multi-cultural/country aspect collectively gave us a broader brain-base for ideas thus also contributing to the spin-off of more projects. But such diverse backgrounds influence the way people think, feel, and act under different circumstances. This may create communication challenges. Establishing effective communication channels is important for a multi-national collaboration project like ours to succeed. Frequent face-to-face discussions and social events allowing team members interact in relaxed and informal setting helped us build mutual understanding, trust and team spirit.

6 Conclusions

This experience report documents ten years of university-industry collaboration between National university of Singapore and ST Electronics (Info-Software Systems) Pte. Ltd. The project was of mutual interest and brought benefits for both sides. In particular, collaboration led to industrial application of variability technique developed at the university. Numerous graduate (PhD and Master) thesis and undergraduate research projects benefited from collaboration. Three students involved in project were subsequently employed by STEE-InfoSoft. We hope that our experiences and lesson learned described in the paper can be beneficial to others.

Acknowledgments

We thank STEE-InfoSoft staff and NUS students who participated in various phases of our collaborative project. Paul Bassett's advice was invaluable in formalizing XVCL and understanding its applications.

References

1. Basit, A.H., Jarzabek, S.: Detecting Higher-level Similarity Patterns in Programs. In: European Software Engineering Conference and ACM SIGSOFT Symposium on the Foundations of Software Engineering, ESEC-FSE 2005, Lisbon, pp. 156–165. ACM Press, New York (2005)
2. Basit, H.A., Rajapakse, D.C., Jarzabek, S.: Beyond Templates: a Study of Clones in the STL and Some General Implications. In: Int. Conf. Software Engineering, ICSE 2005, St. Louis, USA, pp. 451–459 (May 2005)
3. Bassett, P.: Framing software reuse - lessons from real world. Yourdon Press, Prentice Hall (1997)
4. Batory, D., Singhai, V., Sirkin, M., Thomas, J.: Scalable software libraries. In: ACM SIGSOFT 1993: Symp. on the Foundations of Software Engineering, Los Angeles, California, pp. 191–199 (December 1993)
5. Batory, D., Sarvela, J.N., Rauschmayer, A.: Scaling Step-Wise Refinement. In: Proc. Int. Conf. on Software Engineering, ICSE 2003, Portland, Oregon, pp. 187–197 (May 2003)
6. Bosch, J.: Design and Use of Software Architectures – Adopting and evolving a product-line approach. Addison-Wesley, Reading (2000)
7. Clements, P., Northrop, L.: Software Product Lines: Practices and Patterns. Addison-Wesley, Reading (2002)

8. Czarnecki, K., Eisenecker, U.: Generative Programming: Methods, Tools, and Applications. Addison-Wesley, Reading (2000)
9. CPG-Nuke home, http://www.cpgnuke.com/
10. Deelstra, S., Sinnema, M., Bosch, J.: Experiences in Software Product Families: Problems and Issues During Product Derivation. In: Nord, R.L. (ed.) SPLC 2004. LNCS, vol. 3154, pp. 165–182. Springer, Heidelberg (2004)
11. Gamma, E., Helm, R., Johnson, R., Vlissides, J.: Design Patterns – Elements of Reusable Object-Oriented Software. Addison-Wesley, Reading (1995)
12. Jarzabek, S.: Effective Software Maintenance and Evolution: Reuse-based Approach. CRC Press. Taylor & Francis (2007)
13. Jarzabek, S., Li, S.: Eliminating Redundancies with a "Composition with Adaptation" Meta-programming Technique. In: Proc. of ESEC-FSE 2003, European Software Engineering Conf. and ACM SIGSOFT Symp. on the Foundations of Software Engineering, Helsinki, pp. 237–246. ACM Press, New York (2003)
14. Jarzabek, S., Seviora, R.: Engineering components for ease of customization and evolution. IEE Proceedings - Software 147(6), 237–248 (2000); a special issue on Component-based Software Engineering
15. Jarzabek, S., Zhang, H.: XML-based Method and Tool for Handling Variant Requirements in Domain Models. In: Proc. 5th International Symposium on Requirements Engineering, RE 2001, Toronto, Canada, pp. 166–173 (August 2001)
16. Kiczales, G., Lamping, J., Mendhekar, A., Maeda, C., Lopes, C., Loingtier, J.-M., Irwin, J.: Aspect-Oriented Programming. In: Liu, Y., Auletta, V. (eds.) ECOOP 1997. LNCS, vol. 1241, pp. 220–242. Springer, Heidelberg (1997)
17. Pettersson, U., Jarzabek, S.: Industrial Experience with Building a Web Portal Product Line using a Lightweight, Reactive Approach. In: Europ. Soft. Eng. Conf. and Symp. on the Foundations of Software Engineering, ESEC-FSE 2005, Lisbon, pp. 326–335. ACM Press, New York (2005)
18. Rajapakse, D.C., Jarzabek, S.: Using Server Pages to Unify Clones in Web Applications: A Trade-off Analysis. In: Int. Conf. Software Engineering, ICSE 2007, Minneapolis, USA (May 2007)
19. Rajapakse, D., Jarzabek, S.: An Investigation of Cloning in Web Portals. In: Int. Conf. on Web Engineering, Sydney (July 2005); also poster at WWW 2005
20. Tarr, P., Ossher, H., Harrison, W., Sutton, S.: N Degrees of Separation: Multi-Dimensional Separation of Concerns. In: Proc. International Conference on Software Engineering, ICSE 1999, Los Angeles, pp. 107–119 (1999)
21. XML-based Variant Configuration Language, http://xvcl.comp.nus.edu.sg
22. Yang, J., Jarzabek, S.: Applying a Generative Technique for Enhanced Genericity and Maintainability on the J2EE Platform. In: Glück, R., Lowry, M. (eds.) GPCE 2005. LNCS, vol. 3676, pp. 237–255. Springer, Heidelberg (2005)
23. Zhang, H., Jarzabek, S.: A Mechanism for Handling Variants in Software Product Lines. Special Issue on Software Variability Management, Science of Computer Programming 53(3), 255–436 (2004)
24. Zhang, W., Jarzabek, S.: Reuse without Compromising Performance: Industrial Experience from RPG Software Product Line for Mobile Devices. In: Obbink, H., Pohl, K. (eds.) SPLC 2005. LNCS, vol. 3714, pp. 57–69. Springer, Heidelberg (2005)

1ˢᵗ International ICSR Workshop on Comparing Software Retrieval Approaches (CORA)

Oliver Hummel and Werner Janjic

Software Engineering Group, University of Mannheim
68131 Mannheim, Germany
{hummel,janjic}@informatik.uni-mannheim.de
http://swt.informatik.uni-mannheim.de

Abstract. For the first time in more than four decades, the recent advent of the open source movement and the availability of service-oriented architectures has enabled researchers in software reuse to collect a larger amount of potentially reusable software artifacts. Hence, various communities have recently developed a new wave of interesting software and service search, retrieval and matching approaches. However, to date most of these approaches have been created independently from each other and are evaluated on proprietary data only. Thus, their performance is not easily comparable with each other (if at all). The goal of this workshop is to bring together researcher from the above communities and practitioners interested in applying the mentioned technologies in order to establish a common understanding of the challenges involved in evaluating software retrieval systems and a community working on solutions to overcome them. An important long-term goal is the creation of a reference collection with reusable material that can be used as a common baseline for the comparison of all kinds of software search, retrieval and matching tools.

1 Motivation

For more than four decades, immense benefits have been attributed to the reuse of software [1] and a large number of seminal software retrieval approaches have been developed mainly for this purpose [2]. The recent advent of the open source movement [3] and service-oriented architectures has triggered a new wave of interesting research in this direction. Clearly, all kinds of techniques for software search, retrieval and matching form an important foundation for the practical application of software reuse, but obviously, they can be applied in various other contexts as well: a specialized software search that goes beyond mere text matching, for instance, may be beneficial in other areas such as programming, program understanding, as well as for software evolution and maintenance etc. Furthermore, sophisticated retrieval and matching capabilities cannot only be used for source code, but for (binary) components, services and even test cases as well.

However, beyond infrequent initial efforts in collecting potential application scenarios [6][7], there has been neither a systematic collection of such scenarios nor a recent comprehensive evaluation of classic scenarios (such as component retrieval for

K. Schmid (Ed.): ICSR 2011, LNCS 6727, pp. 238–239, 2011.
© Springer-Verlag Berlin Heidelberg 2011

reuse). The last systematic work in this direction is almost 15 years old [2], but since then other communities also recognized that the ability to compare software retrieval and matching tools is important [5].

2 Goals and Conclusion

This workshop aims to bring together researchers and practitioners from numerous communities in order to collate innovative application scenarios for software search and retrieval and investigate effective ways of evaluating them. We especially welcome contributions that work towards a common baseline for a standard collection of software artifacts and benchmarks that can be used for future evaluation of software retrieval, reuse and evolution approaches. Nevertheless new application scenarios for software retrieval tools are as welcome as overviews and investigations of existing approaches and surveys of individual evaluations that have been performed so far.

The concrete goal of this first workshop on comparing software retrieval approaches is forming a platform for researchers and practitioners interested in the mentioned technologies and establishing a first overview of potential application scenarios. Depending on the interests of participants we also aim on discussing concrete evaluation strategies for some of these scenarios. Consider, for example, the recently proposed idea of creating an "internet-scale" reference collection of reusable artifacts [4] that suggests building on previous experience in related areas [5]. Nevertheless, it raises a number of interesting research challenges, such as the questions what are expressive as well as representative and thus useful queries for such a collection or when can a reuse candidate be considered as a relevant result for a given query at all? These questions can only be answered by a community of experts with different backgrounds that agrees upon challenges that can be used for comparing software retrieval approaches in the future.

References

1. Krueger, C.W.: Software Reuse. ACM Computing Surveys 24(2) (1992)
2. Mili, A., Mili, R., Mittermeir, R.: A Survey of Software Reuse Libraries. Annals of Software Engineering 5 (1998)
3. Hummel, O., Atkinson, C.: Using the Web as a Reuse Repository. In: Morisio, M. (ed.) ICSR 2006. LNCS, vol. 4039, pp. 298–311. Springer, Heidelberg (2006)
4. Hummel, O.: Facilitating the Comparison of Software Retrieval Systems through a Reference Reuse Collection. In: Int. Workshop on Search-Driven Development, SUITE 2010 (2010)
5. Küster, U., König-Ries, B.: Towards standard test collections for the empirical evaluation of semantic web service approaches. Int. Journal Semantic Computing 2(3) (2008)
6. Sim, S., Clarke, C., Holt, R.: Archetypal source code searches: A survey of software developers and maintainers. In: Int. Workshop on Program Comprehension (1998)
7. Janjic, W., Hummel, O., Atkinson, C.: More Archetypal Usage Scenarios for Software Search Engines. In: Int. Workshop on Search-Driven Development, SUITE 2010 (2010)

The 2nd International Workshop on Software Trustworthiness (SoTrust2011)

Xiaoguang Mao[1] and Bing Xie[2]

[1] School of Computer, National University of Defense Technology,
Changsha, Hunan, China
xgmao@nudt.edu.cn
[2] School of Electronics Engineering and Computer Science, Peking University,
Beijing, China
xiebing@sei.pku.edu.cn

Abstract. With the pervasive of computing facilities in people's work and daily life, humans run into a revolution in communication and thinking, which brings forward computing thinking and social computing. Humans are socially blind and unsure, and thus, trustworthiness has been put on the spot to answer questions including: Can computing facilities be trusted? Can information systems be dependable? Can unknown people in the other end be trustworthy? That's the motivation to establish a workshop named SoTrust. To assure trustworthiness in social computing, extensive reuse, of various resources such as components, services, product lines, patterns, frameworks and etc, is identified as a critical approach. SoTrust2011 aims at bringing together software scientists, industrial engineers, and researchers from different communities to discuss and exchange their new achievements, novel ideas, experiments, work-in-progress, and case studies in software trustworthiness with respect to reuse approaches. This year, SoTrust focuses on metrics and evaluation of software resource with respect to the property of trustworthiness; techniques and methodologies for the construction, reuse and evolution of trustworthy resources, and industrial experience.

1 Motivation

With the pervasive of computing facilities in people's work and daily life, humans run into a revolution in communication and thinking, which brings forward computing thinking and social computing. In the cyber space, being ties, humans are socially blind and unsure [1]. That is the reason why trustworthiness has been put on the spot these several years [2,3,4,5,6]. Trustworthiness is presented to answer questions such as: Can computing facilities be trusted? Can information systems be dependable? Can unknown people in the other end be trustworthy?

Extensive reuse of software resources has become an important contributor to trustworthiness among computing facilities. These software resources [7] can be components, services, product lines, patterns, frameworks and etc. How can software reuse approaches contribute to the trustworthiness of software systems? How can trustworthy systems rely on reused resources?

K. Schmid (Ed.): ICSR 2011, LNCS 6727, pp. 240–241, 2011.

2 Goals and Conclusion

SoTrust2011 is to bring together software scientists, industrial engineers, and researchers from different communities to discuss and exchange their new achievements, novel ideas, experiments, work-in-progress, and case studies in software trustworthiness with respect to reuse approaches.

SoTrust2011 is the next event of SoTrust2010, which was successfully held with ATC2010 [8] in China last year. The long-term goal of SoTrust is to establish a platform for researchers and engineers to exchange achievements and ideas on software trustworthiness, especially for ultra-scale software systems under the vision of social computing. This year, ICSR brings together outstanding researchers on software reuse, and gives SoTrust an opportunity to delve into solutions, on the direction of reusing various resources adaptively, for software trustworthiness. SoTrust2011 focuses on theoretical foundations, including metrics and evaluation of software resource with respect to the property of trustworthiness; techniques and methodologies, including the construction of trustworthy reusable resources and reuse approaches to enhance trustworthiness; and industrial experience in reusing software resources for trustworthiness. Besides, SoTrust2011 emphasizes reuse and evolution mechanism for the trustworthiness of on-service software systems, after deployed.

References

1. Social computing group of ibm research (October 2010), http://www.research. ibm.com/Social-Computing/index.html
2. Ifip 10.4 working group on dependable computing and fault tolerance (2010), http://www.dependability.org
3. Trusted computing group (2010), http://www.trustedcomputinggroup.org
4. High confidence software and systems coordinating group, interagency working group on information technology research and development, high confidence software and systems research needs (2001),
   http://www.itrd.gov/pubs/hcss-research.pdf
5. Microsoft trustworthy computing (2010),
   http://www.microsoft.com/twc
6. Trustworthiness in wiktionary (2010),
   http://en.wiktionary.org/wiki/trustworthiness
7. The trustie project (2011), http://www.trustie.net
8. The 1st international workshop on software trustworthiness (sotrust, 2010),
   http://www.nwpu.edu.cn/atc2010/Workshops/

The 5th International Workshop on Software Reuse and Safety

William B. Frakes[1] and John Favaro[2]

[1] Department of Computer Science, Virginia Tech,
7054 Haycock Rd., Falls Church VA 22043
frakes@cs.vt.edu
[2] Intecs SpA, Via Giannessi 5, 56100 Pisa, Italy
john.favaro@intecs.it

Abstract. There is one domain in which software reuse is looked upon with suspicion: the domain of safety critical systems. This workshop (http://www.favaro.net/john/RESAFE2011/) addresses the related issues, building upon the results of previous workshops. Updates to current activities in a number of safety-critical domains are discussed, ranging from space and railway to automotive and medical.

1 Safety Relevant Characteristics of Reusable Software

In her book Safeware, Leveson observes that a common problem in much current work in the area is the tendency to consider safety together with other nonfunctional properties such as reliability, availability, and dependability, leading to the impression that improvement in any of the other areas will automatically lead to improvements in its safety-related characteristics. But current standards for safety-critical software development insist on separate treatment of safety, requiring "safety lifecycles," separate safety analyses, and specific process-related roles for personnel among other issues – and special treatment of reuse in safety-critical development.

2 Roadmap for Research in Software Reuse and Safety

One contribution of this workshop is the identification of areas in which researchers can work to advance the state of the art with respect to reuse and safety, improving upon the roadmap developed in the preceding editions of this workshop. Current themes addressed in this edition include the relationship of software safety to architectural frameworks emerging in various safety-critical domains, as well as issues arising from the emergence of model-based development as a paradigm in many of these domains.

K. Schmid (Ed.): ICSR 2011, LNCS 6727, p. 242, 2011.

The Doctoral Symposium of the 12th International Conference of Software Reuse

Leonardo Gresta Paulino Murta

Computing Institute – Fluminense Federal University
Niterói, RJ, Brazil
leomurta@ic.uff.br

Abstract. This short paper provides an overview of the Doctoral Symposium of the 12th International Conference on Software Reuse. Four submissions were received and evaluated by an expert panel composed of five renowned professors. The selected papers were presented in the Doctoral Symposium and received feedback from the expert panel.

1 Summary

This year, the International Conference on Software Reuse continued with its the traditional Doctoral Symposium. The goal of the Doctoral Symposium is to bring together doctoral students working in the area of software reuse and to provide feedback on their current and proposed research. Participants were asked to prepare a 20-minute presentation including a discussion of the main research challenges, solution directions, results obtained thus far, evaluation plan, and research plan towards the completion of their Ph.D. studies.

Four papers were submitted to this edition of the Doctoral Symposium. The two hottest topics in this edition were Software Product Lines and Model-driven Development. All Doctoral Symposium papers were evaluated by an expert panel composed of five renowned professors of software reuse and software engineering in general: Prof. Colin Atkinson, University of Mannheim, Germany; Prof. William B. Frakes, Virginia Tech, United States; Prof. Alessandro Garcia, PUC-Rio, Brazil; Prof. Maurizio Morisio, Politecnico di Torino, Italy; and Prof. Kyo C. Kang, POSTECH, Korea. The selected papers were presented in the Doctoral Symposium and members of the expert panel provided feedback to help students shape their work. These papers are available through the International Conference of Software Reuse website at http://icsr12.postech.ac.kr.

I would like to thank all Ph.D. students that submitted their works, the members of the expert panel that helped in the construction of a productive and useful Doctoral Symposium, Hyesun Lee, who built and maintained the Doctoral Symposium website, Cláudia Werner and Klaus Schmid, who provided extreme helpful and relevant feedback during the organization of this edition of the Doctoral Symposium, and all other people from the organization committee who directly or indirectly helped in making the Doctoral Symposium a reality.

K. Schmid (Ed.): ICSR 2011, LNCS 6727, p. 243, 2011.
© Springer-Verlag Berlin Heidelberg 2011

Pragmatic Strategies for Variability Management in Software Product Lines

Stan Jarzabek

School of Computing, National Univeristy of Singapore, Singapore
stan@comp.nus.edu.sg

Abstract. After general introduction to Software Product Lines (SPL), we focus on variability management, a key technical challenge for effective reuse. We discuss reasons why commonly used variation techniques (pre-processing, configuration files) do not scale well. We present merits (visibility of feature impact on core assets, automation of product derivation, support for evolution and scalability), and trade-offs (need for skilful design and training) in applying uniform variation technique, design specifically to manage variability in SPLs.

Keywords: Software Product Lines, Variability management, Generation.

The starting point for most of the Software Product Lines (SPL) is a single successful software product. This original product evolves into similar products for other customers who need functionality that the original product provides, but with some modifications or extra features. This initial evolution often happens with ad hoc reuse - copy and modify - of source code files of the original product. Versions of source files pertinent to different products are stored under a Software Configuration Management (SCM) tool such as CVS or SVN. As the number of customers and relevant product variants increases, such ad hoc reuse shows its limits: Product size grows as we implement new features in response to customer requests. At the same time, we need maintain all the released product variants, so we have more and more code to maintain. Also with a growing customer base (good for our business!), increasing product variability becomes a challenge for ad hoc reuse: How do we know which versions of source files should be selected from SCM repository for reuse in development of a new product? How should we customize them and then integrate to build a new product? These problems may become taxing on company resources.

We can already start observing initial symptoms of the above problems as the number of product variants reaches 4-5. As maintaining product variants and implementing new ones becomes more and more time-consuming, more systematic reuse practice becomes necessary for a company to exploit business opportunities of a successful product, and to sustain the business growth.

Stabilizing a common architecture for products is the first step in migrating product variants developed in ad hoc way into a Software Product Line (SPL). Reusable SPL core assets – code components, documentation, test cases – are designed around SPL architecture. Conventional architectural design plays important role, as some variant features of products can be nicely mapped into architectural components. Handling such features becomes easy with plug-in components.

K. Schmid (Ed.): ICSR 2011, LNCS 6727, pp. 244–245, 2011.

However, there is a limit to what we can achieve in terms of reuse with conventional modularization, and mechanisms of modern component platforms. Components provide effective reuse solutions at the middleware level. However, in application domain-specific areas such as business logic or user interface, despite many similarities, software is still developed very much from scratch. One of the reasons why this happens is that the impact of features spreads freely across many components, affecting their code at many variation points. To manage such "troublesome" variability, companies typically adopt variation techniques such as preprocessing, manually commenting out variant feature code, parameter configuration files, Ant, or annotations (Java/JEE).

Such variation techniques are simple and available for free. Most developers can understand them without training. But as SPL grows, problems usually emerge: Features get complicated; One variant feature may be mapped to many variation points, in many components, and it is difficult to figure out to which ones and how; Features often are inter-dependent, and inclusion of one feature into a custom product must be properly coordinated with modifications of yet other features.

In the second part of the tutorial, we examine uniform variation technique of XVCL (xvcl.comp.nus.edu.sg) that exercises total control over SPL variability, from architecture, to component configuration, to any detail of code (e.g., variations at the source statement, expression or keyword level). XVCL streamlines and automates customizations involved in implementation of selected variant features into custom products, from component re-configuration, to detailed customizations of component code. The approach replaces the need for multiple variation techniques, and scales to SPLs with large number of inter-dependent features.

References

[1] Jarzabek, S.: Effective Software Maintenance and Evolution: Reuse-based Approach. Taylor & Francis, CRC Press (2007)
[2] Pettersson, U., Jarzabek, S.: Industrial Experience with Building a Web Portal Product Line using a Lightweight, Reactive Approach. In: Europ. Soft. Eng. Conf. and Symp. on the Foundations of Software Engineering, ESEC-FSE 2005, Lisbon, pp. 326–335. ACM Press, New York (2005)
[3] Ye, P., Peng, X., Xue, Y., Jarzabek, S.: A case study of variation mechanism in an industrial product line. In: Edwards, S.H., Kulczycki, G. (eds.) ICSR 2009. LNCS, vol. 5791, pp. 126–136. Springer, Heidelberg (2009)

Software Reuse and Safety

William B. Frakes[1] and John Favaro[2]

[1] Department of Computer Science, Virginia Tech,
7054 Haycock Rd., Falls Church VA 22043
frakes@cs.vt.edu
[2] Intecs SpA, Via Giannessi 5,
56100 Pisa, Italy
john.favaro@intecs.it

Abstract. This tutorial addresses issues and current practices regarding the important topic of the interaction of software reuse and safety. This topic has become very relevant to modern embedded systems in domains from aerospace to automotive, as new architectures are introduced that encourage the development and use of reusable components. The two sections of the tutorial provide first an introduction to the theoretical concepts relevant to safety-related software development, and then an introduction and discussion of concrete examples in today's industry. Current examples of standards regulating reusable software components in safety-critical domains are presented. An example from the automotive industry is presented in more detail.

1 Software Safety and Reuse

Topics covered include: safety definitions, a discussion of software safety myths, presentation of real world software safety disasters, a categorization of types of reuse, an introduction to the most prominent reuse and safety issues, a presentation of the key concept of safety integrity levels, and a discussion of the relationship between dependability and safety.

2 Current Industrial Practice in Software Reuse and Safety

Topics include: an overview of reuse standards and practice in selected safety critical sectors (aerospace, railway, space); a discussion of current safety-related reuse concepts in industry (e.g. problems related to achieving certification, and the implementation of so-called 'proven in use' concepts); and an in-depth presentation of reuse-oriented issues in the automotive industry today, including a discussion of the new AUTOSAR architecture and ISO 26262 safety standard.

K. Schmid (Ed.): ICSR 2011, LNCS 6727, p. 246, 2011.
© Springer-Verlag Berlin Heidelberg 2011

Author Index